THE KNOWLEDGE DIVIDEND

CREATING HIGH-PERFORMANCE COMPANIES
THROUGH VALUE-BASED KNOWLEDGE MANAGEMENT

THE KNOWLEDGE DIVIDEND

René Tissen

Daniel Andriessen

Frank Lekanne Deprez

FINANCIAL TIMES
Prentice Hall

London · New York · San Francisco · Toronto · Sydney
Tokyo · Singapore · Hong Kong · Cape Town · Madrid
Paris · Milan · Munich · Amsterdam

PEARSON EDUCATION LIMITED
Head Office:
Edinburgh Gate
Harlow CM20 2JE
Tel: +44 (0)1279 623623
Fax: +44 (0)1279 431059

London Office:
128 Long Acre
London WC2E 9AN
Tel: +44 (0)207 447 2000
Fax: +44 (0)207 204 5771
Website: www.business-minds.com

First published in Great Britain in 2000

The right of René Tissen, Daniel Andriessen and
Frank L. Deprez to be identified as Authors of
this Work has been asserted by them in accordance
with the Copyright, Designs and Patents Act 1988.

ISBN 0 273 64510 2

British Library Cataloguing in Publication Data
A CIP catalogue record for this book can be obtained from the British Library.

10 9 8 7 6 5 4 3

Typeset by Pantek Arts, Maidstone, Kent.
Printed and bound in Great Britain by Biddles Ltd, Guildford & King's Lynn.

The Publishers' policy is to use paper manufactured from sustainable forests.

René Tissen

René Tissen is managing director of KPMG Knowledge Management and part-time Professor of Business Management at Nyenrode University, The Netherlands School of Business. As an international consultant and researcher, he specializes in advising companies on boardroom-level matters of knowledge management, organization and human resources management.

Before joining KPMG, Professor Tissen held a number of executive and senior management positions in Dutch industry and government as well as abroad.

Daniel Andriessen

As a senior manager of KPMG Knowledge Management, Daniel Andriessen specializes in advising senior management of international companies in the area of knowledge management, knowledge organizations and knowledge systems. He has worked as a business consultant for over ten years and is recognized as an expert in strategy development, policy analysis and organizational audit, as well as the implementation of policy simulations and management games.

Daniel Andriessen received his degree in Administrative Science and Social Scientific Research from the Vrije Universiteit (Free University) of Amsterdam.

Frank Lekanne Deprez

Frank Lekanne Deprez is manager of KPMG Knowledge Management, where he specializes in advising international companies in the areas of operational and strategic knowledge management, as well as creating virtual communities.

Before joining KPMG he was a research associate at Tilburg University and since 1988 has held several management and functional positions as Royal Dutch Airlines (KLM). From 1995 to 1997, he was Manager of Market and Product Development at Galileo Nederland, Ltd.

Frank Lekanne Deprez graduated in Industrial and Organizational Psychology from the Vrije Universiteit (Free University) of Amsterdam.

ACKNOWLEDGEMENTS

Our special thanks go to: Joie van Tilburg-Rose, for constantly adding value and for her ability to visualize our thoughts in wonderful graphic detail. Siemen Jongedijk, for his in-depth research efforts and for finding examples about everything. Jonathan Ellis, for his ability to grasp the ungraspable. Heidi Weisbeek, for always being there at the right moment doing the right things.

Our partners Marie-José, Marian and Petra, for always being enthusiastic, supportive and loving individuals. Our children Jeroen, Marlies, Matthijs, Ceder, Carlijn, Mirthe, Hidde and Siebe for providing us with a meaningful life.

The board of executives of KPMG The Netherlands, especially Ruud Koedijk and Kees van Tilburg, for having the guts to finance and support us throughout.

Our advisory council: André Boekhoudt, Hennie Both, Rob de Lusenet and Pepi Rozendaal, for being committed and enthusiastic.

Sandra Gaarenstroom of Heineken NV for allowing us to use the scenarios that she was so instrumental in designing.

Our colleagues at KPMG: Steven Olthof for being highly innovative in strategizing with us, Daan Boom for keeping us informed and hopefully 'knowledgeable', David Parlby, Robert Taylor and Deborah Hale for helping us to thing multi-culturally. And finally to our publisher, Pradeep Jethi, for his creative and innovative suggestions.

René Tissen
Daniel Andriessen
Frank Lekanne Deprez

CONTENTS

PART ONE

WHAT IS VALUE-BASED
KNOWLEDGE MANAGEMENT?

CHAPTER 1

'What is value-based knowledge management?'

How companies can prepare themselves for greater success in the knowledge economy

If we had written this book five years ago, then we might have started like this:

'The only certainty we have in corporate life is the certainty of change.' This has been a factor for many years. Yet today, change is more rapid, more radical, more overwhelming than at any other time in our history. The increase in the availability of information, the threatening 'glut of information', and in the ease of access is catapulting the world out of the industrial economy into the knowledge economy. The world is developing from a market place into a virtual market space. Global operations are no longer an option, but, increasingly, a requirement. At the same time, managers are being faced with increasingly complex challenges. 'Think global, act local.' 'Produce at low cost, and mass-customize.' 'Don't develop then market. Develop and market.'

Today, however, all this is common knowledge. Uncertainty is the order of the day – and of the next day. Managers are experiencing that as we move further into the knowledge economy, the complexity of decision making will increase beyond our wildest nightmares. For in the knowledge economy it will be essential to act with utmost speed to respond to unexpected and unusual market demands, while at the same time having to juggle the conflicting interests of increasingly irreconcilable parties.

The change is becoming paradoxical as the knowledge economy sets new rules for the way we do business. Companies give away their products for free. The costs and time to deliver an electronic product are nearly zero. The very

Even in the seemingly
traditional area of
furniture, trends are
following each other
more rapidly than ever
before and as a result
product cycles are very
short. When traditionally
people bought furniture
for 'a lifetime', now it is
'until the next trend
comes along'. The
result? Only the fastest-
to-market can hope to
make a profit. In addition,
increased competition
from Asian-based
companies means that
low-cost products are
becoming more
commonplace, allowing
trends to change far
more rapidly. Furniture
retailers are also being
forced into becoming
interior design
companies, as
customers expect to be
able to choose a
complete interior from
one retail outlet and
expect it to appeal to a
very broad taste indeed.

best products get cheaper every year. And the fastest growing companies are the ones with intangible assets.

Pressure no longer comes only from increasing competition and more demanding customers. Public opinion expects companies to make a positive impact on society, as Shell discovered to its discomfort with the Brent Spar. When they announced their plans to sink it, public opinion forced them to hold a full-scale inquiry into other disposal methods. Companies can no longer survive if they are only built to compete; they must now also be built to last.

A bad place to start

Of course, this comes at a time when managers are still reeling from the effects of far reaching reengineering and restructuring projects which were claimed to be the saviour of the situation.

One of the world's leading manufacturers of industrial containers (steel drums) encouraged dozens of employees in their mid-fifties to take early retirement, but when they decided to design and build a future-oriented drum factory using state-of-the-art welding techniques they found out that exactly those people they had retired were the only people with specific knowledge of existing welding techniques. Knowledge that was essential in assessing the suitability of new welding techniques. The result? The company had to rehire them but now pay them high consultancy fees.

Today managers are being forced to admit that this has not had the effect they were promised. Seven out of ten reengineering projects have failed.[1] Even Stephen Roach, the Wall Street guru whose theories of downsizing resulted in over a million employees being dismissed to save costs admitted in a memo to clients of Morgan Stanley, 'I was wrong'.[2] The author Peter Scott-Morgan agrees, 'Knowing what we know now, to persist in the extreme forms of macho reengineering ... is tantamount to management malpractice. It damages the resilience of the workforce to change.'[3]

All this downsizing has been disastrous to companies everywhere in the world. They reduced their workforce – and threw away the intellectual baby with the industrial bathwater. It is impossible to judge how much knowledge has been lost to companies who have felt obliged to downsize because everybody else was doing it. And to make matters worse, they are now realizing that knowledge is irreplaceable and are becoming aware that without the knowledge that they lost when they had to let half of their people go, they are finding it almost impossible to compete in today's marketplace. They need creative vitality – but they've got rid of the people who can provide it.

This situation is aggravated by the fact that most managers have an industrial background. They put their belief in products and production processes, when, in fact, these are no longer the deciding factors. True, speed and surprise are becoming a vital way of creating a difference.[4] Management is being faced with how to get products from the mind to the market as quickly as possible. But speed is no longer simply a benefit; it is a prerequisite for survival. The real challenge is coping with complexity.

The shift is underway

All this means that companies that have developed from an industrial background – assuming that success lies in developing faster, cheaper, and more efficient manufacturing methods – are in the midst of a drastic turn-around in their attitudes to market and customers. They are no longer satisfied by 'just' providing products; success comes from elsewhere.

And so we are experiencing a drastic swing away from industrial activities. Today's focus is no longer on the traditional industrial preoccupation with perfecting existing products. As Kevin Kelly writes, 'Wealth … flows directly from innovation, not optimization; that is, wealth is not gained by perfecting the known, but by imperfectly seizing the unknown.'[5] The future is, Kelly suggests, no longer in computers but in connections. In other words, we are seeing a drastic shift from products to services.

And these services are being put to use to satisfy increasing customer needs. At Andersen Windows, they are proud of their long tradition in providing windows of all shapes and sizes. But the range of possibilities had grown to such proportions – between 1985 and 1991 the number of products offered grew from 28 000 to 86 000 – that the choice left home-buyers totally puzzled. What's more, a price calculation could run to 15 pages. Now salespeople use a computer not only to design the window using a series of 'building blocks' which can be added or subtracted at will, but also to test the design for structural stability

'So, what's new?'
A group of business men – obviously all working for a major European-based electronics company – were enjoying a drink in the bar of an international hotel. One of the men held up his hand and said, 'The game all changed in 1968. That year the first Japanese cassette recorder was marketed in Europe. Until then we had no competition. In fact, my manager said that we could use the milkman to sell our products: he could leave the latest gadget on the doorstep and pick up the money the next time he called.' 'So what's new?' asked another. 'Today, companies give away products to make sure consumers use their services. A global system mobile (GSM) phone is used as bait to hook a customer on a specific provider. Perhaps they should use the milkman, too.'

and to generate an instant quotation.[6] And Matsushita is making use of virtual reality to offer customers the chance of literally 'walking around' in their dream kitchens.[7]

This increase in the attention given to customer satisfaction and customer loyalty goes a long way towards explaining why, during the last decade, the bulk of new employment has been created in services while jobs in industrial sectors have been scrapped by the million. And there are companies which are taking steps to move away from a purely product-based operation towards one in which services play an important role in meeting customer demands. Sony, for example, has announced that it is entering into the field of service provision rather than concentrating on products. With such a step they are underlining the increasing importance of connections and the diminishing importance of products. By providing the services as well as the products, Sony is establishing the sort of integrated value chain which is necessary today to fulfill the total range of customer demands. In fact, it has become part of the company's strategy to be involved in the total media chain – from content and services (music, films, computer games, and telephone subscriptions), via transmission (satellite television and cinemas) to reproduction equipment (televisions, pocket telephones, video recorders and CD-players).[11]

The need for knowledge

It is clear that a lot of knowledge is required to cope with complexity, to provide value-adding services, to encourage

---

The shift is underway

Don't cut me anymore
'Companies are saying, "Don't cut me anymore",' says Bonnie Digrius, an analyst at the Gartner Group.[8]

'In their obsession to cut costs – and people – some companies have perhaps cut too close to the bone, leaving themselves with insufficient resources.' D. Stamps[9]

Sony to provide telecom services
Sony recently announced, as part of its strategic plan to offer more services alongside its products, that it is planning to sell subscriptions for its cellular telephones in England, the Netherlands, and Greece. In addition, it is also planning to offer access services for the Internet as an additional package. 'The telephone service is the first step towards moving even closer to the customer,' a spokesman said.[10]

No downsizing for consultancies
Consultancies have profited from the pervading downsizing and have upsized themselves, assuming responsibilities for which management is paid. The global consultancy market started after the Second World War and has now grown to around $40 billion ($15 billion in the US) and employs more than 100 000 of the most highly skilled people in the world.[12]

---

innovation. And this is why more and more companies are joining forces to combine knowledge. A recent study shows that the most important motive for starting an alliance is to gain access to complementary knowledge. In fact, this is the case in 36 per cent of all alliances.[13]

But alliances are not the only new source of knowledge. It is hardly surprising that business consultancy should have been expanding explosively under such conditions. Managers feel insecure about handling complex issues, and are more eager than ever before to enlist the help of specialized consultancies. Since 1990 consulting services have grown at a rate of around 10 per cent. And, according to Tom Rodenhauser, an analyst with *Consultants News*, the industry newsletter, the revenues of the leading companies have been increasing by as much as 30 per cent.[14]

Knowledge is becoming a product. In some professions – accountancy, the law, and advertising – this has always been the case. Now other forms of knowledge are being marketed by database companies and software houses. When Galileo, one of the three major global airline booking and information systems, was put onto the market recently, it was valued at US $2.45 billion[16] – knowledge as a product.

Other companies are making use of their knowledge of intangibles to create new business opportunities. Mars, the chocolate bar company, saw an opportunity of exploiting its skill in brand management by using its established world brand as the launching platform for a new ice-cream product. The result? The most successful product launch in this industry ever – and the establishment of a totally new category of ice-cream.[18] Similarly, Victorinox, the company which produces the highly successful Swiss Army knife – something every boy dreams of owning – used their brand name to launch a successful range of Swiss Army watches. This allowed a product to be introduced which had great affinity with the brand name, but is now targeted at a more mature public who are less likely to want to carry a pocketknife around with them all the time.[19] And Harley Davidson used their legendary name to introduce clothing, fashion accessories, fragrances, and even trend restaurants.[20]

Marketing knowledge

IBM, the computer company *pur sang*, is recognizing the swing from products to services and is doing everything in its power to increase its ability to advise its clients on a broad front. IBM is very well aware that its clients do not simply want to buy computers and software; but rather, to buy a solution to a business problem. Similarly, Federal Express, the courier service, now sells its core products in the form of systems and advice to companies with complicated distribution and logistical problems. And that means doing a lot more than delivering parcels.[15]

Managing the intangible

According to Joel Barker, a futurist with Infinity Limited, 'Corporate intellectual properties will be more valuable than their physical assets in the twenty-first century.'[21] And as more companies become aware of their intellectual capital – whether patents, process knowledge, technologies, management skills, customer and marketing information, competitor intelligence, new product concepts, customer and supplier surveys, competitor analysis patents, licences, copyrights, process improvement ideas, or procedures – so its management will require on-going attention.

Some companies are already taking on this challenge. Dow Chemical Company has developed an Intellectual Asset Management Model.[22] Arthur Andersen[23] and Hughes Space & Communications Company[24] are managing a knowledge database that contains all past experiences on projects including the clients' reaction to the deliverables. Chevron installed a best-practices discovery team to reveal hidden repositories of knowledge throughout the company. This resulted in a best-practice resource map.[25]

Knowledge is not enough

Does this mean we all have to start capturing all the knowledge we can get? That is what many business consultants will tell you. According to research firm Dataquest, the market for 'knowledge management services, will reach $3.6 billion in 1998 – against $2.6 billion in 1997 and just $400 million in 1994.'[26]

The important factor here is providing knowledge which adds value. It is not enough to generate knowledge, make it available, and hope for the best. This is like offering information on matters which your customer doesn't need to know. Value-adding knowledge is significantly different from indiscriminate information. And companies must be aware of this difference.

The KnoVa factor

The potential which a company has for adding value is called the KnoVa (knowledge value) factor. This shows that in the knowledge economy, the value-adding potential of a company depends on two important ingredients: the service level a com-

Dow: towards a knowledge value management culture

Dow Chemical Company had sales of $20 billion in 1995 and spends approximately $1 billion on R&D. Its present patent portfolio consists of around 25 000 patents. Dow has spent the last four years developing a vision, functional systems, and tools for the 'value management' of its intellectual assets.

Dow now sees other companies as potential customers and licensees for its technology and is exploiting ways of significantly increasing its income from licensing agreements. It is using the intellectual asset management model to make know-how visible and to incorporate it in a database which, coupled with newly created networking hardware and software, will make the right knowledge available to the right people. In this way, intellectual capital becomes the sum of human capital, organizational capital, and customer capital.[17]

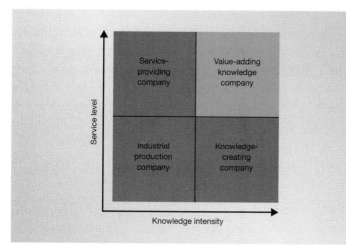

The KnoVa factor

The KnoVa factor

'So we'll put the industrial companies right at the bottom?'
'Of course. They focus on production rather than on increasing services to their customers. And few store house knowledge.'
'So service providing companies are more likely to be successful.'
'For the moment, perhaps. But we have to ask ourselves whether they can really meet customer demands any time, anywhere, and anyway with their present knowledge level.'
'Which means they will have to move further along – to where knowledge creating companies are.'
'But it won't be enough to create knowledge without reference to what customers really want.'
'So it's safe to say that the value-adding knowledge company has the best chance of success?'
'That's the way it looks. And, to be included in that category, a company has to score highly on both service level and knowledge intensity.'
'Are there many of those?'
'Not as many as there should be. But there could be more after reading this book.'

pany provides and the knowledge intensity of the company; and the degree to which a company uses knowledge to produce products or services.

Examples of 'old style' industrial companies are getting ever more difficult to find. Even the production of a simple beer can require an enormous amount of knowledge.[27] This does not mean that many production companies do not have to get more knowledge intensive – they do.

A typical example of service-providing companies are employment agencies. These originally emerged to satisfy the need of many companies for additional staff. It was often time-consuming for companies to recruit such temporary staff by themselves, and would therefore avoid the hassle and turn to an agency. This was particularly true when a member of staff was only needed for a limited period – to take over work from an employee on holiday or on maternity leave, for example – and therefore could not be offered a full-time contract. Today's agencies, however, go a lot further. They have recognized that a high level of service is vital in what is becoming a highly-competitive industry. The way of supplying staff has become more flexible: they can be offered for temporary work but, also, for longer periods on a short contract or even for permanent employment.

The market for employment has since become much more transparent. It is much easier for potential employers to reach potential employees than ever before. The Internet is an example

Best airport in the world markets its knowledge

For many years in succession, Amsterdam Airport Schiphol has been nominated by international travellers as the best airport in the world. On the surface, however, it provides the same facilities as airports anywhere in the world: runways, terminals, service areas. The success is the result of an on-going determination to put the customer first. Attention has been given to matters such as signposting, space, light, train connections and so on. And in the terminal itself passengers can enjoy a wide range of facilities, including shops, offices, hotels, showers, restaurants, and even a casino and virtual-reality golf course. Schiphol Management Services – SMS – has been set up to exploit the knowledge Schiphol has and turn it into a marketable product. It already has a wide range of clients (airports) in places such as Budapest, Beijing, Vienna, Cartegena, Brisbane, Curacao, and Kuala Lumpur.

A particular success story is the renovation and exploitation of John F Kennedy's Terminal 4. Immediate changes – which did not go unnoticed by regular users of the terminal – were flags in the building, plants throughout the public areas, and the absence of

of a new medium which is proving particularly suitable for bringing together employer and employee. The agencies are under pressure; their traditional services are no longer enough to guarantee stability for the future. And so, in order to continue adding value to their customers, the agencies have to become more knowledge intensive – that is, have a greater knowledge of both candidates and vacancies so that the perfect match can be made. For this, increasingly sophisticated information systems are being used. In addition, many agencies are increasing the service they offer to their clients by introducing training schemes for the candidates, organizing seminars, and even establishing training schools and academies for potential candidates.

In their ground-breaking book, *The Knowledge Creating Company*, Nonaka and Takeuchi stress the importance of knowledge creation for modern companies. As the KnoVa factor indicates, this is not enough. You are not in the business of creating knowledge; you are in the business of adding value. The importance of the KnoVa factor is that it shows that if a company is to be successful in the emerging knowledge economy it will not be enough to concentrate either on increasing service levels or on increasing the knowledge intensity of the activities it offers. Success will depend on a two-pronged attack in which both the level of service and the level of knowledge content are increased to allow a company to move on to greater success.

The Dutch company Stork is a good example. It has transformed itself from an industrial production company to a value-adding knowledge company. The company started as a simple machine builder. Engineers spent their days creating the most remarkable machines. Technology was everything, the customer was a necessary evil. But towards the end of the seventies, things went radically wrong with Stork. The decision it made was to concentrate solely on those products about which it had a particular knowledge. At the same time, customers took a central position and Stork began to realize that it would be able to add value by offering a whole range of services connected to its machines – maintenance, repair, modifications, and so on. It also started helping the customer gain as much added-value as possible from its products.

Stork is aiming to master as many parts of the value chain as possible. The disciplines needed for this have either been developed in-house, or acquired elsewhere. Now the company is not only the builder of knowledge-intensive machines – for textile printing and for the food and beverage industry – but also the provider of knowledge-intensive services.[29]

'canned' music. Schiphol is now no longer simply an airport; it is a company that sells its knowledge on an international scale.[28]

CHAPTER 2

'How to use value-based knowledge management'

How companies can use operational and strategic knowledge management to become value-adding knowledge companies

In their focus on becoming KnoVa intensive, a number of companies are already taking some obvious – and indeed necessary – first steps in the area of what has become the end-of-the-century buzz word in business: knowledge management. But the majority of companies are approaching this in an operational way.

Operational knowledge management

Companies already aware of the need to distribute information throughout the organization are making use of a variety of operational knowledge management techniques. Their main concern is to connect people to the system being used for the distribution and transfer of knowledge.

While this may be a good start, companies have found – more often than not – that this tends to become costly, ineffective, and non-productive. Strategic knowledge management gives balance by linking the building of a company's knowledge to its business strategy. Attention is given to the impact of information technology and the need to design the organizational structure accordingly. It recognizes that knowledge professionals are a new breed – a species of workers that finds itself in high demand around the world.

Improving operational excellence

The need for operational knowledge management is often triggered by day-to-day problems. Knowledge may be inaccessible or hidden, meaning that the wheel is constantly being reinvented. Result: low productivity. Or knowledge may only be in the heads of the employees and may be lost when they leave for

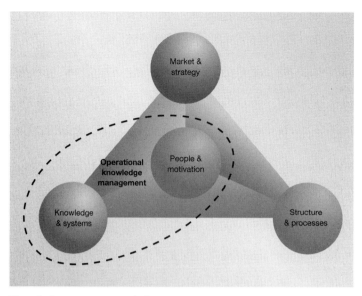

Knowledge management in harmony

another company. Or there may be an excess of information coming at a company from all sides which swamps managers. Problems may not be solved properly – or only partially. Professionals in the company may be putting their own careers ahead of success for the company. And there may be walls between departments, causing long lead times and a total lack of synergy between people involved in the same project.

None of this is particularly advantageous for any company. And once business process reengineering has been undertaken, many managers turn their minds to increasing the knowledge intensity of their processes. Such companies apply a number of tools which facilitate and enable knowledge exchange.

AT&T rolls out knowledge management system The staff of AT&T's Business Communications Services now use an on-line help system to provide faster and more customized service. The system allows a customer service associate to access information from mainframe systems and integrate desktop tools, such as fax, imaging and word processing. When a customer calls, the associate can go into the business mode, click on billing, and find a menu of activities to choose from to resolve the problem. An intranet provides the network foundation that integrates customer information. Before the introduction of this system the information was so fragmented that it was hard for staff to build up a relationship with the customer; now staff see the potential for radically improving response times to customers.[1]

Technological enablers

Gerhard Schulmeyer, President and CEO of Siemens Nixdorf Information Systems, said 'The Internet and global communication technology – and the intranet within a company – are critical factors in a company's success in this new knowledge-based economy.'[2]

AT&T, the world's biggest communications company, is also the world's largest IT spender and is making wide use of the possibilities offered by the intranet. The company has introduced an intranet-based knowledge management system to provide 15 000 customer-service representatives with point and click information to replace the existing paper-based information system. AT&T is also using an intranet to channel customer calls to the appropriate agent, and is spending big money on multiple-terabyte databases and data-mining tools.[4]

In production, Motorola is using an intranet to relieve the pressures of ever faster product cycles. Its new CyberSURFR modem is difficult to assemble and must meet rigorous quality standards. Management decided to set up a factory-floor intranet which provided step-by-step instructions for assembly, testing, packing, and shipping. After initial adaptation problems, employees are now familiar with the system and are making suggestions on how to make it even more efficient. Production problems can be highlighted on the system and employees can make suggestions for changes which can be implemented centrally and be made available to everybody on the floor within seconds. The paperless assembly line may well arrive before the paperless office.[5]

BP's virtual team network

A flat organization is not necessarily a feature of a major multinational. Yet BP believes that business units should run their own businesses. John Browne, CEO, believes that the value that can be derived from sharing knowledge should drive the interactions among the business units. BP's virtual team network is instrumental in this. The network us a rapidly growing system of sophisticated personal computers equipped so that users can tap the company's rich database of information. Everyone at BP can create a home page – BP believes the more the better. And it is experimenting with new ways of making information accessible – for ease of use is essential for knowledge sharing. The network has been used to pass on lessons learned from a project in real time and to inform BP units, partners, and contractors throughout the world.[3]

Cultural enablers

Frank Carrubba, formerly of Hewlett Packard, is quoted as saying, 'If only HP knew what HP knows.'[7] And many companies are in the same situation. Cultural pigeonholing has to be broken. Barriers have to be torn down. The exchange of knowledge has to be made possible within cultures which have grown to be opaque, autistic and non-responsive.

An article entitled, 'Do you have the knowledge?'[8] suggests that it is never simple creating a knowledge culture within a company. One major prerequisite is that senior management is aware of its importance and prepared to advocate and support its implementation.

Several practical routes are suggested: an in-house electronic yellow pages, with information about people, skills and knowledge bases so that an accurate indication can be given of who knows what in the organization. A cheaper alternative is the knowledge fair where buyers and sellers gather to exchange (barter) knowledge.[9] This approach has been adopted by Philips Sound & Vision Division who hold a 'fair' once every quarter, where new projects are presented to other people within the division. It has proved a successful forum for informal communications.

Much of the cultural resistance to the creation of a knowledge culture is based on the idea that knowledge is power. People who know are more powerful than people who don't know. Knowledge is used as a weapon for internal one-upmanship – not for the greater good of the company.

Replacing such a mentality with one of 'Power is in sharing knowledge' cannot happen overnight. Yet many companies are becoming aware of the need to do just that. Rhone-Poulenc SA, France's leading chemical and pharmaceutical company, believes that creating a culture that fosters innovation and creativity is essential for running a twenty-first century company. Peter Neff, the CEO of Rhone-Poulenc's US subsidiary, talks about pushing decision making nearer the customer, breaking down hierarchies and walls and leading people rather than managing them.[11] The success of the company, according to Neff, 'depends on people'. 'Our success in the future will depend on our ability to tap the collective wisdom that is the accumulated judgements, perceptions, experiences, intuition and intelligence – of all our employees.'[12]

'If only HP knew what HP knows'

Hewlett Packard is well known as a largely decentralized organization in which individual business units perform with a large degree of autonomy. Many of the 112 000 employees are technically oriented and are ready to share their knowledge, even though the business unit structure does not offer any organized form of sharing such knowledge and resources. In 1995, however, a number of knowledge management initiatives sprang up in various parts of the company and senior management decided to attempt to facilitate this exchange of knowledge by promoting any activities in this field. At the moment there are more than 20 separate projects. A series of workshops on this topic has been started. Lotus Notes is being used as a technology vehicle, and creative tactics are used to entice submissions to the database. HP Laboratories have introduced a guide to human knowledge resources within the Labs, including a 'nag' feature to urge people to update their entries. And HP's product processes organization (PPO) knowledge management group developed Knowledge Links, a web-based collection of product development knowledge from the various PPO functions.[6]

Leading, rather than managing, is essential, for 'bureaucracy is its own worst enemy. It inhibits people from doing their jobs and stifles ideas that can give customers what they need.'[13]

Buckman Laboratories, a company which has recognized the importance of knowledge by estimating its value, is now actively focusing on engaging the customer. Acknowledging that 'the proper function of a successful sales organization is to provide sales representatives ... with the goods and services necessary to help their customers do business more effectively'[18] – or becoming a value-adding company at the top quadrant of the KnoVa factor – has resulted in a knowledge network which makes it possible for any Buckman employee to take advantage of the knowledge and skills of other employees, including those outside his or her work-group. The network, known as 'K'Netix', includes several discussion forums through which any employee can ask questions and receive answers from any other Buckman employee.[19]

Who pulls the cart?

The impulse for an operational knowledge management initiative frequently arises in a staff department. Managers of IT departments or company libraries and archives see the technical possibilities being offered by, say, Lotus Notes or the intranet and recognize the benefits this could have in their

---

Operational knowledge management has many faces

'Operational knowledge management' has a wide range of definitions. Approaches which can be given this name include:

– valuing knowledge on the balance sheet
– implementing knowledge systems such as Lotus Notes
– competence management
– knowledge process control
– workflow management
– data warehousing and data mining
– knowledge modelling and codifying
– intellectual capital
– managing innovation
– learning organization
– intranet
– expert systems
– extranets
– push and pull technologies (netcasting)

Hoffman-LaRoche: getting started

1. Start by focusing on the right problem. The spot chosen here was closely tied to the strategy of the business and a driver of the organization's future growth.
2. Focus on a process which is undeniably knowledge intensive.
3. Set definitive goals for what the effort will achieve. If possible, these should result in increased profitability.
4. Knowledge management need not be technology intensive, and should not be technology-driven.
5. Bring together the right project team. Keep it small – but make sure every member is the best and brightest available. Remember: 'knowledge is something that is so dear to the company that only the best and brightest can actually bring it out.'[10]

---

own company context. Unfortunately, these initiatives are often seen as departmental hobbyhorses and generally lack support from top management. It is, by and large, an uphill battle to convince top management of the need for such operational knowledge management. It demands costings and hard figures – neither of which can be easily provided.

We believe managers should not be tempted into thinking that operational knowledge management will end their problems once and for all. Certainly it will prove valuable. Yet, they must constantly ask themselves questions about that efficiency. Is the system able to keep up to date with the rapid development of knowledge in a specific area? Does the system support and keep talented professionals? Does it contribute to coherence both among and between organizational units? And does it lead to better use of knowledge in unstructured processes and ill-defined problems where information management is inadequate and automation is inappropriate?

Strategic knowledge management

These questions must be constantly in the mind of the manager. For there is always the spectre of the 'big lie'. Michael Schrage writes, 'the lie says that if organizations only had greater quantities of cheaper, faster, and more useful information, they could increase their profitability and enhance their competitive position in the global marketplace.'[23] And, indeed, it is this misconception which fired the starting shot of the biggest corporate spending spree in the history of business. Because the sad truth is that information – no matter how much or how good – has little or no impact on people's behaviour. Has information about the risks of smoking stopped the world from buying cigarettes? No. The real problem most organizations face is not inadequate information – it is the organization's unwillingness to change behaviour in the face of good information.[24]

Certainly, there is a desire to believe that all problems can be solved by an intranet, an intelligent search engine, Lotus Notes, or whatever. But none of these can ever solve the fundamental problem of relationships within a company. The ability to be able to share knowledge will not break down a determination to keep things to yourself. An intranet will not cause people to work for the good of the company rather than for the good of themselves.

No, systems are not enough. Thomas Davenport observes that collaborative computing does not create collaborative cultures. Collaborative tools must be aligned with collaborative incentives.[26]

This is where strategic knowledge management comes in. Companies use it to manage important relationships within the company and to set the right conditions for collaboration between knowledge professionals.

The first prerequisite for collaboration is to create direction and a shared understanding of goals and opportunities. A knowledge strategy will guide the creation of knowledge that can be turned into market value.

The second condition is the proper treatment of people as professionals whose lifeline is producing valuable knowledge. We must motivate them and provide them with the right competencies. We need to inspire them to use creativity and intuition. To stick their necks out. To be prepared to make mistakes. To be flexible and react faster than ever before.

Superhuman? No – but certainly a new breed of workers, with a totally new book of instructions. A user's manual which will have to be written with particular care and insight.

The third condition is to create a transparent structure, which allows professionals to see exactly where they are in relationship to their company's environment and what the value of their work is to the company as a whole. A structure that is totally process and team based.

Creating direction

Any new knowledge which is created by a company must meet a very simple requirement: it must add value to the company. Only then is it knowledge with a strategic advantage. If the creation of knowledge is to be successfully directed, then so, too, must the people involved in creating that knowledge. And this is why there must be a clear and positive link between the

Information or relationship?

'Consider this conceptual experiment as a way to rethink information ecology. Every time you see the word 'information' in a book or article about technology, substitute the word relationship. Notice how that simple substitution radically changes the design sensibility underlying intranets and other management information systems. When we design networks for the enterprise, are we designing them to manage important information or to manage important relationships? The answer, of course, is both, but our anachronistic Information Age vocabularies distort what is really going on.'
Michael Schrage[25]

1. Map the overall
   business model driving
   the firm's performance
   and profitability.
2. Construct an
   'information map',
   noting the information
   required to support that
   activity and decision
   making.
3. Create a 'knowledge
   map', illustrating how
   information is codified,
   transformed into
   knowledge and used.
4. Create a 'balanced
   scorecard' – a set of
   performance measures
   that top management
   should use to gauge
   the health and progress
   of the business.
5. Create an 'information
   technology map'
   reflecting the
   infrastructure and
   systems needed to
   support the knowledge
   work of the
   organization.
6. Use a holistic
   approach, drawing on
   a whole arsenal of
   people, process, and
   technology-related
   changes.
7. Recognize and
   formulate the roles of
   different kinds of
   'knowledge workers'.
8. Focus processes on
   knowledge creation,
   then define ways in
   which individual
   knowledge becomes
   an organizational asset.
9. Focus technology
   efforts on imposing

business strategy of a company and the development and use of knowledge within the organization.

Monsanto is a very diverse firm with interests in agricultural production, food and beverage ingredients, industrial chemicals, coatings and pharmaceuticals. Sales in 1996 were $9.26 million with a workforce of 28 000 employees. A radical decentralization has resulted in the creation of a number of business units, one of which has been given the task of focusing purely on growth. Its mission: 'to grow existing business ... and create new business by exploiting "white spaces" where core competencies exist to increase the overall profitability of the enterprise'. The 'white space' concept, derived from the work of Hamel and Prahalad, is important but raised immediate challenges. To address this, Monsanto created a web of 'knowledge teams' with the task of creating and maintaining a 'yellow pages' guide to the company's knowledge and serving as points of contact for people seeking information about different subjects. These teams are proactive and creative in thinking about Monsanto's knowledge needs in their assigned topic areas.

Considerable attention has been given to the creation, care and feeding of networks. This has resulted in 'communities of practice'. Networks of people are not only mechanisms for communicating; they help to advance collective understanding by providing a forum for 'sense-making'. In so doing, they create value for their individual members as well as the organization.[28]

A similar approach of identifying knowledge domains and knowledge links has been successfully adopted by Hoffman-LaRoche. In the world of pharmacy, success depends on the speed of new product launches. The faster a product is brought onto the market, the faster a company can recoup its development costs and generate higher profits. In fact, the company had calculated that every day gained in market availability represented a gain of $1 million. In addition, shorter development times mean more new product ideas can be placed in the pipeline, helping to hedge the risk of any of them fizzling out (as many do).[29]

At CIGNA Property & Casualty, a Philadelphia-based insurance company, the aim was to create an upward value spiral for know-how to be shared throughout the company. Information and knowledge contributed by employees is processed by 'knowledge editors' – usually experienced underwriters – and distributed throughout the organization. CIGNA also uses knowledge management to discover and maintain profitable niches and is using the skills and experience of people as building blocks for its success. One important finding is that CIGNA now recognizes that it is not the quantity of knowledge which is important; rather it is the quality of that knowledge which is the key determinant of profitable underwriting. According to Tom Valerio, CIGNA's senior vice-president, 'Every company has a ton of information in its databases; the key to profitable underwriting isn't giving access to every bit of information that's important, it's how you determine which information is relevant and how you tailor it.'[30]

New ways of motivation

Andrew Carnegie once said, 'The only irreplaceable capital an organization possesses is the knowledge and ability of its people. The productivity of that capital depends on how effectively people share their competence with those who can use it.'

Today's new breed of knowledge workers generally has a thirst for knowledge. It is their lifeblood. They eagerly suck it up. Yet they do not easily share it. It is theirs to have and to hold 'until death do them part'. Or so it would seem.

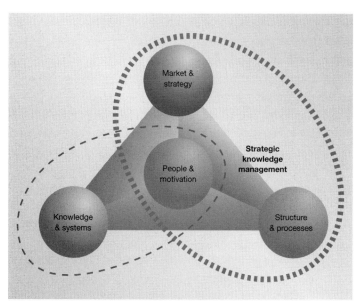

Strategic knowledge management

better organization on knowledge and enabling connections among people and information.[27]

Strategic knowledge management

'Most of us are being advised to practise operational knowledge management, using information technology to organize and distribute information from and to employees.'

'Isn't that a good place to start?'

'Of course it is. Probably the best. The trouble is, you mustn't stop there. You have to add strategic knowledge management.'

'What's that?'

'It gives a balance by linking the building of our company's knowledge to our company's business strategy. Attention is given to the impact of information technology and the need to design the organizational structure accordingly. It recognizes that knowledge professionals are a new breed, a species of worker that is in great demand around the world.'

'And you need both approaches?'

'Of course. That's what makes it work.'

'Operational and strategic.'

'Together. In harmony. That's the answer.'

At Merrill Lynch, the need for a diverse group of professionals to co-operate intensively for a short period has resulted in what they call a spider's web – a self-organizing network which can flexibly combine high specialization in many different disciplines with multiple geographic contact points and a sharp focus on a single problem or customer set. Individuals work with many different colleagues on a variety of projects over the course of a year. All of them submit a confidential evaluation on everyone with whom they have worked closely. People are willing to share knowledge and co-operate because their compensation is attached to this mosaic of peer relationships. And compensation is a major motivating factor in this business.[31]

Another motivating factor is an ever greater challenge. Leaders of the best organizations are often demanding, visionary, and intolerant of halfhearted efforts. They often set 'stretch goals' – for example, Hewlett Packard's William R. Hewlett (improve performance by 50 per cent), Intel's Gordon Moore (double the number of components per chip each year), and Motorola's Robert W. Galvin (achieve six sigma quality).[32]

Successful organizations also frequently feature internal competition and frequent performance appraisal and feedback. At Andersen Consulting, only 10 per cent of the carefully selected professional recruits move on to partnerships. While at Microsoft, the reverse process holds sway: they try to force out the lowest performing 5 per cent each year. Great organizations are unabashed meritocracies.[33]

Management must take steps to motivate workers to share knowledge. At Buckman Labs, incentive, evaluation, and promotion systems are designed to recognize those who do the best job of knowledge sharing and ignore or punish those who don't.[34] Chaparral Steel changed its pay structure to reward the accumulation of skills in addition to performance. It has an absentee rate that is about one-quarter of the industry average.[35] And Pfizer has developed 'competency models' for its treasury executives that call for more than basic financial skills. Knowledge building and knowledge sharing are considered critical for management as they strive to create linkages across the organization.[36]

Support professionals through processes and teams

Many companies are organized by function, discipline or authority. This must change. A successful company will be one organized around processes and teams because a clear and transparent organization makes it easier to share knowledge.

Heineken NV has recently designed a number of scenarios to launch itself into the twenty-first century. One of these scenarios involves structuring the company to become a value-based knowledge organization. From the core, the Executive Board directs and focuses company knowledge that relates to overall performance and strategic and operational decisions. Activities of the operating companies – the OPCO's – and production families called Clusters – will become more process-based as will corporate functions and executive activities. Smart networks connect all functions to each other. It is an example of a knowledge company which is brain-rich and asset poor.

Monsanto has undertaken a radical business restructuring programme. It has designed a new organizational model based on three entities: strategic business units, business services, and steward groups. These redesign efforts are supported by a number of new information technology programmes. This approach is integrated into a knowledge management architecture.[37]

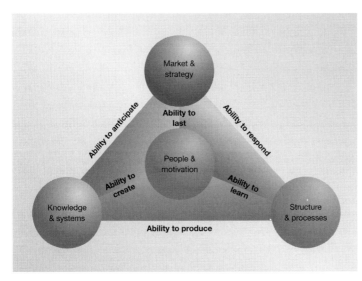

Thrive in the knowledge economy. Integrate the approach

'Our value-based knowledge management approach has four key areas – market & strategy, structure & processes, people & motivation, and knowledge & systems. To integrate these fully, a company needs to develop six capabilities, each forming a link between two of these key areas.'

'Shall we take them one by one?'

'Sure. First, there is the ability to produce: using the right application of knowledge & systems in structures & processes.'

'Then there's the ability to respond: attacking the market, using a decentralized organizational structure.'

'Now, three: there's the ability to anticipate, using (decentralized) knowledge to get the big picture about future market discontinuities.'

'Next, there's the ability to create, getting motivated people (smart professionals) to generate new knowledge.'

'Fifth is the ability to learn; professionals forming a learning organization in which they constantly learn from the experiences of each other clients, and customers.'

'And finally, you need the ability to last, getting professionals to commit to your company by offering a sense of purpose.'

Businesses today have to
face two seemingly
conflicting demands: first,
they must understand and
fulfil the diverse needs of
each individual customer;
and second, they must do
this while keeping their
costs down to an absolute
minimum. An answer is
sometimes found by
linking the internal
business processes to the
information and
communications
architecture. In 1994, Levi
Strauss introduced a new
product called 'Personal
Pair Jeans'. The customer
could pay a $10 premium
and purchase a pair of
jeans which are personally
tailored to fit the individual
measurements along four
dimensions: waist, hips,
rise, and inseam. With the
introduction of 'Personal
Pair Jeans', Levi Strauss
increased the number of
sizes it offers from 400 to
over 4000.[38]

Becoming a KnoVa company

We've said it before: in the knowledge economy the key to a
company's success will be its ability to continuously add value
in such a way that it brings itself into an upwards, ongoing
value spiral. In order to achieve this, companies need to possess six basic capabilities.

1. The ability to produce

Most companies know one thing: how to produce goods and
services. Now they must do this using the right application of
knowledge within the proper structures and processes. This
means using knowledge to control processes which are often
highly complex, demanding literally hundreds of suppliers,
each with their own requirements. BMW has a computer-run
production line which allows customized cars of all the current
types to be produced on a single production line. A computer
ensures that each specific component – including those from
third party suppliers – arrives at the production line at exactly
the right moment.[39] Also look at the success of workflow management systems such as SAP. They really increase an
organization's ability to provide, i.e. to deliver a product to a
customer in the most efficient and effective way possible.

2. The ability to respond

Reacting quickly to market changes is one of the biggest challenges for companies and also one of the biggest opportunities.
Successful companies acknowledge that market responsiveness
is a key to survival.

An approach which allows such responsiveness is the introduction of business units, each placed near to the customers
and the market segment. Authority is decentralized as business
units take all the necessary decisions to meet changing
demand. Asea Brown Boveri, ABB, is a global company that
makes and markets electrical power generation and transmission equipment, high speed trains, automation and robotics,
and environmental control systems. The company has 210 000
employees that are led by only 250 senior managers. When
formed by the merger of the Swedish ASEA and Swiss Brown
Boveri in 1987, one of the earliest strategies was to recognize
and move power from the centre to its operating companies.

The central head office staff was reduced from a total of 6000 to a total of just 150 people with a matrix management structure introduced worldwide. Several layers of middle management were stripped out and directors from the central headquarters moved into regional co-ordinating companies. The company was split into 1400 smaller companies and around 5000 profit centres functioning, as independent operations as far as possible. At the same time, a new group-co-ordinating structure was introduced. Everyone in the company has a country manager and a business sector manager. Locally, about 100 people ran the country business. Approximately 65 global managers ran eight business sectors. The moves were essentially aimed at empowering managers to move closer to their customers. And to give them incentive to act as smaller, entrepreneurial units. Even research and development was decentralized. All dealings between units were undertaken at market prices. However, reporting was centralized: a sophisticated central computer system monitoring unit performance and supplying HQ with monthly updates of sales and orders and quarterly financial results. Thanks to the new structure, the company truly behaves as a transnational. It lives locally and sources globally, developing a network of suppliers for each of its businesses by picking the best worldwide, reducing costs, and cutting on cycle times. It capitalizes on its core technology, unifies it and applies it across all businesses. Its businesses can compete effectively locally, but share technology, innovation, products, and learn globally.[40]

3. The ability to anticipate

Responding to market trends is essential. But not enough. To be truly successful, a company must be able to see the overall picture and not just react to trends, but actually anticipate them. It is important to recognize in advance the discontinuities which will shape the market in which you are operating.

It is sometimes easy for even the best companies to miss a discontinuity and fall behind. Microsoft, for example, did not anticipate the explosive rise of the Internet, and soon found that Netscape, a seemingly insignificant company, had crept in and secured a leading world position for itself.[42] A legal battle has been raging to disqualify Amazon.com (the Net's online bookstore) from doing business. Legal action has failed and Barnes & Noble,

Barnes & Noble vs. Amazon

Amazon.com hit the world with the first on-line bookstore. It provided a slick way for readers to find out about books and order them without ever leaving their home. The result? When floated on the stock market, the company had a capitalized value of $670 million. Now it is receiving stiff competition from Barnes & Noble, US's giant bookstore chain. And B&N are discovering that anything Amazon.com can do, they can do just as well. Amazon.com may have grown thanks to a philosophy of avoiding stocks and physical warehousing – ordering direct from wholesalers when an order was placed – but may have to enter that game if it is to match the speed of delivery which Barnes & Noble, thanks to its physical bookstores and supply logistics, is throwing into the battle.[41]

are attacking Amazon.com, using their expertise as a seller of traditional, hard copy books. The question is, however, whether the largest US bookseller may not actually be cannibalizing its own bookstores by offering its books on-line.[43]

It's important to recognize that a new 'golden rule' of organizational design emerges from all of this, one that indicates that the closer an organization operates to its market, the worse its ability to anticipate is likely to be. Increasing your ability to respond will generally decrease your ability to anticipate.

4. The ability to create

Companies must constantly look for ways in which they can keep the value spiral moving upwards. And this largely depends on a company's ability to create knowledge. Such knowledge creation can take a wide variety of forms. It can mean using R&D to create new products or technologies. It can mean using existing knowledge in a new way – for example, applying CD audio technology to data storage. It can mean gaining new knowledge about customers. Customer loyalty programmes, such as the many frequent flyer clubs, give valuable insight into the habits of major target groups. But most of all it means mobilizing all hidden sources of existing information and knowledge to create 'New Combinations', as Schumpeter has called them.[44]

In the pharmaceutical industry, companies are using IT to transform their data resources into competitive weapons and provide customers with critical information and value-added services. According to Karen Harper of KPMG Peat Marwick's life sciences practice in New York, 'Pharmaceutical companies are becoming knowledge brokers.' Pfizer Inc., a $10 billion firm in New York, has launched a massive sales-force automation programme that enables 2700 sales reps to customize their sales pitches. Information can be immediately accessed about any specific drug, giving doctors details about dosage, side effects and treatment regulations.[45]

5. The ability to learn

Since the publication of Peter Senge's book *The Fifth Discipline*, the concept of the learning organization has become very popular. The concept proposed by Senge stresses how important – and valuable – it is for employees to learn from their own experiences, and from their customers, competitors, and colleagues.

Rover champions learning organization

At Rover Cars in the UK, a revolutionary human resources policy and educational effort has been used to energize its workforce. The Rover New Deal eliminates involuntary layoffs and allows employees to peruse education alternatives of their own choosing. The company places less emphasis on technology and more on learning effort.[46]

This is very much what Stewart calls the 'virtuous cycle'. 'People learn to do things that become stories that become documents that go on a network that people use to learn how to do things.'[47]

Senge pointed out that there are implicit beliefs which act as barriers in a learning organization. Beliefs such as 'They'll never let us do it.' 'Don't get caught doing something different that doesn't work.' 'What really matters around here are costs.' 'If something went wrong, somebody screwed up.' All these throw up seemingly insurmountable barriers.[49]

Yet, it is exactly companies that break down these barriers that become successful. Xerox around the office watercooler encourages the exchange of ideas salespeople. The idea has been further expanded to give salespeople a 'radio watercooler' in their car, so that they can chat and exchange information about customers.[50] National Semiconductor failed to account for learning in communities of practice and laid off the wrong people – the people who apparently were not doing anything. Now the company has come to its senses and gives them semi-official status.[51]

6. The ability to last

As we have seen, knowledge professionals will play a crucial role in the knowledge economy. They will be able to demand better working conditions, greater freedom and increased job satisfaction. This will mean that the knowledge professional will not be easily bound to one company. The idea of employment for life is most certainly alien to this new breed of professional. They will job hop easily, going where they feel they can achieve greatest satisfaction.

But when knowledge professionals walk out of the door, much of the knowledge goes with them. A particularly good example of this occurred in the banking world. Some 60 of the 140 analysts working for ING Barings left the bank and reappeared in the trading room of competitor Deutsche Morgan Granfell Bank.[53] A particularly unwelcome example of transfer of knowledge! Yet, it illustrates a fundamental fact: in the future, policy will not have to concentrate on separation but on attachment. A company will need to develop a way of revitalizing itself – not necessarily by attracting young and fresh people but, rather, by renewing and refreshing its existing workforce.

Shared (mis)understanding?
'The learning organization literature tends to assume shared understanding. This assumption does not always stand up because people might say 'yes' to something they do not understand and 'no' to something they understand.'
T. Garavan[48]

The new job mobility
An analysis of government data by the Employee Benefit Research Institute has discovered that job tenure in the US – already lower than in any other industrialized country – is actually dropping even further. Between 1991 and 1996, job tenure for men between the ages of 25 and 64 dropped by 19 per cent. Although some of this can be put down to reengineering, lay-offs, and the like, there is every indication that job-hopping is on the increase. Workers with skills which are particularly sought after are finding it to their benefit to change jobs every few years rather than spend a long stint with one employer.[52]

BP: from failure to success

One company that has truly balanced operational and strategic knowledge management is British Petroleum (BP). In an extended interview in the Harvard Business Review,[54] John Browne, describes in detail the change through which his company has gone. This interview provides the basis for the following case study.

'BP, the international oil company, is a very different company today than it was a decade ago. Then it was an unfocused, mediocre performer whose business extended to minerals, coals, animal feed, and chicks; today it is the most profitable of the major oil companies.'[55]

'BP is much smaller and simpler than it was back then. It now has 53 000 employees – down from 129 000. It used to be mired in procedures, now it has processes that foster learning and tie people's jobs to creating value. Before, it had a multitude of baronies, now it has an abundance of teams and informal networks or communities in which people eagerly share knowledge.'[56]

BP is now a value-adding knowledge company, mastering all of the six capabilities such a company needs to possess.

The ability to produce

The new BP organization is very flat and based on processes, not tasks or hierarchies. 'Processes linked to a purpose are powerful at changing behaviour because people can see what they're aiming for.'[57] These processes include management processes as well because managing directors and their deputies work as a team in dealing with the business units. When they review past and future plans of the business units, 'the message is sent that performance matters. That's an assurance process.'[58] They also have 'a strategic process for ensuring that the units are constantly creating lots of business options for the future and are constantly sorting through them and improving them.'[59] It is the job of the top management team to stimulate the organization, not control it. Its role is to provide strategic directives, to encourage learning, and to make sure there are mechanisms for transferring the lessons.

The ability to respond

The company was made more flexible and responsive by being split into 90 business units. There is nobody between the general managers of the business units and the group of nine operating executives. The organization is even flatter because 'each of the managing directors works as part of a team in dealing with the business units.'[60]

The ability to anticipate

BP has also put considerable effort into creating direction by ensuring that there is a clear purpose. Because it understands that 'if that purpose is not crystal clear, people in the business will not understand what kind of knowledge is critical and what they have to learn in order to improve performance. A clear purpose allows a company to focus its learning efforts in order to increase its competitive advantage.'[61] For BP, this meant 'instilling the belief that competitive performance matters – that producing value is everyone's job and that to produce value you need to focus so that you don't get distracted by things that aren't central.'[62] These central issues also include social values such as 'ethics, health, safety, the environment, the way employees are treated and external relations.'[63]

The ability to create

BP has 'integrated its technology organization with the business units so that it is working with them, both to solve the most important business problems and to exploit the most important business opportunities.'[64] Over the past five years, it has 'refocused its technology people on application and given them the mission to access the best technology wherever it resides.'[65] For BP realizes that no matter how good a company is, 'it cannot possess more than a tiny fraction of the world's best technology.'[66] It is the 'ability to combine and apply technologies – not the technologies themselves'[67] – that frequently gives BP its strategic advantage.

The ability to learn

People were encouraged to learn by being given challenges and learning has become a major weapon of the company's determination to anticipate the future helping the company identify opportunities others might not see and to exploit them rapidly and fully. BP learns not only from more than its own people. It also learns from contractors and partners such as Shell.

The ability to last

Finally, motivation of professionals is given high importance with the company constantly finding new ways of making them excited and keeping things enjoyable. It has also created an attractive environment for knowledge professionals: it realizes that if BP is 'not regarded as leading edge, then why would graduates join them instead of Microsoft or Intel?'[68] As a result, BP's people 'are highly motivated, understand exactly what they have to do to create great value, can see the results of their actions and have a sense of ownership. They excel at building and using knowledge capital, which means accessing and applying knowledge that exists both inside and outside the company. They excel at forging distinctive relationships.'[69] Because they are convinced that 'you cannot expect others to share their knowledge and resources with you unless you have a strong relationship with them.'[70]

Despite this success, BP is constantly alert to changing markets. It applies smart strategies which offer a series of frameworks to help management reexamine what they are doing relative to what the world can offer and what the competitors are doing. It asks: 'Who are we? What makes our company distinctive?'[71] These frameworks are used to structure dialogue throughout the company, helping leaders talk about strategy with people in the business units. And BP has discovered that this is 'a tremendous way to get people to grasp what is really happening in every component of the company and to help them avoid falling into the trap of thinking of strategy as something fixed or as cash flow analyses with only one answer.'[72] Strategy, at BP, is 'about buying the right options that will give it a shot at competing in the future.'[73]

Creating a new and positive perspective

Creating these abilities implies a new breed of organization – one that is effective and efficient in building knowledge and adding value to both company and individual professionals. Yet, this is not something which is only open to specific organizations – basically, any organization can become a value-adding knowledge company. It is neither enormously difficult nor is it excessively complex. What it does require, however, is the willingness to make decisions which will enable people to constantly add value.

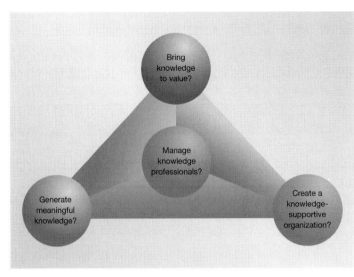

Generate value through knowledge. How do we ...

Four questions for management
'Only four?'
'Yes – but vitally important questions. Ones which will cause a lot of thought and headaches.'
'But worth it if the result is a value-adding knowledge company?'
'Yes. Because unless you are prepared to move your company towards that top right-hand quadrant in the KnoVa factor, you will have a tough time of it in the knowledge economy.' 'Tough decisions or tough operations.'
'That sums it up.'

With all this in mind, management has to deal effectively with four basic questions.

- How can we turn the knowledge we have into something which can add value to the markets in which we operate?
- How can we generate meaningful knowledge rather than simply flooding our organization with indiscriminate information?
- How can we create a knowledge-supportive organization in which everybody is convinced of the contribution knowledge can make to the success of the company?
- How can we manage our people who will increasingly become knowledge workers or professionals, motivating them to generate knowledge and share it with their peers on a structured basis?

It is these four questions that are addressed by a new approach to the management of knowledge: value-based knowledge management. An approach that secures the value-adding power of a company's knowledge without building up knowledge for knowledge's sake. Value-based knowledge management is an integrated and harmonious approach that helps you design and implement the following.

Value-based knowledge management combines strengths of both approaches

'So you think it's all about getting smart, do you?'

'Of course. And getting smart in four very critical areas. First, we need smart strategies, the vision and action plans for bringing knowledge to value. Second, we must have smart organizations, entirely process and team based that know how to manage professionals and profile the purpose for which their corporate centres exist. Third, we must have smart professionals who can work in teams to build, share and harvest knowledge. And fourth, we need an integrated environment that ensures existing and new knowledge becomes smart knowledge.'

'And you have to have all four?'

'Certainly, otherwise there is no integration with no basis for success or, even, survival.'

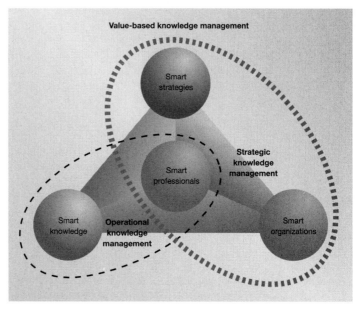

Value-based knowledge management combines strengths of both approaches

1. Smart strategies: showing how to create and leverage knowledge that will deliver company value.
2. Smart organizations: in which the key is to create organizations which are entirely process and team based.
3. Smart professionals: offering the tools with which to shape the attitude and key competencies of professionals with the help of innovative motivation, appraisal, and reward systems.
4. Smart knowledge: showing how to develop knowledge which is fully focused and using the correct management processes to keep it visible.

Creating value through knowledge management

Kevin Kelly, the former but still famous Editor in Chief of *Wired* magazine, fundamentally questions the need for knowledge management. Take a look at the diagram at the top of the next page.

If this is also the way you view the business world, you may want to pick up a different book. For us it's not a question of either/or. We do need knowledge management, and we need it in a value-based manner. There are three ways in which a company can use knowledge management to add value, by making

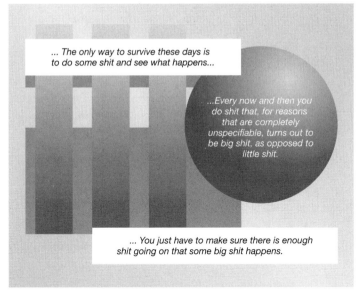

Do we need knowledge management?

its knowledge more efficient, better connected and tremendously innovative.

In other words, companies can get a better grip on existing and new knowledge by improving their knowledge efficiency, connectivity and innovation.

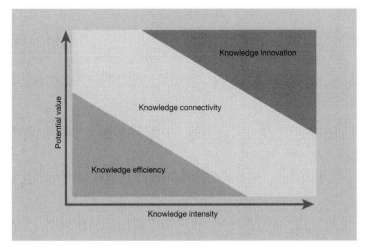

Knowledge management improves efficiency and accelerates innovation

1. **Knowledge efficiency** has to do with carefully codifying and storing already existing company knowledge in (electronic) databases. This type of knowledge is usually extracted from its developer and made independent of that person. The goal here is to *(re)use* this knowledge in order to prevent the company and its employees from reinventing the wheel each time they need knowledge. It is knowledge at your fingertips: just 'click' and it's available. Experience has shown that this type of knowledge management can often result in cost savings of 15 to 20 per cent. And with this return, investment in information technology is justifiable.

2. **Knowledge connectivity** relates to managing knowledge that is, or should be, passing between business and service units. To realize significant synergy between these units, knowledge about company best practices, for instance, would be mutually beneficial to share. This is the strength that holds a company together and improves its business performance. This knowledge, unfortunately, is often not (re)used, mainly because business unit managers lack the motivation to share it. Take for example detailed local knowledge about a global client's purchasing practices. It would interest business units that currently service, or want to service, this client in all locations. This could be especially important when it comes to price negotiations.

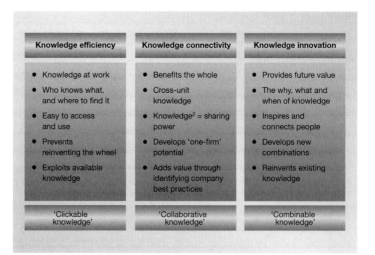

Way to add value with knowledge management

3. **Knowledge innovation** normally involves knowledge that is closely tied to a person or (virtual) team and is shared mainly through direct person-to-person contact. Clearly, improvisation, experimentation and creativity are competencies needed to realize novel and valuable ideas, solutions and services/products. Through new combinations of existing knowledge and/or the development of new knowledge, it becomes possible to renew processes, products and services that reinforce the competitive advantage. Usually, this type of knowledge management does not need to limit itself to improving the management of a company's R&D function.

If knowledge management does all of this, you may be wondering, why do we need value-based knowledge management?

PART TWO

WHY DO WE NEED VALUE-BASED
KNOWLEDGE MANAGEMENT?

CHAPTER 3

'Whatever happened to the Industrial Age?'

Tracing the path from the agricultural economy to the knowledge economy

Almost unnoticed, our world has slipped from the industrial economy into the knowledge economy. And although business men may realize that we are in a transition period between these two economies, many of them are still so involved in the industrial economy, that they are blinkered to what is really happening around them.

This is understandable: many of today's managers have come from an industrial background and that has inevitably shaped the way they think about work, about managing their businesses and about reacting to the challenges which arise in their day-to-day business.

Few people are fully aware of how drastic the current situation is for business. Everybody knows that the importance of agriculture as part of Gross National Product (GNP) has been superseded by industry. Most may acknowledge that today's industry is being superseded by knowledge. But many have yet to realize that knowledge is now becoming big business in itself.

The virtual economy: the Internet changes everything

Over the past century, we have benefited from unimaginable scientific advantages from the microchip to nuclear power, from the aeroplane to radio waves, from distant stars to subatomic particles. While this reflection is inspiring, looking ahead is even more exciting when we consider the rapidly accelerating rate of change and its empowering agent – the Internet.

The foresight of a gene king

Craig Venter was laughed at when he left the academic world seven years ago to collect little fragments of genes. His 'no-brain' work was considered as inspiring as collecting stamps. Even so, Venter found these fragments easy to find, since for each active gene, a copy is available in a cell, which is made of RNA instead of DNA. Soon he had a database of thousands of fragments, the so-called Expresses Sequence Tags (EST's). Venter outsmarted his scientific friends by patenting his collection of fragments. And then Venter found them easy to sell which he did for a cool $125 million. The buyers – commercial companies interested in applying the data in their research. The rest of the story, Venter is now respected for his simple, little collection.

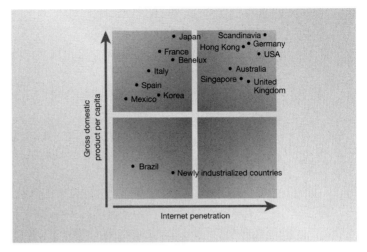

Internet penetration wordwide

Even though the Internet is the product of technology (electronics, telecommunication, power generation, media, computing, networking, software design and information services), its power comes from people using it. Power that increases exponentially as more people get connected. In essence, the web has unleashed the power of the individual – 100 million users worldwide.[1]

The real danger of the virtual economy

Increasingly we are moving into a knowledge-based economy. Instead of fighting over trade routes and raw materials, companies in the future will defend their right to produce and globally market products and to hold intellectual property. It will be seen by many people as a virtual economy – an economy that is intangible and not easily understood. There is an inherent danger in adopting a if-we-can't-grasp-it-let's-ignore-it line of thinking. And remember, the virtual economy does have a physical carrier – the Internet.

We have mentioned the explosive popularity of the Internet, but its actual penetration is still only the 13 or 14 countries that are responsible for the world's GNP, 80 per cent of the world's economy. Compare this to the Internet's potential – more like 240 countries in the world. Not to mention that the Internet is really only a stepping stone to the virtual

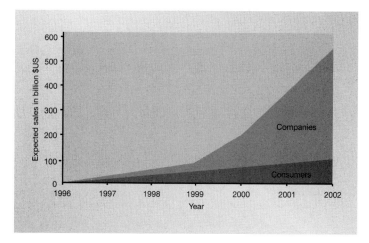

E-commerce is gearing up

economy. It is electronic commerce that will be the power economic driver of the virtual economy.[2]

Barry Riley pictured it clearly in his *Financial Times* column,
'The Internet still has only a modest penetration of the mass
market. Even in the US, it has achieved little more than a
10 per cent penetration of the consumer market. Yet, it is growing fast. New products will be needed to make a further
breakthrough: mobile phones that easily connect to the net,
and standard television sets with Internet facilities. But, within
five to ten years, this will happen.'[3] It's easy to forget that the
Internet is only in its infancy.

Another key feature of the new economy is that it doesn't
require any sizeable capital investment or expenditures to be
economically active and successful. Knowledge is the only
meaningful resource today, ranking head and brains above
labour, land and capital. And, the virtual economy will be an
office-at-home economy, where companies won't base their
image on posh corporate headquarters or a large investment in
machinery and technology, but on knowledge to acquire a
major stake in the economy.

Customers choose for the new economy
Perhaps an omen for the popularity of the Internet was the
dramatic change in the products and services that people

Old key indicators	New key indicators
Motor vehicles 0.3%	Home telephone services 8.8%
Food 0.6%	Entertainment & rec. services 12.4%
Major appliances 1.1%	Cable TV 13.4%
Clothing 2.3%	Brokerage and financial services 15.6%
	Home computers 18.1%

Rise in personal consumption

Average 0.9% ⟶ Average 12.5%

Customers choose for the new economy

wanted and bought. From January 1997 to January 1998, the key indicators changed from cars, food, major appliances and clothing, to more sophisticated products and services like telephone services, cable television and home computers. Personal consumption even jumped from 0.9 to 12.5 per cent.[4]

All in all, the developing new economy would have not been possible if Internet technology had not spread the way it has. It has resulted in a monumental corporate collision that profoundly impacts business and people. Now we are about to witness the full impact of the knowledge revolution.

E-commerce revolutionizes the shopping experience

Amazon.com, once an on-line bookstore, has a vision of becoming the on-line mall for the world. It is set on being customers' first choice for finding and discovering anything they want to buy – online. As the most stellar of all e-commerce stocks, one thing is sure, it will revolutionize retailing and set a benchmark for e-commerce. It's astonished investors by continuously operating at a loss, while raising its market value from a mere $503 million to a grand $22.1 billion as of January 1999, only three years later. That's no surprise, since Amazon is worth more than all American bookstores, including Barnes & Nobel and Borders, put together.

Internet learns the art of sales and merchandising

As Internet commerce matures from the exotic to the everyday, it becomes less about exploiting a position on the frontiers of technology and more about mastering the art of sales and merchandising. Whenever people get the urge for a new product or service, they want it now, wherever they are, just the way they like it, and oh by the way, they want to be entertained while buying and using it.

Amazon caught on to this novelty quickly by stimulating the involvement of its customers with: customer reviews and interviews with authors, and uses the technology to turn the feedback and the suggestions into services tailored to their personal interests.[6]

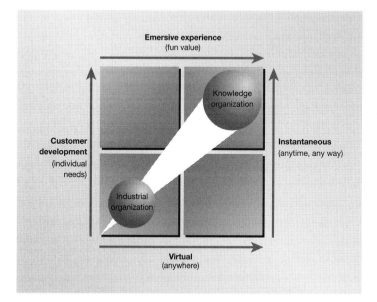

People now expect more

According to Roy Satterthwaite of the Gartner Group, 'Building an e-commerce site is a definite requirement for any midsize to large enterprise that intends to remain competitive during the next two to five years. One of the challenges, however, is that today's state-of-the-art e-commerce site will become outdated in just a few months if the back-end connections and interactive applications do not keep pace with the new technologies that are being developed,' said in its report, 'Survey Results; The Real Cost of E-Commerce Sites'.

'Market Differentiator' websites raise the bar

The Gartner Group has identified three cost categories for Internet players that will emerge: 'Get on the Map' sites cost $300 000 to $1 million, and are adequate but functionally behind the industry; 'Run with the Pack' sites cost $1–5 million and are equivalent to most industry participants; and 'Market Differentiator' sites that raise the bar cost $5–20 million.

Business-to-business leap frogs consumer e-commerce

It is not business-to-consumer e-commerce alone, however, that is changing the way business communicates with and sells to customers. What is changing even faster are the ways businesses communicate and trade with each other – what the *Economist* describes as business-to-business, or B to B, e-commerce. Business-to-consumer electronic commerce remains modest – perhaps $8 billion in the US during 1998, compared with $43 billion of business-to-business e-commerce, according to Forrester, a US consulting firm. Even in the US, business-to-consumer e-commerce will be worth no more than $108 billion by 2003 – less than Wal-Mart's 1998 sales.

Businesses are more likely than consumers to buy and sell on-line. They are better equipped and connected, more used to trading at a distance and more cost-conscious. Once large firms move their purchasing on-line, business partners and suppliers do the same. Boots, the druggist, has already established a purchasing site for its electronic procurement and is securing the buy-in of its suppliers. At a global lighting products manufacturer, e-procurement of machine parts was applied via the extranet. Using the web, buyers all over the world place buy offers and the associated specs. Suppliers view these requests and return bids. In the process, procurement has been reduced from 22 days to eight days.[7]

Not only will trading between companies be transformed, companies themselves are likely to be reshaped. Improvements in efficiency will come from switching paper-shuffling to on-line, from reducing transaction costs, from making information more widely and quickly available, and from using it more effectively. Companies will find it easier to outsource and to use communications to develop deeper relationships with suppliers, distributors and many others who might have been vertically integrated into the firm. Many companies may end up as loose agglomerations: networks of smaller companies or individuals bound together by corporate culture and communications. The diplomatic art of managing *ad hoc* partnerships and alliances will become a key executive skill.[8]

An increasing number of alliances are not about geographic

areas but managerial ones, in particular, about defining where companies begin and end. Typically, a company will focus on one or two core competencies, and outsource what's not to its allies. Even though a modern company will be entirely IT-based, its work will be Information & Communication Technology (ICT) driven, and at its heart – people.

At the heart of the matter is people

A survey of 200 senior executives in North America, Europe and Asia by Andersen Consulting and the Economist Intelligence Unit shows that between today and 2002, companies will predominantly use ICT to learn about their customers. In a shift from finding and attracting new customers to retaining the profitable ones, companies are expecting to make greater use of the Internet along with focus groups, e-mail and call centres. This will enable them to zero in on even the smallest customer segments. While organizations contend that they will continue to rely heavily on the sales force for communicating with and acquiring about customers, they indicated that it is through electronic channels that they expect to grow significantly.[9]

Companies are eager to learn about their customers because they have come to recognize that customers submerged in meaningful and exciting experiences keep coming back for more. And, this will be the key to engaging customers in the future.

A high expectation value seems befitting of a virtual world

Today, individuals and companies are prepared to pay in advance a lot of money to control economic activity on the Internet in the hope that future payoffs will be enormous. While forgoing profit may at first appear to be financial suicide, building mass of customers and advertisers seems to be the direction in which things are heading.

Net companies: do they walk on the wild side?

Although few now doubt that electronic commerce has a thrilling future, people differ over what, and how profitable, that future will be. The top three Net-companies are Yahoo!, Amazon and America On-line. Their stock gains inspire either visions of easy wealth, or from the sidelines, plain old envy – maybe even revulsion at the excessive greed.

Yahoo!, the search engine that was valued at $8 billion at its Initial Public Offering (IPO) on the NASDAQ late in 1988 was expected to generate an enormous advertising income in the future from the 95 million customers that use the search engine as a portal to the web. Already in 1999, Yahoo! has begun to deliver profits as 320 million people use the site each day. One wonders, however, how long it will take the consumer to realize that s/he doesn't need Yahoo!, but rather an intermediary that can help in making the best buy on the web?[10]

Amazon, the on-line bookstore that wants to sell everything to everyone everywhere, has made it clear that it intends to invest heavily to build dominance of the market. Will its shareholders, however, continue to hurl their money at the company on the hunch that its managers' investments to build a brand will be enough to head off the legions of copycats who are already taking advantage of the Internet's low cost of entry.[11]

AOL, American On-line, must have dipped into some deep pockets, to the tune of nearly a half a billion dollars, for advertising and distribution costs before making its first dollar. And it has paid royally – 17 million subscribers and advertisers ready to serve them. In 1999 according to analysts, AOL will reap $380 million while its competitors weep. Although this service provider-cum-portal is worth more than Disney or Time Warner, what can it do against free Internet services that have been set up by large retail groups in Europe? These Internet portals are fast becoming a commodity business and not an activity that will make huge profits. Only somewhere, in a linked business, somebody will.[12]

Technology-driven companies are growing

In the US technology-driven companies, with a major knowledge component, were outgrowing almost every other company: America On-line had grown by 215 per cent in just one year. Mcafee Associates had grown by 110 per cent, while healthcare companies such as Oxford Health Plans and Healthsource had grown by 130 per cent and 93 per cent, respectively.[13] All of these were modern start-up companies, that did not have to drag the tradition of industrial operations with them. They were free to act in the knowledge economy in the way best fitted to it.

Knowledge products on the increase

Another sign of the emergence of the knowledge economy is that many traditionally industrial companies – those designed and built to produce physical products – are being forced to produce knowledge products and services. A logical step, because knowledge is where the future is. And so it is understandable that many companies are being pressurized, purely for self-preservation, to move into knowledge products and services. Without being particularly well-equipped to handle the new demands which are made on them. For example, today's car industry is almost a part of the electronics industry. The value of the electronic content is higher than that of the steel.[16] And more and more functions in the car are being controlled and maintained by electronics. Some companies see the knowledge content of existing products increasing dramatically. And whether in computers or airlines, again it is electronics which are the enabling factor. For it is the growth of electronics, and the growth of things which can be handled by electronics, which are changing some product areas beyond recognition. And then there are companies which are actually moving into producing intangible products. The money industry, for example and the information industry.

The rise of the knowledge professional

Knowledge professionals will become the dominant factor in the knowledge economy, just as farmers were the dominant factor in the Agricultural Age, and workers in the Industrial Age. This is both logical and inevitable. In the Industrial Age, workers had first been sought for their hands and for their sheer strength. But as the application of electronics took hold of industry and business in general, so workers were eagerly sought for their minds – their ability to think and solve puzzles which could then be put into operation by a machine or some pre-programmed robot.

The law of connection: embrace dumb power
Today you can literally have chips with everything. The price of chips means that they can literally be used in anything – repeat, anything – we make. Smart cards are as sophisticated as bankers. And very soon we'll have chips in basketball shoes, in hammers, in lampshades. And by the year 2005, there will be 10 billion grains of working silicon. And the challenge will be not to produce them – but to connect them. The result? Safe air travel, for example, by letting aeroplanes communicate among themselves and pick their own flight paths. *Kevin Kelly*[14]

The new economy of value-adding work:
'All work activities can be classified into three types:
– value-adding work, or work for which the customer is willing to pay
– non-value-adding work, which creates no value for the customer but is required in order to get the value-adding work done
-waste, or work that neither adds nor enables value.' *M. Hammer*[15]

When companies began expecting people to think, they started the process which blurred the lines between employees and management. Between staff and line. It sounded the death knell of the functional organization. The days of regarding workers as tools were finally ended. What's more, people were being hired because they were smarter than their boss. Because they had the knowledge which their old-style boss may never obtain.

For many managers it seemed that the tail was wagging the dog.

Increasing complexity

The increase in complexity resulted in a growing need for specialization. Yet what many had predicted had not actually happened: we haven't yet seen the emergence of the individual; instead, we are seeing that individual professionalism is becoming more team-directed than ever before. It is integrated into the total workforce and fully focused at the target in hand.

And this trend will only increase. Simply because the knowledge sector is where the jobs are. US figures show that between 1980 and 2005 over 85 per cent of all new jobs will be in knowledge services, creating 29 million jobs, and by 2005, the sector will employ close to 48 per cent of the total workforce.[17] As a result, the workforce will consist largely of people in knowledge services – in sectors such as financial, insurance, real estate, and business services, community services. These

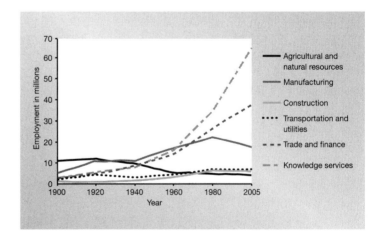

US employment: rise of knowledge services[18]

are the growth sectors. This is where the majority of employment opportunities are and will continue to emerge.

Decreasing employment

But this means that other sectors are decreasing in line with the increase in knowledge services. Employment in agricultural and industrial sectors are expected to continue to decline losing over 6 million jobs over the period 1980–2005.[19] It is a tough blow for people who are often considered 'unskilled labour' – people such as operators, fabricators, labourers, and precision production, craft, and repair workers – who, it is predicted, will account for 1 million of these lost jobs. But it is also inevitable as automation and information technology has an ever-increasing effect on production processes. Not surprisingly, however, one area in manufacturing will certainly show an increase – and that is for computer analysts and other computer-related occupations.

This loss of employment is one of the spectres hanging over business managers. In fact, many are convinced that the loss of employment will be dramatic. Machines have already taken over a large amount of routine work from people, and this trend, they assume, will accelerate rather than decrease.

Knowledge-intensive services are flourishing

If we look back at the developments leading today's economy, then we see that worldwide agriculture peaked in 1890, when farmers, hunters, foresters, and fishermen produced close to 30 per cent of Gross National Product. By the 1990s, however, agriculture had declined to no more than 8 per cent of GNP. The same fate awaited the Industrial Age. Industries such as manufacturing, construction, and public utilities all grew phenomenally during the 1970s – but now they have gone into a decline, slipping back to a little over 35 per cent of GNP.

Just as industry rose to supersede agriculture, so services are emerging to take over in importance from industry. Communications, trade, finance – these are some of the services which now, with 57 per cent of GNP, are leading world economic growth.[20]

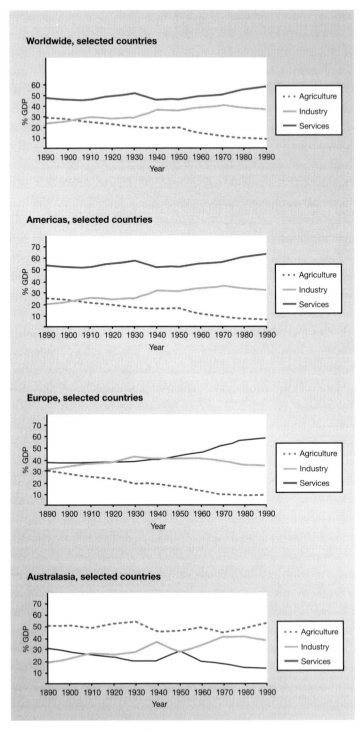

Towards a service economy [20]

In Europe, strong industrial-based economies are declining and in many countries – including France, Germany, Italy, the Netherlands, Spain, Sweden and the UK – services are providing a significantly larger share of GNP. In many leading countries of Australasia, which experienced the economic boom of the industrial age a lot later than Europe, agriculture is still responsible for a significant part of GNP. But it is highly unlikely that this will be the case for very much longer. In the Americas, services are continually providing a larger and larger portion of GNP – and, at the moment, these economies are ahead of the world in the services race.

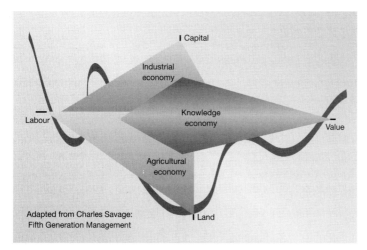

Ride the third wave to value

The quest for value

If we are to enjoy success in the knowledge economy, we will need to change our perspective. We must adopt a new one that is based on four guiding principles. First, we must strive to enhance the overall intangible market value of our company. To accomplish this, we need to help improve our customer's market value as well. At the same time we need to improve our value to society. And in order to do this, we will want to increase the value that we offer to the men and women who stand as the success backbone of our company.

Ride the third wave to value

'Agriculture depended on the ability to harvest and work the land; Industry depended on the skill to combine capital, machines, and workers. What's the key to the knowledge economy?'
'Combining people, knowledge and technology to enhance, the customer and the market, and the societal value of the company.'
'But hasn't it any physical, any tangible product?'
'Of course not. It doesn't require a lot of capital or labour. It's knowledge-intensive, which is why small companies are often the stars today.'
'The ones without an industrial history.'
'Right. They haven't got the heritage of industry to weigh them down.'
'So what about the good old industrial companies?'
'They'll have to take a giant leap forward. They'll have to produce knowledge-based products and services. Some are moving into producing new, more intangible products; others are increasing the knowledge content of their existing products. They have to realize that future profit is in knowledge based products and services – not in manufacturing.'

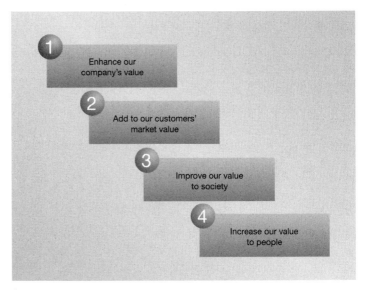

To compete in the knowledge economy, adopt a new perspective

1. Enhance our company's value

Some companies are fully aware of the growing importance of knowledge, and are exploring ways of measuring and monitoring intellectual capital. The fact of the matter is that every single company has in-house knowledge. And every manager should know how much the knowledge in his or her own company is really worth. It should be calculated by every single manager, because once they have done that, they will appreciate just how important knowledge is and how important it is to manage that knowledge.

This has far-reaching implications. Although the importance of knowledge is increasingly being recognized by many companies, it remains an intangible asset, one which does not allow itself to be protected in the same way as more physical assets. The security and protection of knowledge is therefore becoming critical in any company's strategy. Knowledge can simply get up and walk out of the door. This happened to ING Barings Bank, which lost half of its very successful Taiwanese team, which had achieved record trading on the growing Taiwanese stock exchange to Merill Lynch.[22] All this, of course, increases the likelihood of companies trying to acquire knowledge by foul means or fair.

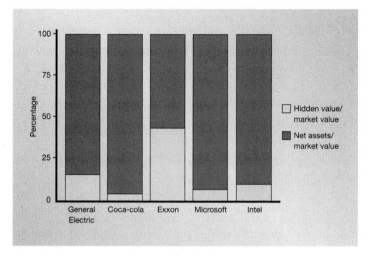

Growing importance of 'intangibles' in business

A company's economic potential matters most

It's companies that continuously focus on valuing knowledge that are expected to excel in the knowledge economy, even though, there is little management information about this intangible. Peter Drucker was noted in the *Wall Street Journal* a few years ago as saying that nothing in a financial statement measures the main things that govern today's business. There is no column to measure market understanding or technology strength. These deficiencies only show up on a balance sheet after the damage is done. Daily, the rise of the knowledge economy, which promotes a company's intangible assets as its basic building blocks for prosperity, widens the gap between the traditional financial statement and reality.

Of course, some of the difference in market value between companies is intrinsically due to the psychology of the stock market, i.e. when investors and analysts brand a company as being 'sexy', that in itself can connote value. The difference that matters, however, has to do with the company's economic potential: the future earning capability that a company has outside or above the regular business forecasts. Key is a company's power to quickly and skilfully develop new products and services. What better way to speculate on the value-adding potential of a company?

There is a growing interest in putting intellectual capital on the balance sheet

At first, companies were interested in doing this since increased assets send a desirable message to the shareholders. That was until they realized that it is also a red flag to the tax authorities. And, the existing methods for making intangible resources transparent have their limitations. They focus on the past rather than the future and contain few indicators that identify a company's real reasons for success.

So what is the real reason why your company stands to thrive in the new millennium? Because it has secured ample resources? It's recognized in the market as an industry leader? It's been in business for over 50 years? Sorry, but in this high-tech, fast-paced knowledge economy, these traditional roads to success are no longer enough. If yours is like most companies today, you are standing at a crossroads asking yourself: Can we value our company based solely on the classical balance sheet? Or, must we forge ahead with a new core strategy, one that leverages intangible assets based on core competencies that outperform the competition.

To answer this '$64 000 question', corporations, governments and professional associations from around the world convened at the Organization for Economic Co-operation and Development (OECD) international symposium in Amsterdam, May 1999. In their search for a break-through methodology that could measure intellectual capital, they listened intently as the more than 20 research teams presented their findings. Was it fate, or intuitive planning, that caused this meeting to be held in the original building of the Dutch United East India Company – the first company in the world to issue stocks.

The Value Explorer focuses on a company's economic potential

One method in particular, seemed promising – The Value Explorer©.[23] This approach assigns a company's intellectual capital a monetary value based on its economic potential. It also provides the information needed to manage it as an asset. In this age, making the 'right' decisions is the kiss of death, if they are made too late. Knowledge to guide timely strategic decisions comes from a deep understanding of the market, not of finance.

The Value Explorer focuses on a company's intrinsic strength by analyzing the intangible assets hidden in core competencies.

Three value indicators supply additional insight

Three indicators give your stakeholders insight into the value of your intangible assets, without revealing any confidential information.

1. *The knowledge intensity indicator* marks the importance of your intangible assets compared with your tangible ones.
2. *The potential indicator* gives you insight into the future economic potential of your company.
3. *The balance sheet indicator* shows to what extent your balance sheet represents the true value of your company.

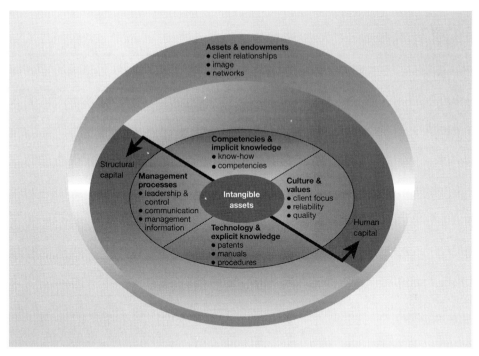

Identify intangible assets

By measuring these strengths, it can rate the intangible assets that make up your company's intellectual capital.

First, The Value Explorer identifies a company's core competencies. Second, it identifies strengths and weaknesses for each of these competencies using five different tests. The first test looks at the value the competence adds for customers. Test two determines how competitive it is. Test three evaluates its future potential. Test four concludes its sustainability. And, Test five assesses its robustness – how well the competence is anchored in the organization.

Third, The Value Explorer measures the value of each of your company's core competencies. One challenging aspect is that the value of a core competency, like that of any intangible, is not fixed. In fact, its value is constantly changing based on current market conditions and in concert with your business strategy. Whenever a company finds a new and promising application for one of its core competencies, its value increases. Most current accounting practices use historical costs to appraise the value of intangibles, thereby completely missing the point.

1. *Establishes a strategic
management agenda*
The board and a
company's CEO use
The Value Explorer to
evaluate the reports on
intangible assets and
core competencies
supplied by
management.

2. *Directs investments*
Since The Value Explorer
quantifies core
competencies in dollars
and sense, managers
use it to decide which
ones should be
strengthened and which
ones warrant no further
investment.

3. *Leads mergers and
acquisitions*
Companies, and their
bankers, use The Value
Explorer to guide them in
assessing the strength of
core competencies and
in determining the value
of companies they buy
and sell. Knowing a
company's strengths and
weaknesses, when it
comes to intangible
assets, provides the in-
depth insight needed to
make winning
combinations.
Once The Value Explorer
ascertains this for both
companies, it identifies a
synergistic match based
on strategic comparisons
and combinations. What
better way to fruitful
mergers and
acquisitions?

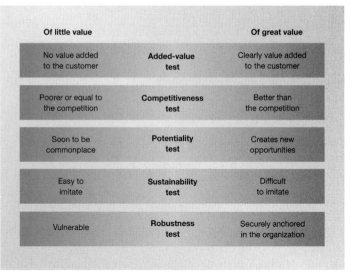

Of little value		Of great value
No value added to the customer	**Added-value test**	Clearly value added to the customer
Poorer or equal to the competition	**Competitiveness test**	Better than the competition
Soon to be commonplace	**Potentiality test**	Creates new opportunities
Easy to imitate	**Sustainability test**	Difficult to imitate
Vulnerable	**Robustness test**	Securely anchored in the organization

Test the strength of your core competencies

There is no doubt that in the knowledge economy new tools will be needed to determine a company's value. It is only astonishing that, up until now, no tool has been available to assess a company's value in the light of this new era.

The value dashboard shows the value of a company's core competencies
Below is an example of a company's value dashboard produced using The Value Explorer. It shows the value of this company's five core competencies (a company may have more or fewer competencies). For each competency, the strengths are expressed on a scale from one to five. The value of all the competencies combined equals the value of the company's intangible assets, as shown in the centre of the visual below.

Life time of customers – the new financial yardstick
Access to the customer and the management of this relationship is such a key element of e-commerce that *Fortune* suggested that the lifetime value of a customer has become an underlying yardstick for valuing Internet stocks. This value is based on advertising revenues and expected transactions fees on various forms of e-commerce. Stewart Alsop, of New Enterprise Associates, used AOL as an example, 'With 15 million customers, most of whom pay $22 per month, the

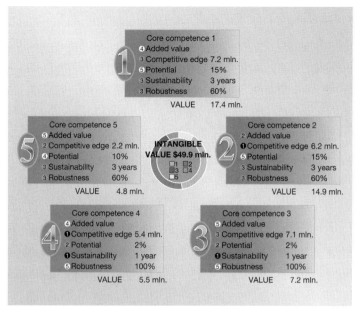

ENERG's knowledge value

company can charge higher rates to advertisers and licensees. If AOL's customers last two years on average, the subscription revenue alone could mount up to $528 and the advertising and licensing revenues could be $300 or so. In total, this would make a hefty investment in acquiring new customers when the company knows each can generate $700 or $800 in two years. Equally, so, the market value of the company divided by the number of subscribers rated AOL customers at $5300 (March 1999). This doesn't look completely insane, if you believe that AOL can persuade customers to stick with the service longer.'[25]

2. Add to our customers' market value

The challenge actually goes even further. It is not just a matter of managing knowledge, but of using knowledge to create value for your customers. This demands a much more active approach than just calculating the value of existing knowledge in your company and then doing everything possible to ensure that it increases in value. It means working with knowledge as a source of competitive advantage. For in the knowledge economy, companies which make use of knowledge in that way will be the companies that are successful. The famous French scientist and

ENERG's[24]: energy potential

As a successful research and engineering company serving electric utilities for years, ENERG, Inc., had become quite comfortable. The company only needed to introduce new R&D concepts and implement new technologies on a regular basis to keep its competitive edge. Suddenly, the privatization of the utility industry changed ENERG's market dramatically. The good-old-utility market changed from being totally technology oriented to being focused on financial assets. ENERG's market collapsed along with its profits forcing ENERG to scout out new entries into new markets. With The Value Explorer, ENERG was able to determine its core competencies. It determined which ones offered unique and innovative potential – the competencies sufficient for conquering the competition. The company then developed a strategic management agenda that outlined the necessary tasks for supporting and expanding the selected core competencies. A strategy to conquer new markets was born.

consultant Claude Fussler, said what most companies are now starting to do is making their success dependent on the manner in which they serve their clients. For the continuation of this success, these companies must know what their clients will want in five to ten years. He then added the key issue, 'that the big question is how to determine a demand which at the present doesn't seem likely. [Especially] if your current customers are satisfied, you still make a profit, and have a stable company.'[26]

This is an enormous challenge to companies with an industrial background who think in terms of products rather than in terms of satisfying customers. And that challenge is going to become even greater as we move further into the twenty-four hour economy. Business is becoming global. The world never sleeps. So we have to be prepared to do business anytime, anywhere and anyway.

3. Improve our value to society

The knowledge economy is developing today, pushed forward by the events taking place in the world around us. Certainly technology is instrumental in pushing this development. But there is also the pull of organizations that focus on achieving a positive impact on society – rather than concentrating on the self-serving interests of increasing shareholder value. And this is one of the indications that shows that business is changing fundamentally. For it shows that companies are now realizing how the way they do business impacts on society and that society, more than ever before, strikes back when something is wrong in this respect.

This realization has far-reaching implications. If a company acknowledges the impact it can have on society – by providing work and jobs and ensuring a stable economy – then the focus of a company's ambition must change to reflect this radical thinking. It must change its focus from being competitive to securing its lasting future. The principle of being 'built to compete' would have to give way to the principle of being 'built to last'. And as the marketplace expands to cover the world, so the presence of companies will also change and become more globally focused than at any time in their past. But it will be a global focus with a domestic orientation. The sustainable companies will become, in short, globally domestic. For this will be the litmus test for success in the knowledge economy.

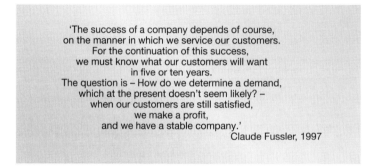

'The success of a company depends of course,
on the manner in which we service our customers.
For the continuation of this success,
we must know what our customers will want
in five or ten years.
The question is – How do we determine a demand,
which at the present doesn't seem likely? –
when our customers are still satisfied,
we make a profit,
and we have a stable company.'

Claude Fussler, 1997

Enhance customer worth

We are already seeing that cities throughout the world are looking more and more alike. Whether we walk down the streets of London, Paris, New York, Moscow or Tokyo, we are sure to pass a Body Shop, a McDonald's, the same banks. We use the same credit cards to make our purchases, and we listen to the same news broadcast, especially geared to global business people.

But will this continue? CNN is realizing that a single programming for all parts of the world is not the answer and is introducing, instead, regional programming to appeal to local global needs. For this is what people want, what they expect. They do not want to travel thousands of miles to find more of the same or hear more of the same. They expect local and global news to be more respected, go more hand in hand than they do at the moment.

Add customers to the balance sheet

In 1994, Skandia Assurance and Financial Services published its first report about intellectual capital as an appendix to the annual report. It was the first fruit of a process which the company had been following for several years based on a firm belief that the value of a company can be split up into two areas: financial capital and intellectual capital. According to Skandia, 'Intellectual capital is the possession of the knowledge, applied experience, organizational technology, customer relationships, and professional skills that provide Skandia with a competitive edge in the market.' It is the basis from which all financial results are made.

Although this intellectual capital contributes to the market value of the company, that was not the main reason for calculating it. More important was the wish to make the in-house intellectual capital visible so that managers would have a broader base for their decisions. Skandia has developed a model known as the 'Skandia Navigator' which not only sets a value on intellectual capital, but also navigates this capital. One of the innovations in the Navigator is the recognition of customer capital as an asset. For a bank, the relationships with customers have a value. The customer is where the cash flow starts. The strength of that relationship and the loyalty of the customers are indications of this value.[27]

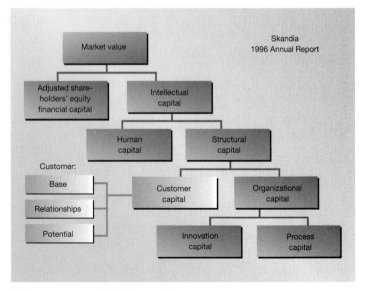

Add customers to the balance sheet

All this will increase the complexity, which any business has to handle. Change, for example, may no longer be predictable or progressive. It could very well prove chaotic, unpredictable and paradoxical and that adds complexity: a whole lot of complexity. This is compounded by the need to balance and react to often opposing wishes from an ever increasing number of stakeholders in the business. They will increase in variety and internationality, so that decisions can no longer be taken on a simple 'either/or' basis, but require a degree of 'and/and' subtlety in their handling such as has never been known in the past.

Only in this way can a company become a positive influence in today's society. And start the process which will transform a company from simply being built to compete to one that is also built to last.

4. Increase our value to people

The workforce is changing. The knowledge economy will not be a full-time employment, but a right-employment economy. Most companies have already started to look at workers as professionals who possess the ability to think and act independently. In the industrial economy, people were seen and

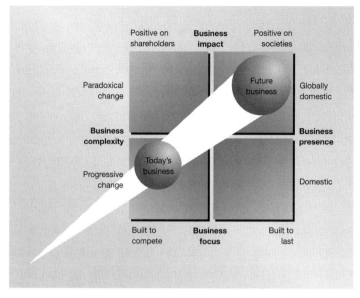

Increase value or disappear

treated as workers as typified by the old saying in the UK, 'Workers need to check in their hands every morning, not their heads'. In the knowledge economy, people will instead be asked to not only check in their minds but also their hearts. Another and perhaps most important fundamental difference is that professionals will be able to act independently.

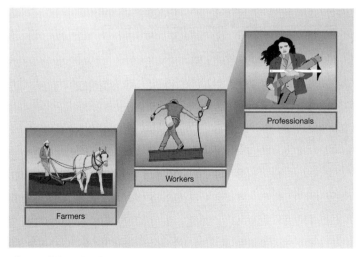

The workforce is changing

Workers surely had hidden resources in the industrial economy, but we simply didn't expect them to use their brains. Managers were the ones to think and decide. Employees were supposed to work and do what they were told, not to be creative and innovative, let alone use their talents. Traditional job classification systems were designed to make sure people would not do more than what they were told. In the new economy, the exact opposite holds true. People are valued for being able to use all of their resources. Managers will now have to learn to manage them. Companies, on the other hand, will have to fight to hire them.

The nature of work has dramatically changed

With the advancement of information and knowledge technology, the very nature of work has changed. Work has progressed from being repetitive, to requiring the independent judgement of a professional. There is also a new objective to stop working within existing frameworks, and make the most of ever-changing realities. The focus of work in general has shifted from accomplishing tasks and set objectives to connecting with customers and exploring new opportunities. Individuals performing specific functions have been replaced by teams working in a process structure. Of course all of the improve-

Left to right brain
The webpage entitled 'The Next 20 Years', predicts, 'By the year 2020, computers will have taken over all 'left-brained', or computational, tasks from humans. Conversely however, people with right-brained skills such as relationship building will be in high demand for new jobs to come forth in the 'personalized services' arena.'[28]

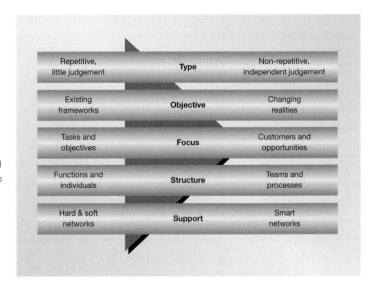

The nature of work has changed

ments would not have been possible without the support of 'smart networks' that integrate technology with people.

As far as jobs go, it is predicted that by the year 2005, 35 million extra jobs will be created in Europe for talented people who are expected to fully use their creative and innovative spirit.

CHAPTER 4

'Power to the people – or to the machine?'

Will there still be work for people
in the knowledge economy?

So what will be the role of people and work in the knowledge economy? Will it mirror what Rifkin predicted? In *The End of Work*,[1] he states that we shall soon see a division of the working population into two segments: those who know and those who don't know. But this now seems unlikely. Technology is going to develop to such an extent that skills to work with that technology won't be necessary any more. At least, not the sort of manual skills – and intelligence skills – that we know at the moment.

Machines are taking over

Today, machines are gradually infiltrating traditionally non-machine areas. The way ATMs are cropping up everywhere seems to prove this better than anything else. At first they appeared outside banks – as if still expecting people to 'go to the bank' for their money. Whether they went inside to get their money or stayed outside seemed irrelevant. Now ATMs are appearing elsewhere, at strategic places where people need money. A favoured location is outside supermarkets, as if stressing the fact that shopping costs money – and that people want access to it right at the place they are going to spend it. Although, of course, a supermarket which does not accept electronic payments would be difficult to find today.

These developments have had far-reaching consequences for employment in the banking world. Initially it was thought that people would object to doing business with a machine; now it is becoming increasingly obvious that in many situations they actually prefer it. After all, a machine offers anonymity, something people want when handling their

Electronic banking bad for jobs
A recent study carried out by Coopers & Lybrand on the consequences of electronic banking calculated a possible redundancy of bank employees of 35 per cent in the Netherlands, 44 per cent in Germany and 44 per cent in Belgium.[2]

financial affairs. Many banks are therefore increasing the tasks they give to a machine and reducing those handled by people. Wells & Fargo is actually reducing the number of branches and setting up small service kiosks in their place.[3] A reduction of human work – but an increase in intelligent efficiency.

Computers are making jobs routine

But then, the computer is making jobs that had previously been considered specialized almost routine. Even at the beginning of the nineties, giving advice about a mortgage was still considered a specialist job. Today, computers can almost instantly produce a comparative cost picture and make a recommendation based on little more than a few basic details. It is probable that very shortly an intelligent terminal will replace today's mortgage advice centre.

This implies that machines will not only threaten simple non-skilled repetitive jobs, but will soon also encroach into skilled areas. The white-collar sector is now just as threatened as the blue-collar one had been by the arrival of automation and robots.

Human creativity will be at the heart of the knowledge economy

Machines will increasingly act on brain-level complexity representing the 'hard side' of knowledge. Meanwhile people, professionals, will contribute to the 'soft side' with intuition, feeling and emotion. None the less, there are 'machine pirates' looming around the corner with what we call 'machine creativity'. That's when machines take on the ability to address the soft approach. As yet it is not well-advanced, but it does evoke a silent fear of people that their jobs will be replaced by machines.[6]

This fear may be founded in the fact that when the agricultural economy took over, machines took over manual work. In the knowledge economy, we are already seeing the beginnings of machines taking over mind work. And in research we can easily speculate about the coming of the quantum economy, where computers take over human work. But we'll take up that discussion in Chapter 6. You can then judge for yourself if this

The increase in artificial intelligence in the banking world
Artificial intelligence has already become an important factor in the financial world. Mortgage providers in the US such as Fannie Mae, Freddie Mac, Countryside, G.E. Capital, and United Guaranty all introduced artificial intelligence systems to handle the assessment and approval process for mortgages. Swiss Bank has introduced artificial intelligence to manage risk throughout their operations, from making decisions on individual transactions to control of portfolio diversity. In the field of credit cards, American Express uses artificial intelligence to automate authorization of purchases on their no-limit charge cards.[4] And Citibank uses a system that can predict currency trends, based on various past market conditions. Since the introduction of this system in 1992, Citibank has earned 25 per cent annual profits on currency trading – far more than it ever did when employing human traders.[5]

is a realistic perspective and if people's underlying fear is grounded.

Less time to adapt

The speed of innovation in the area of information technology is so rapid that companies – and society – are allowed increasingly less time to find ways of replacing jobs which have become redundant through IT innovation.[7] And this problem will grow: today, artificial intelligence is eating into the traditional white-collar skilled job area. In fact, more than 70 per cent of America's top 500 companies are already using AI applications in commerce, industry, and the professions.[8]

Other traditionally labour-intensive sectors are also being affected by automation. Agriculture – once the most important employment area of all – is now automated almost to a point where workers are no longer needed. In the US, twenty harvesting machines, each run by just three people, provide more than one half of all the carrots needed by the American market.[9] Sixty people producing more than half of the domestic demand for carrots in the US! And the same road is being followed in the industrial area causing Eckhart Wintzen, the famous IT guru to say, 'If we continue in this way, we will

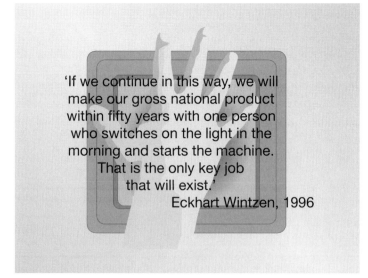

'If we continue in this way, we will make our gross national product within fifty years with one person who switches on the light in the morning and starts the machine. That is the only key job that will exist.'
Eckhart Wintzen, 1996

John Q. Public vs. John Q. System

make our gross national product within fifty years with one person who switches on the light in the morning and starts the machine. That is the only key job that will exist.'

Employment – a burning issue

Employment is, indeed, one of the biggest issues facing our modern manager. Larson & Zimney are quoted as saying, 'We don't need people. We need brains.'[10] And although on the surface this may offer some comfort, it is nevertheless debatable. The field of artificial intelligence is progressing rapidly by the day. Manual labour has already been largely taken over by the machine. The time is getting closer when the machine – the computer – would take over mental labour.

History has shown that this is a logical progress. Each new era in society has been heralded by a discontinuity: a period of upheaval brought about by a major destabilizing event such as the sudden introduction of a new technology (e.g. the Internet) that triggers new business opportunities. Such a discontinuity happened at the transition from the agricultural to the industrial era. This was the first man-machine discontinuity. Now the signs are all pointing to a second man-machine discontinuity – when computers take over routine mind work, and herald us into the knowledge economy. And it will not be too long before a third man-machine discontinuity heralds the transition from the knowledge economy to the quantum economy. A time when work carried out by humans will largely become machine work.

Knowledge is becoming 'routinized'

Part of this will be the routinization of knowledge. And that is already progressing. The second part, however, will require developing machine creativity to take over from human creativity. That is farther away. But with the progress of information and knowledge technology, it will not be too long before this is achieved. And that, indeed, will bring work into a totally new, even more challenging perspective.

The knowledge economy has caused people to redefine work. All work is considered to be knowledge work. But knowledge work which could be divided into a number of different categories, each of which demands a different level of education and training.

Low intelligence work

The first is no or low intelligence work. Generally this is work which is routine, but which still requires a high level of education in order to handle it. For example, a process operator in the chemical industry requires a high level of education – but the actual work he does is fairly routine and repetitive. It is done within prescribed boundaries and parameters. The operator may control the system, making sure it continues operating, but he or she doesn't actually add any knowledge. When the system is out of control, the operator must intervene – but then he has to follow the rules and regulations laid down in advance to cover such eventualities.

Pilots would most probably not take kindly to people saying that their work requires little or no intelligence. Yet this is the case. A pilot is highly trained and educated – but he is not expected to use his knowledge and skills other than in a control mode. A pilot is required to follow procedures even in the most dangerous of situations. His work – like most work in this first category – follows strict procedures. Of course, aeroplanes require nearly error-free operations all the time. During

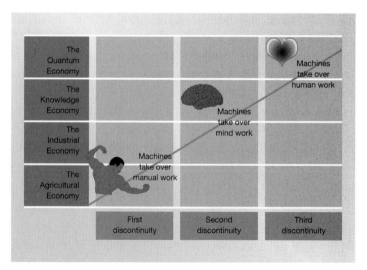

New technology precedes a new age

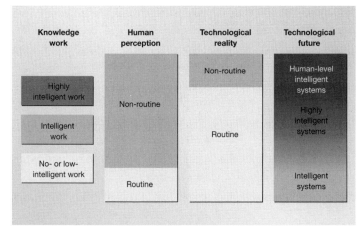

Knowledge work	Human perception	Technological reality	Technological future
Highly intelligent work	Non-routine	Non-routine	Human-level intelligent systems
Intelligent work		Routine	Highly intelligent systems
No- or low- intelligent work	Routine		Intelligent systems

Computers take the drudgery out of work

emergency situations, the collective mind[11] of the aeroplane cockpit crew will harness the knowledge gained and experience available to amply deal with the problem. But then we doubt whether passengers would appreciate a pilot who 'does things differently' at every landing!

Normal intelligence work

The second category could be considered 'normal' intelligence work. It is work in which the contents and routines differ from one day to the next. The best example of this is a manager. A manager knows within which boundaries he or she works, but is allowed freedom in deciding how actually to carry out the work within these boundaries. It differs from the lower category because it does not involve repetitive routine work, but instead demands a higher level of creativity.

High intelligence work

The third and final category is work of high intelligence, where high demands are made on people. For example a CEO. They are not only expected to be creative, but also to redesign the framework in which they operate. And because it is just as importantly, they have to have the ability to do that redesigning. To think outside the box and to work outside existing frameworks.

Computers take the drudgery out of work

'In the knowledge economy, we can distinguish three categories of knowledge work.'

'Machines are already fully accepted for low-intelligence knowledge work, such as a process operator in a chemical plant. And much of the work we see as intelligent is already routine from a technological view, and can be replaced by intelligent systems, such as a loan advisor at a bank. But what about the future?'

'We think that in the future, even the small portion of work we call highly intelligent knowledge work, non-routine and requires tacit capabilities of creativity, emotion, and intuition, will be handled by human level intelligent systems.'

What is routine?

Traditionally, routine work consists of highly repetitive, predictable activities. In human perception, only low intelligence work falls into the category 'routine'. Yet technological reality is different. For even most intelligent work is repetitive and routine if we can uncover the patterns. To uncover the patterns of routine work, we make use of 'problem-solving strategies'.[15] This means that, in the near future, intelligent and highly intelligent systems will be able to take over this kind of work. In the foreseeable future, human-level intelligent systems will be able to perform even non-routine highly intelligent work.

The great divide

There will, however, still be a divide – not between those who know and those who don't know. Rather, it will be a divide between what we could call the commodity group and the talent group. The key competence of the latter will be the ability to sell themselves to the highest bidder. They will be able to work and participate in jobs. They will have the practical ability to get people to hire them.

There is already evidence of a shift from what we can call cold technologies to warm ones such as face recognition, voice recognition, thermal fingerprints, retinal scans, DNA analysis and so on.

This shift in work will mean that the group of commodity workers will have to operate in a market which has totally new parameters. We are already seeing how companies are out-sourcing a lot of their activities. This was traditionally to suppliers in the neighbourhood for it made sense not to waste the savings made by using external suppliers on high transport bills. But now information technology has made the world a whole lot smaller. It is no longer necessary to outsource to somebody in your neighbourhood – or even to a company on the same continent. Companies will be able to insource exper-tise from literally everywhere. Especially the sort of expertise offered by those workers in the commodity group. A few years ago, KLM Royal Dutch Airlines considered taking steps to insource its ticketing operation – using a telephone link between Holland and New Delhi to handle all its ticketing that way. In the end, the plan came to nothing as society objected out of fear for massive job losses. Yet we must wonder whether this can ever be stopped. Spanish companies are already wrap-ping up Dutch Christmas presents, the Dutch-based temporary employment agency Randstad is recruiting British tradesmen, and call centres are being opened outside the country in which the company operates.[17]

Outsourcing and insourcing

Nor will it only be a case of companies outsourcing commod-ity workers. They may also decide to insource talent workers. For example, one of Holland's automobile parts manufactur-ers, has set up a technology centre in Eastern Europe and will be insourcing the high end of the production instead of out-sourcing the low end. There is a whole batch of Russian scientists who are offering their services via the Internet. And the same is true of software developers in Eastern Europe and India. The physical location of expertise is, thanks to the developments in information technology, becoming increas-ingly irrelevant.

Office without hierarchy

Thanks to electronic products and services such as fax, e-mail and GSM, people are no longer tied to one work area. Instead, a 'flashcart' is now being introduced, which can hold all the files, pens, and papers of one employee. When the employee has to be in the office, the 'flashcart' can be moved next to any desk that happens to be free at that time. The result is a space saving of 30 per cent. But even more important is that this new office setup is being used as a model for a more flexibly organized way of working which is much more concerned with results. 'Many people working here,' said a spokesperson for the Dutch Ministry of Social Affairs, who is piloting the project, 'have reached agreements with their superiors about the results they should achieve. They can then decide how best to achieve these results. A strict hierarchy is not in the least suitable for this method of working.'[18]

Talent becomes the core

'Physical strength powered the agricultural economy. In the industrial economy it was our ability to increase the speed of mechanized repetitive processes. Now, as the knowledge economy emerges, computers fundamentally reshape our working lives and increasingly capture repetitive mental tasks.'

'This means the economic driving force shifts from routine to talent. Companies focus on creativity and search for people who are resourceful in every sense of the word. This demands people who have the skill to deal with knowledge complexities and paradoxes and it could actually lead to a shortage of workers…even inspire the invention of Machine Creativity!'

Incidentally, all this demonstrates another important matter: that so-called third world economies will no longer be shut out of a global marketplace but will be able to participate fully in it. Whether they supply outsourcing commodity facilities or by being the physical location for production activities in which the high end is insourced.

The battle for talent has begun

All this, however, will require one essential ingredient to make it all happen: the talent group. They are the diametric opposite to the commodity group. They are highly talented and recognized as such. They are innovative – and are expected to be. They add value to a company by creating the difference. They will represent a lot of money, because they will be in a sellers' market. They will be able to pick and choose who they want to work for. And they may not always allow the sweet smell of money to be the decisive factor. They will attach as much importance to the job they are offered, to the people they work with and to the challenge that they will find in that job. And although their main competence may be their ability to earn

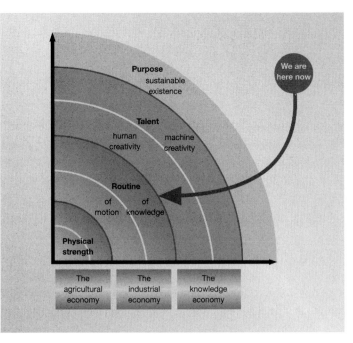

Talent becomes the core

and command large salaries, they may very well opt for less money and greater satisfaction.

So the debate will not be about whether there is a divide between those who know and those who don't know, but rather between those who can earn money and those who can't. Nor will it necessarily be the least educated who are automatically at risk in the changing world. They will not automatically be the ones who lose their jobs because of automation or the introduction of artificial intelligence systems. But, it may very well be their fate that if they do lose their jobs, they could have a difficult time finding new ones.[19] The jobs suitable for the lower educated will evaporate like dew in the morning sun.

This shift has already signalled the start of the race for talent. For people trying to find the right sort of professionals to handle the new work on offer. Professionals who can think for themselves, who can be creative. Professionals who do not simply focus on content knowledge, but also on human competencies, such as emotion, feeling and teamwork. Everything else can be automated, everything. And that makes the future not only challenging, but also rather forbidding. After all, if it were possible to automate the production of accountant's audits, then what would you have to do with all those accountants. Will they be out of work in two decades?

By the time our children go to work, the economy will have become an economy of creativity, which helps us to generate ideas, concepts, content and theories. Creativity based on human talent. That is where the opportunities will lie.

Already we see that there is an increasing need for work in the Netherlands – one of the strongest economies in Europe. The lack of personnel is already affecting some industries and, according to recent figures, this need will increase in the coming five years 'like an oil slick on water'.[20] At the same time, companies are seeing that knowledge is a critical factor for their success. And as a result, knowledge workers are becoming more powerful. They are, according to a degree research project undertaken by Han van Driest, demanding more say in company policy while expecting a greater degree of freedom for themselves.[21]

The softbots are coming

Experiments are taking place in Cambridge, England, with so-called intelligent agents. The researchers had created 22 'softbots', and had taught them to play football. They first told the two 'teams' that the object of the game was to get the ball into the opponent's goal at the other end of the field and sent them away to 'play'. And they played like two groups of school children – all chasing after the ball in a pack. So then some more of the rules were explained – for example, that one of the players should remain in the goal area to stop the ball when it was kicked, and then they were sent away to play again. Gradually, as more of the rules were explained, the teams began to develop their own strategies. They learned from their experiences. There is a website which makes use of softbots. It gets to know your likes and recommendations about music or films you might be interested in.

'If it is so difficult for
companies to find the
right people, how can
they attract employees?'
'We need to give them
what they need to
perform: time, support,
purpose and space.
Time to perform and to
reflect, but also time to
take leave. You know,
time to be and time to be
off?'
'Exactly, but that's
difficult in our 24-hour
economy. Furthermore,
we need to give them
support: access to
professional know-how,
the corporate memory
and to various ways to
transfer knowledge.'
'It sounds like creating a
community around the
professional to make
work easier' (see
Chapter 8).
'Then, we need to give
them personal space and
freedom to act like true
professionals - freedom
to be and to be different.'
'And finally, we need to
give them a clear
purpose that's in line with
their personal goals.'

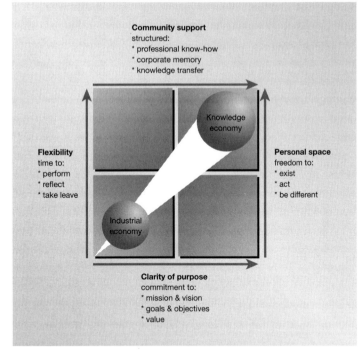

How companies attract employees

The dividing edge

This future economy is much nearer than many people think
possible. And when it arrives, the world will change more
rapidly, more drastically than ever before. This is not a totally
carefree picture – for how will the world cope with this new situation? Crime has been kept at a relatively constant level for
many years – but with employment chances decreasing, the
result might very well be a more violent, more criminal society.
Work is a stabilizing factor. And so too are emotions, sex. Give
this to machines, and the very fabric of society may become
unglued. With all the consequences that would imply.

But there is also another destabilizing factor: we cope with
new situations by trying to make them routine. What, then,
will happen when a significant part of our daily lives has been
turned into a routine? Will we be able to cope with new situations? Or will we become disorientated? Estranged from
ourselves? For that is a very real danger. Strength was the driving facilitator in the agricultural age – and this was the first

thing which people made routine. This continued in the industrial age, where Charlie Chaplin, in *Modern Times* sharply portrays motion becoming routine. Robots in car production repeated ever more complex movements with greater accuracy and dexterity than any human being could hope to copy.

And now that urge to make work routine is being continued into the knowledge economy. Motion has been turned even further into a routine, and now a start has been made to submitting knowledge to the same process. And that is where we are at the moment: on the dividing edge between what can be called the routinization of motion and the routinization of knowledge.

The interesting catch, which we are already seeing, is that most information and knowledge in organizations is purely routine. Not routine of motion, but routine of knowledge made possible by technology. This, however, is not the core competency of technology, but of talent! The more we make using information and knowledge a routine, the more time knowledge workers will have for creativity and innovation.

All this will mean that we shall constantly have to reassess our definition of work and the relationship between man and machine. That relationship will never be the same again.

CHAPTER 5

'Will global companies solve the paradox?'

*How mega-power companies lead
the way in the knowledge economy*

We are living in a time when global companies are becoming world-class role models for doing business in the new economy. Their sheer size, power, and turnover puts many of today's leading corporations ahead of the majority of the world's national economies. They are already so large that they have become economies unto themselves. Companies like General Motors, Ford, Itochu, Shell, Exxon and Mitsubishi all operate on a global scale. They don't operate in different local markets – they operate globally. In their operations they ignore national borders. They have made the world into one giant marketplace – or perhaps we can nowadays better call this a market space. And this has made them more powerful than we could ever have imagined.

This can be easily shown by looking at the sales of the world's largest 200 companies. Together their sales are greater than the economies of all the world's countries put together with the exception of the top nine economies. Just imagine that: 200 companies have a greater combined turnover than 182 countries together.[2] In economic terms, using data from 1995, Shell is as large as South Africa, General Motors is as large as Argentina, and the world's biggest corporation, Mitsubishi, is twice the size of Hong Kong and flexes more muscle than the GNP of 78 countries combined. Together, sales of the top ten companies in 1995 equalled the Gross National Product of 125 countries combined. Sales of the top 100 corporations account for more than 20 per cent of worldwide economic activity.[3]

'Many companies feel
the pressures for both
increasing globalization
and for increasing local
responsiveness. Those
that only go for
globalization become
global companies with
the same products and
formula all over the
world.'
'You can eat the same
hamburger and shop in
the same Bodyshop
almost everywhere.
Cities all over the world
look more and more
alike.'
'National companies that
have responded to those
local needs by mergers
and acquisitions become
conglomerates of many
different local companies,
often lacking the
economies of scale
global companies have.
Internationals have many
local companies which
are copies of the original,
not even hiring local staff
or managers.'
'So, becoming
transnational means a
true integration of global
presence and local
responsiveness?'
'Yes, and that's what you
see happening with
companies like Asea
Brown Bovery and
Philips.'

Rank 1996	Rank 1995			$ mil.
1	4	General Motors	U.S.	168,369.0
2	7	Ford Motor	U.S.	146,991.0
3	2	Mitsui	Japan	144,942.8
4	1	Mitsubishi	Japan	140,203.7
5	3	Itochu	Japan	135,542.1
6	10	Royal Dutch/Shell Group	UK/Neth.	128,174.5
7	6	Marubeni	Japan	124,026.9
8	9	Exxon	U.S.	119,434.0
9	5	Sumitomo	Japan	119,281.3
10	8	Toyota Motor	Japan	108,702.0

Today's Giants[1]

Becoming transnational

Global corporations, despite their seeming supremacy, are confronted with an enormous contradiction: how to be global and
act local. Expanding across borders doesn't necessarily mean a
company can export everything into a new situation. Of course,
there are companies that do that – think of McDonald's, who
sell exactly the same hamburger in New York and Moscow,
Amsterdam and Beijing. Think of Coca-Cola or Pepsi Cola. They
are all global companies – but none of them take much account
of local requirements. In fact, you could say they prove that
there are no local requirements in certain products. There is

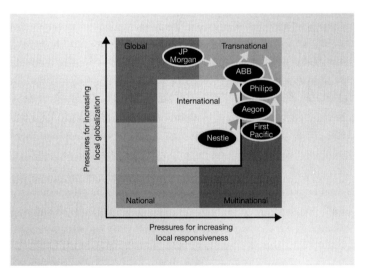

Strategies gravitating towards transnational

little need to be locally responsive – and so they concentrate on being globally integrated. It is a mentality that largely arises when the background of a company is in manufacturing or logistics, aiming for standardization of products and processes. And these companies are often the ones which decide to go global. But will this be sufficient for very much longer?

The use of the word 'global' is intentional for there are a number of different ways of operating in a world market. Global is one of them. And so, too, is multinational.

Multinationals

A multinational company – even one which operates in all parts of the world – is, however, different to a global one. It is generally a conglomeration of many different local companies – often acquired over the years to obtain a foothold in specific markets and the result is that frequently these local companies have a large degree of autonomy. They operate as if they are companies in their own right and only make use of their multi-national membership when it suits them. This can often lead to undesirable situations. Take, for example, one of the world's leading drum manufacturers. They have companies – both marketing and manufacturing units – throughout the world, and each has a large degree of independence. Each business unit – for that is the way they are organized – is fully responsive to local needs, but has little interaction with the other business units. It is very much that sort of 'go it alone' setup which is typical for a multinational. This can be very successful, for it means that local needs are fully satisfied. But it can also be a drawback, which is exactly what it proved to be for this drum manufacturer.

At a certain moment, two of its drum-manufacturing plants – one in Rotterdam and the other in Antwerp – both wanted to invest in a new lacquering line. Now this is the most expensive part of the drum-making process, and when the board received, virtually at the same time, two requests for such a facility, they wondered whether this was good commercial sense. After all, Rotterdam and Antwerp are only about 60 miles apart, and one lacquering line could easily handle the production of both plants. This was the sugges-

Typically multinational

Philips, the Dutch multinational electronics company, had to downsize enormously in the nineties and withdraw from several market areas. But even today it is still not focusing on the value at its knowledge – and with 15 000 inventions and over 60 000 patents to its name, it has an enormous knowledge content but more on achieving shareholder value. The biggest problem Philips faces – and one which many large companies also have to face – is that Philips doesn't know what Philips knows. Nobody has a true understanding of the value of the knowledge which is already present and available in the company. If this knowledge could be exploited and turned into market value, this could allow Philips to achieve new success in the knowledge economy.[4]

tion made to the local companies. But it was rejected out of hand by both plants. There was no way, they both argued, that the two different countries – each with their own cultures and customs – could possibly make use of the same lacquering plant.

It is exactly this sort of thinking that has resulted in such wide-scale problems for many multinationals, particularly those in fast-moving consumer goods. They have often developed into little more than a lose confederation of local companies, concentrating very much on the local market, and adapting their actions and market plans to meet the needs of the local market.

The good ones are extremely responsive to local needs – but the drawback is that they do not make the most of their mutual strengths. The local perspective can actually blind them to good business judgement.

Internationals

The third type of global company is perhaps best called 'international'. These companies do not really take into account local needs – but rather, offer a local company which is a copy of the original, generally national, company. A good example is the Banco de Bilbao in Spain. It is one of the country's most powerful banks but with minimal foreign presence. The strategy followed was to establish branches of the Spanish bank in all Spanish-speaking communities, starting in Latin America. The staff – both managers and employees – were all Spanish. They didn't use many local staff and they didn't hire any local managers. They were a Spanish bank – and all the employees had to be Spanish. In fact, the chairman once said, 'You only understand how a Spanish bank works by being Spanish.'

Transnationals

The last type of global company is the one which companies will have to emulate if they are to be really globally oriented and locally responsive. Such a company balances a maximum of local responsiveness with a maximum of global representation; the transnational. It does, in fact, what many managers consider impossible. The transnational is the conundrum of modern business reality.

The problem is, however, that two things are lagging behind: management development and knowledge management. Management development is needed to develop and control a company through a family of key people that are skilled and committed. Knowledge management is what ties these people together without physical barriers. It provides an architecture to work together on adding value without actually being together. Many managers might want their company to move from a national to a transnational company, but not if it means losing its identity. In other words, they don't want to lose control themselves. There are many examples of how this can affect good business sense. The Dutch-based ABN AMRO Bank is the largest foreign bank in the US – but there are no US citizens at top board level. Until recently the board of Philips was made up exclusively of Dutchmen – Dutchmen who had spent their entire working career with the company or who were relatives of the founding family. When DASA took over Fokker, the Dutch board made it very clear that the company would not accept a German as President and, as a last resort, accepted a Dutchman who had spent the last 25 years working in Germany. Yet when the ING Bank took over Barings in the wake of the Leason affair, the first thing they did was put 20 Dutchmen into key management and executive positions –

Develop senior management with the transnational MD wheel

'If we want our company to be truly transnational, we have to make sure we develop our management to behave transnationally. Senior managers can learn to make decisions with a transnational mind-set, postponing judgement and using a deep understanding of other cultures.'

'This will be difficult since every manager carries his local frame of mind with him.'

'But they don't need to learn all on their own. It's more important that the different nationalities are represented on senior positions, thereby forming a transnational team. And the decision process structures and systems of their organization should be designed in such a way that views from many cultures are used. Getting points of view from different sides. Listening to experts who work in the regions concerned.'

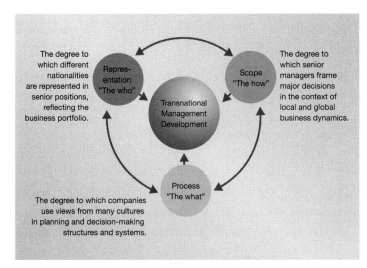

Develop senior management with the transnational MD wheel

and they were praised for doing it. Global by intent, national by management. This seems to be the watchword of many of today's emerging global companies.

Transnationals demand a new mind-set

This will have to change in the future. A transnational company will have to accept a totally new mind-set. The board will need to become a transnational board, reflecting the full diversity of nationalities within the company. But at the same time, that diversity will also have to reflect the portfolio of the business. A board will have to be a sort of matrix, reflecting nationalities on the one hand and the portfolio on the other.

All this will have three distinct effects on the way the board of a transnational company will have to approach its business.

First, it will have to frame its decisions in the context of both global and local business dynamics. Both will have to play an equally important role in the decision-making process. Not just global – not just local. But a balance between the two. And that's difficult because all companies have their roots in one country and their decisions tend to reflect what they think might be best for the home front. That's no longer true in our global marketplace. The home front is the world. And that requires an enormous swing in attitude and insight.

Second, board decisions will have to be based on views from different cultures. The knowledge a company has about these cultures will have to be put to better use than ever before.

And third, senior management will have to reflect the different nationalities of the countries in which its company is active.

Three challenges, but each more difficult to put into practice than ever before.

Transnationals demand global knowledge access

For a transnational company to be both globally oriented and locally responsive, it must have its knowledge act together. The complexity of decisions requires both an insight into worldwide trends and developments and in-depth knowledge of local situations and habits. So the decentralization of authority to local business outlets in the form of business units needs to be accompanied by a centralization of knowledge. Not in terms of physical centralization of brains or central planning and control of knowledge flows, but in terms of direction, accessibility and sharing. A centrally managed knowledge strategy guides and directs the creation and application of strategic knowledge, worldwide accessibility of available knowledge and a strong leadership supporting the sharing of vital knowledge.

Open to criticism

As companies grow larger and more influential, they also lay themselves open to public criticism. People are finding it increasingly difficult to tolerate large corporations who think only in terms of shareholder value. People and societies are increasingly expecting companies to act responsibly. They expect them to understand that, with the influence they have on the world economy, they must show they are prepared to accept the responsibility which automatically goes with authority. Social issues cannot be ignored by companies of this size. They can no longer justify plucking profits from small countries to pad the wallets of shareholders living elsewhere.

There is a steady increase in companies which are responding to this changing environment. Levi Strauss, for example, is no longer using exclusively natural cotton, but is replacing it with

The Brent Spar paradox

The Brent Spar paradox shows that companies can no longer make decisions separate from other related developments. The solution to sink the oilrig into the ocean may have been the best economically; it nevertheless proved socially unacceptable. Environmental concerns expressed by action groups such as Greenpeace and the ensuing public pressure eventually forced Shell to reconsider its decision and look for new solutions to the proposed sinking. As the company's president Herkströter said at a seminar in Amsterdam, 'Our technological background which told us that problems have to be identified, isolated and solved works well with technological problems, but isn't very useful when confronted with softer problems. Whereas technical problems may only have one solution, the search for solutions to social and political dilemmas generates many possible answers, and they're almost always a compromise.'[5]

Under pressure

Leading companies are becoming aware that their very scale and the impact this can have on society not only gives them enormous power, it also makes them ideal targets for public opinion. Public opinion swayed the mighty Shell in its decision on how to dispose of the Brent Spar. Companies such as Heineken are criticized extensively if they open or continue operations in countries seen as less politically correct. When a major environmental disaster such as the Exxon-Valdez occurs the company will face a bill of many billions of dollars not only for cleaning up the results of the accident but in repairing the damage done to the corporate reputation. It will take a long time before Exxon can enjoy the sort of trust that Levi Strauss is laying up for itself by its environmentally friendly core values.[6]

biologically grown cotton. They are also pioneering activities which will allow a gene to be introduced into the cotton to give it the right shade of indigo blue in the field. The result means that the whole production process of jeans is becoming increasingly environmentally friendly. Yet, significantly, for it shows how fundamental this sort of thinking is to Levi Strauss, jeans made of this new material are no more expensive than those produced using traditional fibres. Nor does Levi Strauss promote the fact of biologically grown cotton in their marketing. All this demonstrates that environmental issues are no longer part of a fashion trend but simply a necessity within our society.[7]

Shareholders supreme

This flies in the face of the attitude adopted by many companies that it is difficult, if not impossible, to reconcile the demands of shareholder profit and social responsibility. In fact, visionary companies – companies like 3M, Merck, Citicorp, Ford, Sony, Marriott, Walt Disney, and Johnson & Johnson – all value the positive impact they can have on society. Their performance proves that the seemingly irreconcilable not only can but must be reconciled. That is the challenge we all have to face. That is the way we can show we are committed to the future, rather than clinging desperately to the past.

In 1997, Arie de Geus, former head of strategic planning for Shell, wrote a now famous article entitled, 'The Living Company'.[8] In it he states that most corporations are underachievers and exploit only a small fraction of their potential. The premature failure of so many corporations is, according to de Geus, due to the fact that they base their strategies on economics rather than recognizing that a company is a community of people. A society unto itself. And if that society is to continue, then it must be prepared to develop. It must become a living company. 'The living company,' concludes de Geus, 'stands a chance of living longer.' This seems very much in line with the ideas of Collins and Porras who, in their book *Built to last*, wrote that companies that are value focused and are creative in finding solutions are adaptable to change. 'They see it,' they wrote, 'as a challenge to find pragmatic solutions and behave consistently with their core values.'[9]

No place to hide

Of course, the development and spread of information technology means that companies can no longer keep hidden things they would rather not have known to the public. In the 1960s, the Dalkon Shield was introduced in a flawed version, and the company managed to keep this from the public for six years. In the 1990s, when Intel introduced the Pentium Pro processor, the design fault was known worldwide within six weeks[10] thanks to the Internet.

What about employment?

Although global companies are impacting society more than ever before, this is not supported by figures from other areas. Although in 1995 the top 100 companies accounted for a little over 20 per cent of the world's economy,[11] they employed less than 0.5 per cent of the world's workforce, assuming the total workforce in the world is a little over 2 billion. Less than one half of one per cent of the world's workforce produces more than 20 per cent of the world's sales. What's more, two-thirds of the world's population can never hope for a job in one of these companies, nor they will never be able to afford to buy their products.[12] This imbalance may no longer be tolerated by society. In 1955, although sales of the top 100 corporations plummeted to $5.5 trillion and profits soared to $113 billion, their impact on employment stayed largely the same.[13]

Yet the problem is that this imbalance will be compounded even further. With the rise of the knowledge worker and the decline of the industrial worker brought about by the transition to the knowledge economy, the trend is towards fewer jobs, not more. In addition, there is a trend which reverses the traditional job security which is at the foundation of many countries' economies. No job is safe. Employment is no longer guaranteed. Between 1979 and 1992, the largest US industrial corporations cut a total of 4.4 million workers from their payrolls.[14]

Importance of national states declines

Social issues are increasingly becoming the responsibility of global corporations. As their importance increases, so the importance of national states declines. Finance, employment, and knowledge are all areas being managed now by corporations – and this leaves less manoeuvring space for national governments to influence working conditions and to provide a sustainable environment. The power of corporations over national states will only further increase: if a corporation does not agree with rules and regulations proposed by a national state, it can simply move its operations elsewhere. It is therefore very doubtful whether national states will retain the ability to enforce social and ecological policies. What's more, the wealth of nations could be drained by corporations eager to appease shareholders if companies are determined to stick to their desire to put shareholder value before social responsibility. If they do continue to do this, then our future living and working climate is firmly in their hands.

Global corporations will be the first to be faced with the new rules emerging in the knowledge economy. They will become world-class models, and will take their position as leaders more seriously than ever before. Their leading position, however, will mean that they will be carefully watched by other companies to make sure they toe the line expected of them.

CHAPTER 6

'No time to rest'

How the knowledge economy will be
superseded by the quantum economy

Today we are living in a transition period. A transition period between the last days of the industrial economy and the first of the knowledge economy. We are moving from automating motion to automating knowledge: machines will take over such work. The service industry is becoming the focal point of our attention. Employment in that area is increasing, while in virtually every other area it is decreasing.

Yet the changes we are witnessing as we move from the industrial economy to the knowledge economy are only a foretaste of the radical change we shall all be facing when the knowledge economy gives way to the quantum economy. Representing the far side of our knowledge economy, quantum computing allows us to resolve conflicting paradoxical business issues with meaningful knowledge. This results in the 'best of all worlds' for shareholders, stakeholders and society. It will start, as is generally the case in each major change from one economy to another, by affecting the very top of the workforce and then filtering down to other parts of labour.

The high end of the knowledge economy

On paper it always looks so neat to show how one economy stopped as another started; how the industrial economy took over from the agricultural economy. And how the knowledge economy took over from the industrial economy. Yet in reality, there is no definite dividing line between the one economy and the next. It is a more gradual, evolutionary process.

At the moment the knowledge economy is making itself felt by taking over the top end of the industrial economy. But that does not mean that the industrial economy has suddenly ceased to exist. We are still right in the middle of it and would most probably remain in some form of industrial economy for the foreseeable future. But the difference would be that knowledge would play an increasingly important role, first at the top end of the industrial economy, and then gradually filtering down until it affects all levels. And the same will happen as the knowledge economy moves into the quantum economy: the quantum economy would first be felt at the top end of the knowledge economy and gradually work downwards, filtering through to the very lowest level. And undoubtedly, by that time, a new economy could very well emerge which again would start at the top of the quantum economy and filter downwards. It is a perpetual motion which is kept moving by its own momentum.

What will happen is that societal and business issues will get so complex that new technology is needed for businesses and societies to achieve sustainable existence. Societal issues will range from shortages of water and energy to environmental pollution. Future business issues will focus on paradoxes: having to have both a positive impact on shareholders *and* on society, making decisions from both a domestic *and* a global perspective, in organizations that are both built to compete *and* built to last, with people that are accustomed to both single *and* multi-reality decision making.

The Tyranny of OR

Companies with vision no longer allow themselves to be restricted by what Collins and Porras called the 'Tyranny of the OR'.[1]

The Tyranny of OR implies a rational view which does not easily accept a paradox and cannot live with two seemingly contradictory forces or ideas at the same time. The OR thinking mode pushes people to believe that the solution must be A OR B. It cannot possibly be both. Successful companies, however, which have broken free of the tyranny of OR know that often the solution can be A *and* B. It is an ability to embrace extremes, to resolve seeming contradictions. Instead of finding that they are forced to choose – to make an OR decision – they decide to make an 'and' decision, doing both things at once. It is not a question of balancing one with the other. It is simply a matter of doing both of them. And doing both of them very well indeed.[2]

For example, in the quantum economy, companies will have to move from being suspected to being respected. Ecologically-friendly products will not need a special label, for consumers will expect a company to participate to the full in environmentally-friendly practices, products, and production methods. Indeed, consumers may very well demand a label for products which are not produced in an ecologically-friendly manner! Decision making will not be able to exist with strict rules and patterns; it will demand creative, lateral thinking. Creative solutions will be expected. Traditional thinking will be scorned. We will 'routinely' be asked to go outside the box, to look beyond the logical, to the seemingly illogical solution. We will be asked to use our brains not in a machine-like, ordered fashion, but in a capricious way that is only possible, at the moment, with a human brain.

An immediate result will be that decision will be taken with the particiaption of groups outside the board of the company concerned. Society at all layers will become involved in running corporations. Not simply an obligatory works council, but rather groups which will actually be pro-actively involved in the expected consequences of decisions.

Decision making more complex

All this means that corporate decision making not going to get any easier – but will become complex increasingly. So complex and so mind-shattering, in fact that many people will wonder whether it can actually be handled by human beings.

Today, the corporate decision-making processes are much more narrow: they are aimed at building companies which can compete and which can deliver shareholder value in a rapidly changing and globally domestic market. The decisions revolve around constantly recurring issues such as speed, surprise, flexibility to business change, and the agility to handle such change.

Society's character	...on life	...on the economy	...on society	...on values	...on management abilities	...on work	...on the essence of life	...on children
The quantum economy	Sustainable existence	Meaningful knowledge (wisdom)	Globally domestic	Shared universal values	Providing purpose (sense-making)	Machine-machine	The eternal	You must be better
The knowledge economy	Change	Knowledge	Multi-domestic	Shared community values	Providing talent (creativity)	Man-machine	The spirit	You must know better
The industrial economy	Progress/growth	Goods products	Domestic	The individual	Providing stability (routine)	Man-man	The religion	You must learn better
The agricultural economy	Salvation	Food	Local	The community	Providing strength (physical)	Man-animal	The church	You must eat better

People's orientation →

People and societies matter most in the future

The decision-making process is analytical, based on facts and involves straightforward trade-offs aimed at a single thing: making profit. It is making companies ruthless, making them go to extremes, making them adopt killer strategies, making them take risks, making them break rules and making them shy away from nothing which could gain them a competitive advantage.

Decision making, however, will move (or be pushed?) from dealing with a single reality to dealing with multiple realities. It will mean that every single decision will be based on a relationship, an interconnectivity to a score of issues worldwide, and will have to take into account the repercussions any decision may have on local and global affairs.

Information becomes meaningful knowledge

This is illustrated by the way we handle information. In the industrial economy, information technology was used to provide information while people were needed to make sense of it. This will change in the knowledge economy. We will still be bombarded with information – but it will actually have become knowledge. Through knowledge technology,

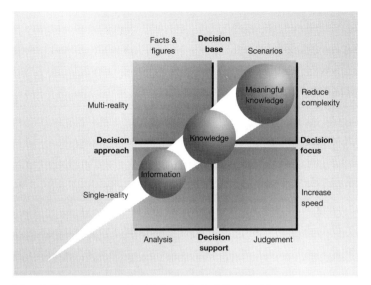

More information or valuable knowledge? You decide

machines will have already largely made sense of it for us. But from a fairly limited perspective. Too limited to help reduce the complexity facing a manager required to reach a decision in the quantum economy. Managers will not just need knowledge – they will need meaningful knowledge. And that is a crucial distinction. Meaningful knowledge is not fact driven, but scenario driven. It isn't the result of a deep analysis but, rather, of intuition. It doesn't deal with evolutionary and progressive change, but with paradoxical change. And it isn't rational – it's emotional.

More information or valuable knowledge? You decide

'Meaningful knowledge is the most important asset for any company wishing to cope with complexity. It allows multiple-reality decision making in business situations where paradoxes prevail and human-level decision making falls short.'

'In the Industrial Age, people used information technology to provide information. People made sense of it. But this will give way to knowledge technology, in which machines will make some sense of information.'

'Agreed. And there's a new technology called quantum technology. It will decrease complexity to a level where effective human decision making can take place, allowing companies to make decisions that have a positive impact on society and shareholders, that are globally domestic in companies that are built to last.'

'That's a good thing, because executive decision making will become so difficult, paradoxical and complex that the knowledge complexity level required to handle it will go beyond our human potential.'

'As Sherry Turkle wrote, "Meaningful knowledge is needed that makes it possible to decide effectively, to make a successful whole from complex, interrelated, dynamically changing, and sometimes even conflicting parts".'[3]

The quantum economy will demand a complete U-turn from managers who survive positively to it. Even today, companies are realizing that managers will need to have something of everything in order to provide added value to their employer. Increasingly comprehensive demands are being made on prospective employees as well.

It is here that computer technology based on quantum theoretical principles will play an enabling role in providing a way of solving such complex, paradoxical problems. The commercial availability of such systems will push the economy rapidly into the quantum age. An age in which it will be possible – in fact imperative – to provide answers to complex issues which take into account the seemingly contradictory needs of society on the one hand and shareholders and stakeholders on the other.

The power of technology

As with any new economy, the trigger will be technology. The role of technology will become so powerful it will fundamentally shake the way we look at ourselves. This, however, is not new. We have seen it several times. According to the MIT philosopher Mazlish,[4] the first time was when Copernicus found out the earth was not the centre of the universe. The second time was when Darwin found out we are descended from apes. When Freud said there is more to humans than what we see at first glance, that we have inner forces that sometimes go beyond our control, mankind was again shaken to the core. It happened again in the forties when Alan Turing laid the basis for the modern computer.

Now we are on the edge of what could turn out to be another discontinuity in the relationship between man and his environment: a significant shift in the relationship between man and machine (the computer); and this time it may very well turn out in favour of the machine. But with this important difference: for the first time, a technology may help us cope with the complexity it causes because, for the first time, we might be able to emulate human-level complexity.

The main thrust of computer technology so far has been to emulate brain level complexity by increasing the storage capacity and the processing speed of the computer. The main

The 4th discontinuity

underlying question has been: 'does a human being have some sort of algorithm we can emulate?' Although many scientists say this is not the case, some of them believe it is. One of these is Frank J. Tipler who regards a human being as nothing more than a particular type of machine, the human brain as nothing more than an information processing device, the human soul as nothing more than a program run on a computer called the brain.[5]

Computers with brain level complexity

Let's assume for the moment that the brain does have an algorithm, only a very large one. Bekenstein has calculated that human beings can be in one of $(10^{10})^{45}$ states at most (its 'storage capacity' in bits), and can undergo at most 4×10^{53} changes of state a second (its 'processing speed' in flops [floating point operations a second]). If we compare this with the current state of developments in computer technology, that technology still has a long way to go.

A more positive picture emerges when we only look at the human brain. Measurements by neurophysiologists indicate that the actual amount of information stored by the brain is between 10^{13} and 10^{16} bits for children and between 10^{14} and 10^{17} bits for adults.[6] Notice how little the difference is. Computers that can code 10^{15} bits are already available, so speed is the real barrier to emulating the brain.[7] Tipler estimates that 10 teraflops would be required to simulate the entire brain (a teraflop being 10^{12} flops). In 1986 the fastest supercomputer then available had a speed of one gigaflop (10^9

Conventional computing has its limits

'People have been trying to use conventional computing to reach human-level complexity with a computer that can deal with non-brain-like processes: feelings, intuition, and the ability to deal with paradoxes.'

'Yes – but these efforts have only been marginally successful. Even alternative methods of computing will probably not get us there.'

'I know. But Moravec, the famous MIT technology forecaster, expects computers to reach brain-level computing by the year 2030. Expectations are now being revised to the year 2015.'

'Perhaps by using the experimental quantum computing method, which offers the promise of achieving the human-level complexity needed in the quantum economy. Infinite data may be stored on atoms and retrieved through nuclear magnetic resonance. Computers may enter a non-physical world, allowing businesses to embrace the Paradox Paradigm.'

'That will mean that companies can then turn paradoxical quandaries into valuable decisions, bridging the complexity of an anytime, anywhere, anyway economy. And offer options and solutions to create the best of both worlds.'

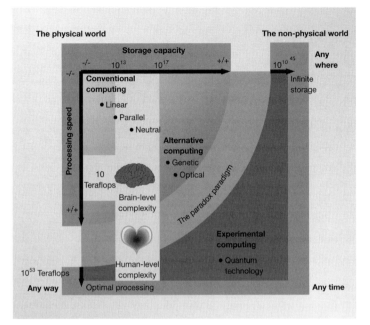

Conventional computing has its limits

flops). In 1990 it had reached 10 gigaflops and in 1992 100 gigaflops. Like a number of others, Tipler predicts that we will see computers with brain level information processing capacity by the end of the twentieth century.[8] By the year 2030 Moravec expects this computer to be available at current personal computer prices of a few thousand dollars.

So we will see computers that can think faster than a human brain by the end of the century. That's perfect for helping us cope with speed as the shift from the industrial to the knowledge economy requires us to do. But the quantum economy demands that we can deal with complexity, with change that is no longer linear but paradoxical.

Towards human-level complexity

If we need to cope with complexity, we need to use more than our brain capacities. We need to be able to handle paradoxes and for that we also need intuition, feeling and emotion. Only these help us combine paradoxes which appear to be irreconcilable, to make and/and instead of either/or decisions. Computers that help us with this will need to have more than just brain-level complexity, they must reach near human-level complexity.

Conventional forms of computing will never be able to do that. Parallel or neural computing are perfect for increasing speed but will not get us anywhere near human-level complexity. Alternatives computing, like genetic or optical computing won't do the job either. These computers can be considered as speeded up abacuses.[9] There is a new technology coming up, although still at a very experimental stage, called the quantum computer.

Cueing the qubits

The quantum computer stores its data on atoms and – because there is almost an infinite number of atoms in the universe – has therefore almost an infinite storage capacity. A second advantage is that the computer is subjected to the rules of quantum physics and therefore uses the quantum combination of states. A classic computer stores and shuffles binary numbers (the digits 1 and 0 that resemble 'on' and 'off' positions); the switches in a quantum computer can be 'on' and 'off' simultaneously which is a paradox in itself.[11] A computer that uses paradoxes for its calculations must be able to help us handle our own paradoxes.

Source: Vincent Icke, 1997

Paradoxes: are they real or aren't they?

Paradoxes: are they or aren't they?

'We have all probably experienced a paradox in action. At night, when you look out of your window, you see your reflection. But a passer-by saw you.

Quantum computing takes advantage of an atom being in two states at the same time. It's called the super-position of atoms. As strange as it may seem, the paradox occurs only when we observe it.'[10]

Until recently there was one problem with the experiments so far: the information stored on atoms could not be read again because the reading itself upset the delicate balance. This problem has just been solved using nuclear magnetic resonance (NMR) spectroscopy. Instead of putting information on a single atom, Dr Gershenfeld and his colleague, Isaac Chuang of Los Alamos National Laboratory in New Mexico, stored their information in molecules. Molecules consist of atoms and the nuclei of atoms act like tiny magnets. These magnets can point up or down which can be the equivalent of 'on' and 'off'. With NMR one can measure which way most of the molecules point. If the reading itself upsets some of the atoms, the majority would still point in the right direction.[12]

Getting the right answer out of a cup of coffee

The final problem was to get the right answer out of the quantum computer. Because of the paradoxical positions of the switches in the computer, lots of quantum computers usually give lots of different answers, so a corrective calculation is needed. Dr Gershenfeld and Dr Chuang found out that the quantum computer can perform this calculation by itself. Using the carbon atoms in a molecule called alanine, they have built a computer that can add one and one and give the result. If they start using more complex molecules – according to *The Economist,* if they start using more complex molecules, the caffeine in a cup of coffee is a good candidate[13] – they hope to make a 10-qubit device which could divide the number 15 into its factors.[14]

Why might quantum computing help reduce complexity?

Why would quantum computing help to solve the paradoxical, societal and business problems of the future? The answer to this is probably the most speculative content of this book since the technology is still highly experimental. The answer lies in the fact that the human brain has been so conditioned that it can only appreciate a limited degree of complexity.

One of the best examples of this is still the mystery of 'light'. This has characteristics of both matter (particles) and waves.

Since our brain is conditioned to think in terms of 'either/or', it is almost impossible for us to understand that light is both a wave phenomenon and a particle phenomenon. Or take for that matter, the issues of 'what was there before the Big Bang?' It is simply beyond our comprehension that a primordial explosion arose out of nothing, giving birth to matter, space and time. Either there is time, space and matter or there isn't.

Quantum computers will probably be able to calculate in terms of 'and/and'. The fact that the paradoxes of quantum physics are at the foundation of its calculating powers may make it possible to use the quantum computer to find solutions to paradoxical problems. The computer can then be used to make 'and/and' calculations with paradoxical knowledge complexity, which are completely incomprehensible to the human mind, and then present the results of these calculations in terms of 'either/or' decisions which are much more understandable for human beings. The difference is that these solutions will have been built on much firmer foundations. By repeating this process several times, increasingly meaningful knowledge can be obtained.

Perform a 'quantum' experiment

'A simple experiment using quantum physics explains why the quantum paradox is true. When we shine light at a 50/50 mirror, classical physical understanding is that 50 per cent of the light will go through the mirror and 50 per cent will be reflected. What actually happens is that 100 per cent goes through the mirror and 100 per cent is reflected. When researchers used conventional mirrors to capture both the reflected light and the light going through, the total reflection of light came back to 100 per cent – not 200 per cent as we might expect. The quantum paradox is proven.'

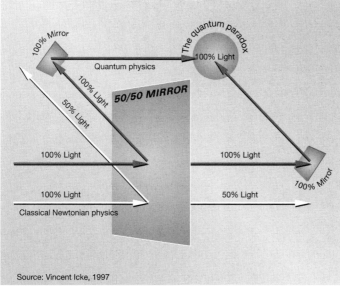

Source: Vincent Icke, 1997

Perform a 'quantum' experiment

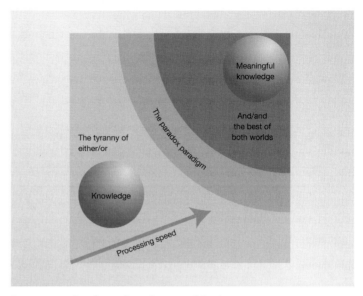

Quantum technology triumphs over either/or

Why quantum computing could lead to a fundamental change

But if quantum computing can help solve paradoxical social problems, will that be so substantial that we can talk of a fundamental shift of both society and economy? Optimists assume that social problems are not paradoxical in themselves but become paradoxical because of the way ideology translates them. This ideology pollutes carefully balanced human judgements. Quantum computing can help make rational assessments of an almost infinite complexity which will leave no place for ideology. In the multi-reality decision making, ideology is being replaced with meaningful knowledge. Meaningful knowledge will enable us to reach sustainable existence in a global world. This means a total shift towards a quantum economy based on meaning.

Realists believe in the unknown possibilities of new technology, including quantum technology. Such technology, according to them, will be able to reduce the knowledge complexity of social problems on a world scale to such a degree that ideology will have less hold on them. The underlying idea is that the more we know about a problem, the less we need ideology. Of course, ideology will *never* disappear completely.

After all, we can always differ in our opinions about fundamental norms and values. And so, realists expect an improvement thanks to quantum technology, although radical than the improvements expected by the optimists.

Pessimists believe in the law of perpetual misery: each new technology will cause as many problems as it solves. In their eyes, the quantum economy will never be a Brave New World.

What has this to do with value-based knowledge management?

We should remember that none of this may happen as the technology involved is still largely experimental; it is, however, developing rapidly. The only thing we do know for sure is that after the knowledge economy, a new economy will appear at the horizon. But what has all this got to do with value-based knowledge management?

Value-based knowledge management is needed to prepare ourselves for any new economy that is based on knowledge. It gives us the ability to control and nurture the fourth production factor: knowledge. It ensures that all employees within an organization are focused on the importance of knowledge as a value-adding factor. This will create the conditions for new technologies – knowledge or quantum technology – which will enable us to take an important step forward in multi-reality decisions.

To reach the top end of the knowledge economy, companies need to pass a threshold. Value-based knowledge management helps them to pass it. Without value-based knowledge management, the introduction of knowledge technology is not as productive as it could otherwise be. Because it balances both operational and strategic knowledge management, value-based knowledge management helps to generate value with knowledge. Without value-based knowledge management, the introduction of quantum technology is useless. It prepares the groundwork that enables us to generate meaningful knowledge and solve paradoxical societal and business issues.

But remember, most companies are still only at the stage of experimenting with operational knowledge management. Only

Towards global governance
In politics, the movement which believes in the possibility of a rational solution to paradoxical social problems is evident in supporters of a 'world parliament'. They see the European Parliament and the United Nations as predecessors of a single institution that will be capable of using rational decision making to achieve global governance.

a few are really skilled at it; some of which are used as examples in this book. Only a few of these companies are able to combine operational knowledge management with strategic knowledge management to become a true value-adding knowledge company. So most companies still have a long way to go.

PART THREE

HOW DO WE APPROACH VALUE-BASED KNOWLEDGE MANAGEMENT?

CHAPTER 7

'Smart strategies'

*How companies should use every eye
and ear to create mega opportunities*

As the world in which we operate moves from the industrial economy into the knowledge economy, we must realize that unless we radically change our way of operating, we will simply have no chance of lasting success in this rapidly changing business environment. This means we must be prepared to stop operating in the ways we found effective in the industrial economy and adopt new approaches which are better suited to the new situation.

One of the reasons value-based knowledge management offers a positive perspective for management and employees is its ability to create new and multiple strategies on a continuous basis.

This may sound simple, yet it demands a radical break from the obsolete production-oriented mind-set. Having the CEO devise a strategy once every four years and supporting this with tactical business plans for each unit may have been suitable when we were operating in fairly calm and predictable conditions; now that we have been thrust into turbulent seas, we have to be prepared to adapt quickly and constantly as new challenges emerge, using all the eyes, ears, and knowledge we can mobilize.

So what makes smart strategies different to traditional ones?

Well, first of all, there is never one single smart strategy. There must always be more. One is never enough, because the risk of failure is just too large. It is good to hedge your bets, and ensure that you have complementary strategies which support you without being totally dependent on each other.

Second, smart strategies are always based on a company's unique knowledge. The knowledge which is unique to your

At Sony and Sharp, they ensure that their technicians and marketing specialists are fully informed about the companies' competencies. Any employee who has an idea for a new product can request access to these competencies. If management is convinced of the potential of the idea, it forms a team which has the right to involve the very best people from anywhere in the world. Sharp uses urgency project teams for which the very best competency resources in the company are reserved. Sony makes use of gold badge teams. By reserving the best competency resources in the company for these gold badge teams at Sony and urgency project teams at Sharp, these companies ensure they stay focused on growth opportunities.[3]

company – whether new knowledge, or existing knowledge. In the knowledge economy, a company that possesses valuable knowledge can gain a temporary competitive advantage. If, in addition, competing companies face a cost disadvantage in trying to emulate this knowledge resource, organizations with these unique, company-specific capabilities can obtain sustainable competitive advantage.

As companies come to realize the importance of knowledge, so some are entering into alliances with each other, hoping to expand the knowledge resources they can have at their disposal. Motorola, IBM and Apple have formed an alliance to create a new design of computers based on semiconductors. The alliance was very much directed at creating knowledge which would be of benefit to each of the participants.[1] In a more industrial area, General Motors entered into an alliance with Toyota under the name Nummi. The aim was to help GM learn about Toyota's unique manufacturing methods.[2]

Third, in traditional thinking about strategies, the word 'strategy' is used as a noun. It was a thing. In smart strategies, it is a verb. 'I strategize, you strategize, we strategize.' And we do it actively and continuously. A strategy is not something which is done once then put into a cupboard; it is a frame of mind which ensures we discard old, faded strategies, and replace them with new ones. It ensures that we are on a constant lookout for new opportunities.

And fourth, smart strategies are not devised in isolation: they involve everybody. Not just managers, not just employees but also vendors, customers, and even competitors. Only if we do this can we be sure that there is sufficient support to make things happen. At Chrysler they have involved their vendors in a project aimed at reducing costs. Each supplier is asked to analyze its internal process to see what measures can be taken to reduce component costs without reducing quality. In addition, vendors are involved at an early stage in the design so that they can make a contribution from their own competency. The result has been savings totaling several billion dollars.[4]

Wonder glue

Smart strategies are an essential cohesive factor in keeping the elements of the value-adding knowledge company together.

First, the strategies connect the company's goals to their professionals by giving them a clear sense of purpose. These professionals feel committed to creating and sharing knowledge since they see this as a meaningful way to contribute to company success. As we will see in the next chapter, smart organizations provide a supportive framework for these professionals to be able to do this in a truly value-adding manner.

Thus, in the virtual market-space, smart strategies offer new opportunities that help focus the minds of a company professionals and give them exciting opportunities for realizing new business opportunities. In today's world, it's no longer a question of doing things better; we have to do the right things, anytime, anyway, anywhere.

Second, smart strategies help create, structure and harvest company knowledge. Once we know where we want to go and in what area of expertise our new opportunities can be found, we have a much clearer idea of what knowledge needs to be created and structured. We also have some idea how it can be best harvested to add value to our company. If we understand this – and it is a very crucial point indeed – we can avoid building up knowledge for knowledge's sake. We must create an important tool, a knowledgemap, to help us develop knowledge which is appropriate for our needs.

Don't solve problems

'Wasting time and being inefficient are the way to discovery. In the network economy, productivity is not our bottleneck. Our ability to solve our social and economic problems will be limited primarily by our lack of imagination in seizing opportunities rather than in trying to optimize solutions... When you are solving problems you are investing in your weaknesses; when you are seeking opportunities, you are banking on the network.'
Kevin Kelly[5]

Organizational architecture

The organizational architecture is ... 'the collection of formal structures and informal relationships that give their company a particular feel and functionally.'
Nadler and Tushman[6]

Make the connection think smart

'Smart strategies are the glue which hold the value-adding knowledge company together.'
'So what are they?'
'Well, they're essential for creating new market opportunities. For helping create, structure and harvest company knowledge. For giving a sense of purpose to knowledge workers. And the driving force behind the companies' organizational design.'

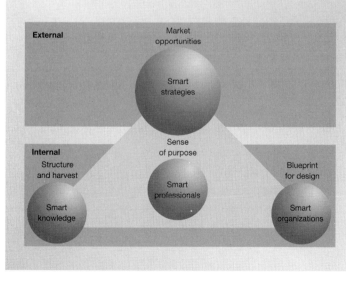

Make the connection think smart

Third, knowledge professionals are not the easiest people to manage and it is vital for a company to find out exactly what makes them tick. One thing is certain: knowledge professionals will run fastest and farthest for a company that has a clear idea of where it is going one that has a vision which most closely parallels the personal plans of the professional. If the company and the professional click, this can result in a formidable weapon. If they do not, then action has to be taken. But what? We could try to change the professionals' focus – but that rarely works. We could offer them a higher salary – but that rarely works either. We are left with two options: either we make our company vision and strategy much clearer, much better defined; or we agree to part company.

And fourth, smart strategies are the driving force behind a company's organizational design. If we have clearly defined our vision and know what strategies our company has to deliver its products and services, we can think about defining the organization which will get the best out of our people and help them reach our goals. This is the right way to go about things. Once we know this, we can start answering other key questions. What operational processes have to be in place? How can we organize people around these processes? What are our main strategic processes – and can we organize the headoffice around them? Is it useful to make a distinction between front office and back office? Do we need competence centres so that we can organize our people around knowledge domains?

Responding both internally and externally

But smart strategies are more than glue. They are also the engine which keeps the company moving. Which ensures that the company is constantly fuelled with enough energy to move forward. And they continuously have to reflect necessity to take into account external market forces – the market – and internal forces. Three essential ingredients are required: vision, mission and multiple strategies.

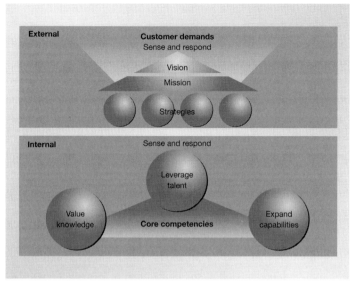

Start your value-creating engines

The importance of vision

Vision has lost a lot of credibility because of its overuse in management literature. We could almost be forgiven for thinking that all we have to do is design a vision of the future – and the rest will take care of itself. The problem is, the future doesn't exist. At least, not one single, immutable future. So we cannot predict it. What we need to do is develop a clear idea of the important characteristics of the future in which we would like to operate. This means that we have to look at trends which can affect our world and our business.[7] Are we, for example, going to be faced with the same disruption of the business chain that is taking place in the world of insurance, where insurers are now approaching customers directly rather than relying on a network of agents? Is our added value as a temporary employment agency getting less because of the way the Internet is being used to offer jobs? Will people start to work from home rather than spending half a day in traffic jams? And if these trends combine, what discontinuities can we see for our business and our company's present position? – perhaps most importantly – if we look at a possible future scenario, what sort of opportunities are presented to us? And what will we have to do to make the most of those opportunities?

Start your value creating engines

'Companies should begin leveraging their knowledge by providing a clear vision of the future and letting their people own it. They should define their mission, decide what their main purpose is and the kind of organization they want to be, and then determine the strategies that their company should follow to add value to the marketplace and the society in which it thrives.'

'Externally, market strategies sense and respond to both current and future demands.'

'Yes, and internally, smart strategies uncover a cache of brilliant gems – a company's own competencies. This priceless combination includes a constant source of potential as well as existing dynamic talent, valuable knowledge, and organizational capabilities. All are virtually limitless when they continue to value, leverage and expand them.'

Such a vision of a possible future can be an enormous source of energy and enthusiasm and provide an impulse to seek new opportunities. It will do something more: it will help us think the unthinkable.

Stating our mission

If we learn to think the unthinkable, there is little that can stop us from becoming successful. But there is a danger that we might find ourselves so far removed from reality that we need something to bring us down to earth, back to reality. The reality of what we want our company to be in this new and possible future that is mapping out in front of us.

'Mission statement' is another of those over-used terms which have lost their meaning. This is largely due to the fact that many people think a mission statement is an end in itself. The true value of a mission statement often lies in the discussion which leads to its creation. It is an ideal opportunity for everyone to reassess the company's strengths and weaknesses, its strategies and its stated vision. It can lead to a fuller understanding of why we do things the way we do and what value we finally add for our customers.

Nevertheless, a mission statement can be a powerful rallying point for any company. At least if it meets a number of criteria.

- It should express to the environment the added value of our company.
- It should assume a vision of the world around us.
- It should be written by management and members of the organization.

But ...

- A mission statement is not independent of time or circumstances.
- It should be reassessed and revised at regular intervals.

A successful mission statement is one which captures the imagination of all the stakeholders in the company – employees, suppliers, shareholders, and customers. To do this it needs to contain a certain number of elements.

- It should make clear the business in which our company is and will be involved.
- It should state what customer focus our company has.
- It should say what ambition we have.
- It should state how we plan to achieve that ambition.

A single strategy is not enough

In today's rapidly changing market we must develop multiple strategies. A single strategy is not enough; that would make us far too vulnerable to possible changes in the market. No, we have to develop multiple strategies which we can use to guide our company's knowledge in different ways, each of which can create new value. Amsterdam Airport Schiphol, for example, is building its continued success thanks to three strategies: operating the world's best airport; participating as manager but also as financier in the development of foreign airports; and selling knowledge to other airport companies. 'But success is never final.'[8]

Shine the light

When building these smart strategies, we must take internal as well as external factors into account. They must be like the beam of a lighthouse: it passes over the sea and over the land. Like the lighthouse. When we are shining our light over the sea we are, in essence, scanning the market, trying to ascertain future market demands. Trying to detect how our customers will react in the future. Most of the time we may think we are searching in the dark. But by using the knowledge we have in our company, we can create a light which can help us detect the subtlest changes in the market landscape. It will help us detect changing customer demands. Illuminate markets and market segments we may never have reached or considered before. It may even light up some new opportunities for turning today's emerging products into tomorrow's cash cows.

But, for half the time, the light must also shine on the land – on the internal workings of our company. What is there in our backyard which has been left there, ignored? Could it be a diamond? Or a whole mine of diamonds? What talent have we left unexploited? Unchallenged? And what are the organizational capabilities which have not yet been exploited?

The light must shine – not for a few moments, but constantly. Shining the light must become a habit. Only then can we rest assured that we will see the slightest change overland or oversea, either internally and externally, which could give an indication of a new way to move forward. Alertness, flexibility, adaptability – these are the key words.

Creating smart strategies

Over the past years many companies have taken steps to become more responsive to customer demands. At Asea Brown Boveri – (ABB) – a totally new business unit structure has been implemented. Head office staff have been drastically reduced in favour of regional leadership in home markets. This allows the company – which is active in 66 different sectors – to avoid duplication of energy, something always a real problem when managing a company with such diverse operations and to be nearer the customer to respond effectively, efficiently, and quickly. It is a strategy which ABB is convinced will fit them for continuity into the future.[10]

Nevertheless, this nearness to customers may have helped decrease the time to market of many products – it has not particularly helped increase the ability to anticipate the future. If anything, this is even worse now than it was in the past.

Seven mega-strategies

As we have already seen, smart strategizing – remember, it is a verb – means moving away from a single charismatic CEO developing his or her idea alone in some corporate ivory tower. It means company-wide participation in which every member of the company at all levels is where appropriate, involved in the formation of the strategy and certainly informed of it so that they can be actively involved in its implementation. Obviously this means that we must all move away from the tactics, politics and devices we have used to develop strategies in the past. This is where our seven mega-strategies come into the picture. Because these seven trends can help radically change the way you put together a strategy which is right for the knowledge economy. Let us look at each of these strategies in somewhat greater detail.

Global, but then local?

The need to appeal directly to local markets is something which CNN initially thought unimportant. A pan-global news service would appeal to every business man, was the ruling opinion. But now that has changed. CNN is now entering a period of localization in which the needs of world 'regions' are more clearly acknowledged. For CNN-News the world is now split up into a number of regions, each with its own editorial and presentation staff. This allows CNN not only to present global news from a local perspective, but also to provide local news specifically geared at that market. Using this strategy, CNN is becoming a true transnational organization.[9]

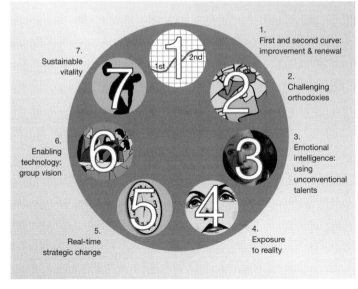

Seven mega-strategies to mega-smarts

Improvement and renewal

We must think about improving our business, while at the same time, we must visualize which brand new business we can develop. We must learn to see these two actions as two sides of the same coin. It is not 'either/or' but rather 'and/and'. We must learn to improve and innovate at the same time. By doing this, we can hopefully anticipate changes in the market and already adapt our thinking to meet those changes before they occur.

In the traditional S-curve theory, we have learned that there is a natural process of rapid growth, stabilization and decline. It is important that we start concentrating on a new S-curve before the existing one has gone into decline. In this way, we can ensure the continuity of our business. To give an example: the rise of the Internet – and the fact that many people are now turning to e-mail – may convince the postal companies that there is little future in a traditional mail service, no matter how efficiently that may be run. So, while continuing to milk the existing curve, they would do very well to put their minds to the second curve, to create a new source of business and income for when the existing curve goes into decline.[11]

they really matter.'
'And that's all?'
'Yes – so go do it!'

KPMG managers challenged

KPMG's Strategy Integration Team (SIT) felt it was important that the 300 directors of KPMG The Netherlands were confronted with their assumptions and convictions about the company in which they participated. The SIT felt that too many directors had lost touch with developments which were taking place in various parts of society. The central question for the SIT was how to create a context in which a major paradigm shift could take place. Their answer was to invite the 300 directors to a dinner in a converted gas factory. There were 100 tables there, each with a guest from a particular sector of society – politics, art, press, business, research, philosophy and so on. Between each course, the directors had to stand up and move to a different table. They were given a single assignment: ask the guest questions exclusively about his particular world. The questions could be about the present and the future. They were not allowed to use the word 'KPMG' or refer to the activities of KPMG. The central message was, 'Listen and open yourself to the world of the guests.'[12]

Challenging orthodoxies

Second, we must actively challenge all those orthodox theories which have taken hold of our thinking. All too often, a company gets locked into traditions – into an attitude of 'that's the way we've always done things' or 'that's what brought us success in the past and you should never change a winning team' or 'this company grew big because of our involvement in x, y or z, and we must remain faithful to our inheritance'. All very noble sentiments – but no longer applicable in an age where knowledge means more than tradition and where a successful past offers no guarantee for an equally successful future. Divesting a company of adherence to orthodox and often traditional ways of thinking is essential for creating a strategy in the knowledge economy.

In the Netherlands telephone calls have traditionally been billed per unit or part of unit used. These units were generally 45 seconds. Then a new company on the Dutch telecom market – Libertel – introduced 'billing by the second'. This immediately broke with the existing tradition. The 'established' Dutch Telecom (KPN) had, coincidentally, just installed software which could also handle 'billing by the second', so they were able to respond to this challenge within just two weeks.

All this means that many long-held beliefs which are the very basis of present strategies have to be shaken and broken down by reality. For example, there is a stubborn belief that cost leadership must necessarily be at odds with high added value. But this has to be overturned so that cost leadership and flexibility and high added value all go hand in hand. An organization's ability to last will be threatened by choosing one or the other.

Emotional intelligence

The third mega-strategy is to open yourself up by using emotional intelligence to allow unconventional talents to lead you to respond to unique opportunities.

In business, we have all learned to be rational. To collect data, create information, and make decisions based on proven knowledge. Yet in reality, we all know that intuition and feeling are more important. There is a story that one day people in the Philips Nat Lab – one of the largest privately-owned research laboratories in the world – were discussing the apparent failure of their laser-based video disc system. Somebody asked when the market would 'see the light' – an interesting little pun on the fact that the system was based on a laser reading digital information encapsulated in a glass disc. Someone said, 'Perhaps they don't need to see the light – perhaps they should hear it instead'. The coin dropped. The result of that remark was the invention of the compact disc.[13]

Neuroscientist Roger Sperry and Robert Ornstein of the University of California Medical Centre discovered that the two sides of the brain differ in the kind of intellectual actions they undertake. The left side of the brain is primarily involved in speech, logic, numbers and analyses, while the right side is more concerned with rhythm, music, imagination. When creating strategies, it is this right side of the brain that we have to unleash – the emotional intelligence.

But there is another reason for using emotional intelligence. It is becoming increasingly apparent that the most successful teams are those that share a common element in their individual passions. Knowledge professionals will create synergy when the purpose 'feels right'. When we create new strategies, we have to manage our teams in such a way that they feel inspired to tap into this hidden source of power.

Hewlett Packard has fostered an environment in which taking chances is applauded. Even if this means that people get things wrong. Everybody within the company is encouraged to talk to customers to find out exactly what they want. They can make suggestions, try out new ideas, and suggest new products. No limitation is put on them. Rather, everybody is encouraged to make use of their emotional intelligence.[14] The Polaroid Lands camera was born from such a flash of inspiration: the inventor, Dr Edward Lands, was taking a picture when his three-year-old daughter asked why she couldn't see the photograph straight away. Why not, indeed.[15] All this underlines what Marcel Proust once wrote, 'The true journey of discovery is not about looking for new landscapes; it is about looking with different eyes.'[16]

When Jan Timmer took
over as President of
Philips, he started a
company-wide process of
change under the name
Centurion. One of the
opening meetings of
Centurion was held in a
conference centre in
Holland and was attended
by the top 100 Philips
managers worldwide.
When they entered the
hall, Timmer distributed a
press release. It stated
that Philips had applied for
bankruptcy. 'This will be
sent out to the
newspapers later today',
said Timmer, 'but I wanted
you to see it first'. It was,
of course, a piece of
fiction, but it made the top
management of Philips
uncomfortably aware of
what could very well
happen if the company
did not improve its
performance. Later, the
concept of Customer Day
was evolved, during which
the whole Philips
community – more than
250 000 people
worldwide – was
confronted with the state
of the company. It was a
major tool in creating
company-wide awareness
and involvement. During a
question time at the first
Customer Day, a manager
asked Timmer whether he
was expecting everybody
to become 'Japanese
workaholics'. Timmer
smiled and replied: 'No –
workaholics is enough'.[17]

Exposure to reality

Once you have opened yourself up by using new talents, you will then be able to make use of the fourth mega-strategy: exposure to reality. Or better, expose yourself to the realities that come from unfamiliar directions and manifest themselves in unfamiliar ways.

There are many such realities which become increasingly important when developing new strategies in the knowledge economy. There are the realities which come from top-down; those that come from bottom-up; those that come from out-side-in; those that come from inside-out. No matter where the realities come from, we have to be prepared to examine them and make use of them in our strategy development. We can never have enough eyes and ears to gather important knowledge which can help us design our own future.

Other concepts, too, will have to be allowed to offer seemingly conflicting knowledge: a future watch will ensure that we learn about the future wishes of customers as they emerge – and often even earlier. It is not simply a question of 'forewarned is forearmed' but rather a question of 'not closing the stable door when the horse has already bolted'. In today's market, horses get out in a wink of an eye!

We must also be prepared to break compromises. No matter where they arise. To compromise anywhere is to compromise our future. Again it is the essence of smart strategies to think in terms of 'and/and' rather than 'either/or'. Shell, in the wake of the Brent Spar affair, has adopted a new method of developing strategies which means involving a whole range of parties from the very start and developing a strategy which takes into account all the conflicting needs of each party. It is called the 'Triple D model' – Dialogue, Decide, Deliver. It means that dialogue is maintained with governmental, societal, and other groups so that wide public support for any decision can be achieved. It requires courage from a company like Shell because it is required to lay its cards on the table at an early stage and this makes the company vulnerable to shareholders and other external parties. But the pay-off is considerable: the preparation time is shorter, the opposition to a proposal is kept to a minimum, and there is less frustration for all parties involved.[18]

Companies must also learn to recognize the imminent emergence of discontinuities and use this information to their own advantage. Ideal design must also be adapted so that companies no longer impose its ideas on the market, but allow the market to impose its ideas on them. Trend diving must be undertaken on a regular, ongoing basis so that patterns can be mapped on which to base strategic thinking.

Real-time strategic change

Our fifth mega-strategy is to use real-time strategic change.[19] We must learn to make use of all the ears and eyes we can get so that we can use large-scale change events that include everyone involved with the company. Not only internally, but also externally. Suppliers and even competitors. Because involving as many parties as possible will allow us to apply strategic solutions as they occur without the need to spend time on long-winded strategy implementation.

Already there are a number of leading companies that are making use of large-scale events. Boeing Corporation, for example, First Nation Wide Bank, Ford Motor Company, Marriott Hotels and United Airlines.

At the Philips Customer Day in 1997, suppliers were invited to participate in the various sessions. The core session involved discussions using prepared sheets. Groups of around ten people – including suppliers where appropriate – were asked to discuss the role of suppliers in the company, how the relationship between suppliers and Philips could be improved, where improvements could be made in the suppliers' operation and where bottlenecks could be removed.

There are a number of issues involved in this mega-strategy, many of them familiar to us from other areas. The time when we were managers is now behind us; today, companies need leaders. Leaders with a vision must empower local managers to mobilize their teams to survey and serve the market. We must also encourage discovery, an active search for knowledge which can help manage the process of change and uncover new areas of potential profit and success. We must help to design and implement issue-based networks which again can be instrumental in our determination to create systems and strategies

Business planning: into the future with Group Vision™

A software company, with around 60 employees, experienced an explosive growth. One of the partners produced a business plan which was then subjected to scrutiny by 25 employees. Using Group Vision™, an agenda for the meeting was prepared and each point became the subject for a brainstorming session. During these sessions the client became aware of several deficiencies in his company and a decision was taken during the session to appoint an interim manager. Changes to the management organization were agreed and together the basis for a business was constructed. The results of the day session were a list of short-term measures and the main lines for further growth in the future. But the facts were not the only result: spending a day intensely discussing the company's business without falling into gossip and chitchat was of enormous benefit.[20]

which add value to our knowledge base so that we, in turn, can add value to our customers.

Enabling technology: Group Vision™

Much strategic work is about creating ideas using brainstorming techniques. This process can be speeded up and made more efficient by using electronic brainstorming software. Group Vision™ helps to capture all the ideas that are generated. Participants are linked to one another via a network of laptop computers. The ensuing electronic dialogue facilitates a rapid and effective exchange of ideas, knowledge, experiences and opinions. As all communication remains anonymous, fear of unconstructive criticism is virtually non-existent. In addition, the output of this process of 'thinking aloud' is broadcast onto a central computer screen, with the result that the ideas, Thomas Ives, and not the personalities behind them, become the focus of attention. Rank, standing, titles, positions and powers of persuasion have absolutely no bearing. The participants learn to relax in an open atmosphere of true brainstorming.

Group Vision™ has also been used very successfully for interactive customer panels. Groups of between 10 and 25 customers – clients, agents, end-users – are formed and supported by Group Vision™. This allows them to structure their aims, the dialogue, the order of questions and give priority to them. The data collected from such sessions can be distributed electronically and processed when necessary.

This system has been successfully used by a whole range of clients and disciplines. It has helped companies to evaluate team members, create a vision and help with strategic planning, working out a basis for working towards results and how to reward them, and ascertaining the consequences of introducing a new product.

Sustainable vitality

And finally, we must adopt the seventh mega-strategy: switching our attention to sustainable values. We must change our mind-set from 'built to compete' to 'built to last'. To do this we have to infuse sustainable vitality into our employees, our company and our society.

Today many leading companies are accepting their responsibility to society and are prepared to state it. De Bijenkorf – a Dutch holding company with several chains of department stores – has a company statement which says, 'By obtaining a good return, we create a stimulating work environment. Our social responsibility is demonstrated by our rejection of child labour, an active environmental policy, consideration for minority groups, and using our influence with our business partners to persuade them to adopt the same principles. And a good social policy which gives our employees and their families/partners maximum support when necessary.' Rank Xerox is to the point saying, 'Waste-free products from waste-free facilities'.[21] Bruce Pharriss, President of Celtrix Laboratories, says, 'Our aim is to improve the quality of human life with innovative therapeutic products'. And Apple stated as early as 1980, 'Make a contribution to the world by producing tools for the mind which stimulate human progress'.[22]

Out of the box

For too long, our strategic thinking has kept us confined to the box. It is now time to jump out of that box, to jump out and grasp the future, not as something which is inevitable and

Jump out of the box into the future

'Whereas old companies tried to create a strategy fit, new companies seize the initiative by setting the rules of the game and defining the field of play. It's this strategy stretch that creates the future.'

'What do you mean?'

'I mean that we must embrace the future as we create it. First, we sense upcoming discontinuities that provoke new customer demands. These will point the way to a wide range of new customer needs which will develop into new concepts that can create new products and services...and even new ways to deliver them to the customer. Now, by relying on our core competencies, we can create the future. Start with developing new products and services and value chains. Then continue the process until a new discontinuity is created.'

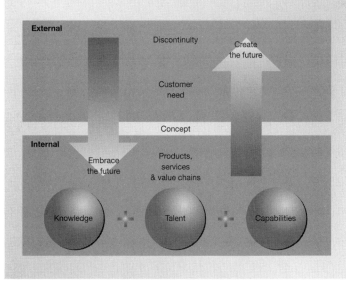

Jump out of the box into the future

Four myths:

1. Excellent companies have charismatic management.
2. Excellent companies look for profit maximization.
3. Excellent companies develop big strategy plans.
4. Excellent companies differentiate themselves by their core competence.

Eight golden rules

1. Let people know what they're making and how.
2. Profits ain't all.
3. Stick to a core ideology, but stimulate change.
4. Who doesn't dare, doesn't win.
5. Develop a sect-like culture.
6. Try everything and keep what's successful.
7. Select managers from the company's employees.
8. Nothing is ever finished, everything can always be done better.

James C. Collins and Jerry I. Porras[23]

beyond our control, but rather, as something we actually create. It was Goethe who wrote, 'A wish is the first indication of what we are actually capable of achieving'. Now it is up to us to put that into practice.

Traditionally, companies have tried to create a strategy fit, allowing the existing rules of the game to colour their strategy. Today, however, the only rule is that there are no rules. Companies create their own playing fields and set the rules to allow them to play the games of their making. Our strategy must be to get the most out of our company's knowledge by embracing the future at the same time that we create it.

Create and embrace at the same time? Certainly. This is another of those paradoxes which litter the knowledge economy. But without such paradoxes, our thinking will be firmly rooted in the past – not in the future where it belongs.

Strategy as fit: anticipating the future

We can only embrace the future if we can anticipate it. One of the ways we can do this is by using the concept of discontinuities.

A discontinuity occurs when two or more trends reinforce each other, fundamentally changing the rules of the game. One such discontinuity could be that traffic jams around city centres and the growing availability of IT could cause a discontinuity in mobility: a shift from moving people to moving information. Another example is the combination of the emergence of the 24-hour economy which has created a need for anytime, anywhere communications and the standardization of mobile communication which has created a discontinuity from a permanent infrastructure to a mobile one.

It is exactly these sorts of ideas which can give us a new insight into the future and can help us get a better feel for the needs of customers in the coming years. For example, if people work at home more than they do at the moment, what consequences will this have? They will need furniture – and a number of project designers and office equipment manufacturers have already broadened their product range for private individuals and have introduced products designed for the home office. They will also need telecommunication – and telecommunication companies are offering high-speed data telecommunication lines for individuals. How to supervise knowledge professionals who work at home is a question which is leading consultancy companies to offer advice on managing homeworkers from a distance.

Or what about new customer demands which will arise because of the explosive growth of mobile telephony? How can you be informed that somebody is phoning you without disturbing everybody in the vicinity? A vibrating telephone could be the answer. How can you carry your phone? Do customers want holders made out of plastic or high-class crocodile leather? How can you keep telephones out of places where they are not welcome? Electronic transmitters can make it impossible to receive a signal for a mobile phone in places such as hospitals or concert halls. A matter of 'no admittance of mobile telephones!'

Using the concept of discontinuity and customer demands in this respect can give us a new slant on the world which is before us. It can help us:

– look back at the present from the future;
– look at what our own market is offering from the point of view of the customer;
– stop using just rational thinking to generate ideas by allowing imagination, feeling, intuition, surprise and creativity to play a bigger role than ever before;
– teach us that there are a lot of opportunities for us and not just a whole range of threats;
– and finally, it can help us challenge our own orthodoxies, so that we avoid doing things 'because that's the way we've always done them'.

If this approach is to be fully successful, we have to do things differently to the way we did them in the past.

– We must have an open mind which can use the right side of the brain to think in terms which we may never have dared to do in the past.
– We must use dialogue to communicate ideas. It is no good telling people what we want to say – it's telling them in a way that makes them want to listen and participate.
– We have to learn to use all our creativity. Creativity isn't something which other people have; we all have it and we must learn to use it.

Knowledge creation in the telework context

Organizations adopting telework will have to provide their organizational members structurally with opportunities to socialize. Socialization has the potential for creating both tacit and explicit knowledge.

A work area where the organizational members are able to meet face to face on a somewhat regular basis will provide an opportunity for collegial learning to occur. Socialization is also important for those mobile workers who have a high level of interaction with customers and are able to accumulate tacit knowledge through these contacts. The organization as a whole is likely to benefit if these mobile workers are given the opportunity to share their knowledge with each other.
S. Raghuram[24]

And they thought Netscape was crazy

Who gives away something for nothing in business? Netscape does. It makes its software available free to customers thus adding to its value. Consequently it has become locked in. At the same time, it is adding to its own value by being recognized as the company which sets the standards in its chosen field. Today Netscape is a multi-million dollar concern. And it achieved this by giving its product away for nothing – and making exceptional use of its knowledge.
Kevin Kelly[25]

What's my core competence?

Telephone company or telecommunications company? Manufacturing garage openers or entrance technology? Training and development office or advice consultancy? Radio manufacturer or miniaturization specialist? Airline or transporter of people? Office equipment manufacturer or helping to increase office productivity? Vacuum cleaner manufacturer or a company that helps create a cleaner environment? Exhaust pipe repairer or car service organization?[27]

– We must think out of the box, look for unexpected solutions, and allow ourselves to think the unthinkable.
– We must stop thinking in terms of solving the puzzle. The future isn't a puzzle which can be solved. There is no single solution to the question, 'What will the future look like?' There are many answers, each just as possible as the other.

Strategy as stretch: creating the future

'Strategy as stretch' means creating the future to our own design by setting the rules of the game. It means leaving the passenger seat and sitting behind the steering wheel. It means changing the rules of the game. Setting the standard for the industry. All this is happening in the knowledge economy. Companies give away their knowledge in order to gain a competitive advantage. It is an expression of faith in the uniqueness of their own knowledge.

In his 'New Rules for the New Economy', Kevin Kelly defines the 'Rule of Generosity: Follow the Free.'[26] 'If services become more valuable the more plentiful they are, and if they cost less the better and more valuable they become, the extension of this logic says that the most valuable things of all should be those that are given away'. Yet, sensible companies often use 'free' to sell other products. A sprat to catch a mackerel. A GSM phone is offered free – as long as you take a three-year subscription on the network. Netscape offers its web browser free – and this helps sell commercial server software. Getting something free makes people pay attention – and with more and more products and services vying for the fixed time at a person's disposal (even today there's no way of making a day last longer than 24 hours), a freebee can be the hook which catches the attention – and sales.

The first step in creating a strategy for stretch is to identify our core competencies: the combination of unique knowledge, talent and organizational capability. What is the strength of our company? Which knowledge is unique? Do we have any unused patents? Do our people possess specific talents? Does the way our organization is structured result in us having unique capabilities in, say, R&D or logistics or sales?

The next step is to take our core competence and rephrase it or rename it so that it is no longer a reflection of our present business but independent of it. This will make it more expandable. That is exactly what Sony did when it said that its core competence was 'miniaturization'. Or what KPMG The Netherlands did it when they worded their key competence as 'offering reliability' or 'giving managers a good night's sleep'.

This ability to think of our activities in terms of concepts instead of products is an important step towards creating a future. In *Mission Possible*, Ken Blanchard and Terry Waghorn give a classic example of this. Imagine, they say, that at the time the car made its appearance on the market, you had asked the manufacturer of horse-drawn carts what market need he satisfied. If he had replied 'We satisfy the need for good carts', then his company would most probably have gone into liquidation. If, on the other hand, he had replied 'we satisfy the need for transporting people', then he might very well have gone on to transforming his company into a car manufacturer. It is also better if you avoid too narrow a definition of what your company does. Suppose you are a stock broker and you think this means you are in the business of stocks and shares? You could very shortly be shutting down. With the arrival of the Internet, everybody can have access to the same information you have as broker. On the other hand, if you think you are in the business of financial planning, you could suddenly see a long-term future for yourself. You are the only person who can limit your company's future.

Beware of the knowledge trap

If some knowledge is good – isn't a lot of knowledge even better? No. Definitely not. One sleeping pill can be beneficial – but taking a whole bottle isn't.

Too many companies faced with the awareness that knowledge is a good thing fall into the trap of gaining as much knowledge as possible. Whether this knowledge is good, bad or indifferent. Knowledge which isn't needed is just that – not needed. The effort spent gathering it is wasted effort.

Managing the acquisition of knowledge is an important task in any organization, and while individual business units may have the initial task of creating and capturing knowledge that is needed at an operational level, it is the responsibility of the corporate centre to make clear exactly what knowledge is of strategic importance to the company. It is its job to create the circumstances in which knowledge can be created and to be fully aware of what knowledge adds value to the company. It does not have to create knowledge itself; it has to ensure that what is created by others is the right sort of knowledge within the company's strategy.

And so we see that the provision of knowledge needs two players: the providers of content (generally the business units or those operational sections of the company which are near the customer) and the directors of content (usually the corporate centre).

Using a knowledge map

It is important to know what you want to know. This is the first step to ensuring that the knowledge you collect is the knowledge you need. A helpful tool to assist you in deciding which knowledge you need is a knowledge map. It shows which domains are critical to the future of the company. It also breaks this knowledge down into smaller units that act as links between the individual knowledge segments.

The first step in creating a knowledge map is to translate your business strategy into key knowledge areas. These should be those areas you have defined as essential for realizing your

Knowledge maps prevent knowledge for knowledge's sake

'It's the best way of preventing the accumulation of knowledge for knowledge's sake.'
'Is that a possibility?'
'Certainly. And it's a trap many companies fall into. Like Oliver Twist, they want more.'
'And a map helps avoid this?'
'Yes. First we identify knowledge domains that are the centre of our quest for knowledge. Then we establish knowledge links that glue together and strengthen related knowledge so that we take advantage of its synergy. Then we define knowledge segments as everything knowledge professionals and systems know about a specific subject that relates to achieving the business strategy.'
'This sounds a bit like the Heineken NV organizational design.'
'It does, doesn't it? In the Heineken example, the company's strategic processes are also the knowledge domains for which the corporate centre is responsible.'

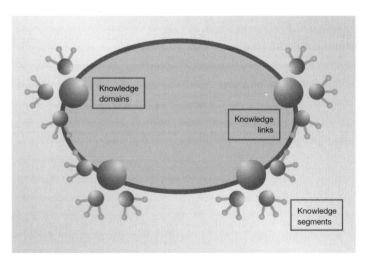

Knowledge maps prevent knowledge for knowledge's sake

The strategic journey of KPMG the Netherlands

Change is always difficult, especially for those companies used to success (e.g. IBM, Philips, General Motors, Kodak and, perhaps, also KPMG). Success makes the focus internal ('Look at us!') and short term ('What can happen to us?'). If success continues or failures aren't directly visible, people are encouraged to do more of what they did in the past which, in changing environments, results in missing opportunities, losing customers and profit and missing the boat.

The only way to escape from this 'death spiral of success' is to initiate fundamental changes. To find new competitive space, to discover new competitive advantages, to set the rules of the business and to be so creative and fast that the competition is left behind. This calls for a fundamental rethinking of the mission and strategy and a drastic organizational transformation. Under the mission 'Vision 2000 Reinventing KPMG,' 100 directors and employees are challenged to use all their knowledge, skills and creativity. The goal is to study new opportunities for KPMG in order to become the most client-oriented advisory firm, with our people and showing pride having fun adding value to the customer. The group met regularly over a three-month period before publishing an in-depth study. One team sketched the most complete possible outline of future developments in society, information technology, culture, politics and economy as well as the way in which these will influence one another. A detailed picture emerged of 18 changes in discontinuities which will have an effect on the market, on its clients and on KPMG. An inventory of our current portfolio of services based on David Maister's '3 E-theory' resulted in a matrix of KPMG services clustered according to 'efficiency', 'experience' and 'expertise'. This led to a summary of all KPMG core competencies and latent competencies and a description of the skills underlying them.

A third group concentrated on identifying the existing and the desired culture within KPMG. Attention was also paid to the possible models which could be used to achieve cultural changes within KPMG.

The result was a strategic architecture. It determines the direction of KPMG's future development: the directions of growth; not only opportunities which follow naturally from the direction in which KPMG is already developing but also the blank spaces where KPMG can occupy a leading position. There is also an ambition, a strategic intention, which not only lies in the realization of the growth directions, but also in the developments which KPMG should experience in the field of organization culture.

Six new business opportunities (KPMG Knowledge Management is one of them) show the value which the strategic architecture of KPMG and the Vision 2000 process have for everyday practice. These six are only a selection of the many opportunities which can be observed on the basis of the work of 'the 100'. The continuous repetition of this process connected with the general strategic architecture is the driving force behind the realization of our business ambitions, particularly for discovering new markets and services required by clients.

strategy in a manner which creates value for your company. These areas are knowledge domains. They are instrumental in focusing the attention of your professionals on building and sharing knowledge which is defined by these knowledge domains. Knowledge which falls outside these domains is knowledge which has no strategic value and should be ignored.

The knowledge domains should be divided into a number of sub-sections. These we refer to as knowledge links. They link the work of individual professionals and teams working within a knowledge domain together so that it is possible to realize business objectives. The knowledge links serve as knowledge enhancers and connect and strengthen the separate streams of knowledge segments flowing into the knowledge domains.

More than a strategic tool

A good knowledge map is an important tool for managing knowledge. Its usefulness goes far beyond that of helping define strategy.

First, it can help focus knowledge creation. For example, once we have defined knowledge domains, we know where to direct our R&D efforts. It will ensure that we do not expend energy on areas which have not been defined as strategic important. The map also can highlight white spots – those areas where we may be lacking knowledge.

Second, the knowledge map can help us see where our knowledge management initiatives have the greatest added value impact – in the domains we have defined as having the greatest strategic importance. This is where we can initiate a pilot knowledge management prospect, so that we can gain a better understanding about how this can work and what results we can expect from it.

Third, it will give us a perfect blueprint for our intranet. We can, for example, give each knowledge domain a specific icon on our intranet. This leads us into deeper water where we reach the knowledge we are after in a specific knowledge segment.

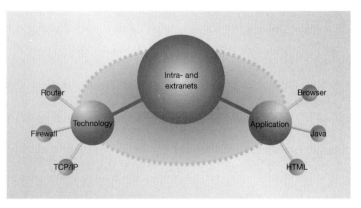

Knowledge domains are at the core of smart strategies

Fourth, it can be a useful aid to showing where the responsibilities for managing our knowledge should lie. Each knowledge domain could, for example, be made the responsibility of a specified board member. Knowledge organizers could be appointed to be responsible for capturing and sharing the specific knowledge links. And individual knowledge workers could be given the responsibility of keeping specific knowledge segments up to date and accessible to others.

Fifth, it can indicate how we can organize our knowledge into competence centres or centres of excellence, so that each centre can cover a specific domain or knowledge link.

Sixth, it can be combined with a 'source map' which can list knowledge sources (whether people or systems or a combination of both) within specific knowledge segments. In this way we can see where specific knowledge segments are located within the organization. It can also show what knowledge is missing and what knowledge is superfluous.

And finally, it can be an important tool in helping to manage the competencies of knowledge workers better. It allows us to compile a 'competence profile' for each knowledge worker. This can indicate clearly what knowledge, skills and attitude is needed for a specific function. Under 'knowledge' we can list a number of segments which we have already defined on our knowledge map. The knowledge worker can then be required to gain the appropriate knowledge listed here. This can further be linked to a competence development plan as part of their balanced individual scorecard with an appropriate training and education schedule.

Mapping knowledge for better client access

Many companies have discovered how powerful a knowledge map can be in getting the most out of the knowledge they need and have. At Teltech, a company in Minneapolis that manages a knowledge network of external experts, they are aware that there are different ways of naming the same thing. The same is true of knowledge. An expert may define something one way, while a client who rings in for information may define it in another way. The solution to this was to replace the traditional 'knowledge model' – with a tree structure that had proved difficult to navigate – with a knowledge map based on the principle of a thesaurus. An on-line search and retrieval system called the Knowledgescope is a thesaurus of over 30 000 technical terms. For each technical entry there is a preferred usage and a series of synonyms. The aim of Teltech is to use those terms that are used by its clients rather than by its professional experts. In this way, the knowledge is made far more accessible.[28]

CHAPTER 8

'Smart organizations'

*How companies become knowledge
intensive, people rich*

Creating an organization used to mean nothing more than creating an organizational chart. 'A place for everybody and everybody in his place,' was the motto. What's more, the organization – and its archetypal structure – seemed to impose order not only on the structure of the company, but also – and more destructively – on the decision process.

It is obvious that such a strict, hierarchical structure is the worse thing to have when the conditions of the knowledge economy are demanding speed, surprise, flexibility and responsiveness. Demanding in fact, an anytime, any place, anywhere mentality which is the very thing in danger of being smothered by a desire to 'organize'.

What's hot and what's not in smart organizations	
Hot	**Cold**
Heavy on know-how	Asset-rich
Light on resources	Brain-poor
Decentralized decision process	Centralized board of management decision making
Centralized knowledge management	Leaving knowledge where it is
Sharing knowledge	Keeping what you know to yourself
Process-and team-based organization	Functional organization
Intellectual capital shared by knowledge professionals	Intellectual capital reserved for managers and CEOs
Unlimited access to explicit and tacit knowledge	Limited access to explicit knowledge
Smart sourcing	Outsourcing[1]

A smart organization moves radically away from the familiar ideas which most companies carry with them. There is, according to Mintzberg,[2] no 'tops or bottoms' in an organization. There isn't any single right organization either. The litmus test is to cover the name of the company on the organizational chart and then work out what it actually does. Nor does a smart organization necessarily deal with jobs. In fact, the job, which Bridges considers a social artifact inherited from the industrial mindset,[3] is a fixed thing with a job description and salary attached to it and a fixed place in the organization, and therefore of little relevance in today's world which uses a different organizational logic – that is, a logic that is not job or function based but, rather, team and process based.

Too often, we have allowed ourselves to be carried away by the enormous amount of information which is now at our disposal. Let's get at it! has been the call of many companies. And this has frequently added to the chaos which is already surrounding us. If this chaos is to be mastered, companies will have to find a new purpose to the way knowledge is employed and focus on improving the way it is accessed, shared, managed and – most importantly – how it adds value to the company. That's where smart organizations come in.

Paradigm shifts

Barker wrote in 1993, 'When a paradigm shifts, everyone goes back to zero.'[6] And companies are being faced with this rule time and time again. When we move into a new age, a new race starts. Barker continues, 'By zero, I mean that regardless of what your position was with the old paradigm – number one in market share, leader in technology, best reputation – you are back at the starting line with the new paradigm. Because of this change in leverage, the practitioners of the new paradigm have a chance to not just compete with but defeat the titans of the old paradigm.'[7]

Why, then, is past success no guarantee for the future? Why do companies not have the ability to work in the new system? Why is change so difficult? It is often because of a major sickness called *'paradigm paralysis'*. Companies have become so attached to the way they have always worked that

The future that has already happened

'The information needs of businesses and of executives are likely to change rapidly. We have concentrated these past years on improving traditional information, which is almost exclusively information about what goes on inside an organization … In fact, approximately 90 per cent or more of the information any organization collects is about inside events. Increasingly, a winning strategy will require information about events and conditions outside the institution: non-customers, technologies other than those currently used by the company and its present competitors, markets not currently served, and so on.'[4]

New races, new rules

Philips is a company which has survived many paradigm shifts. At the beginning of the century it was a leading manufacturer of radio valves – and then the paradigm shifted, and the transistor made its appearance. Philips changed, and became one of the world's top eight companies in transistors. The paradigm shifted again, and today Philips Semiconductors is a major top ten chip manufacturer. But each time, the race had to be run against new competitors – and with new rules – even though each of these new races was based on technological expertise and manufacturing adaptability.[5]

it becomes almost impossible for them to change and become players in the new game.

As we stand on the divide between the industrial economy and the knowledge economy, it is good to pause and take stock of the old paradigm and see how the new paradigm differs from it.

In 1917 the number one company in the US was US Steel. Its product was typically 'Industrial Age': heavy in weight and light in know-how. In today's terms, it had assets of $30 billion, three times greater than those of the next largest company, and employed 268 000 workers.

Let's move to today's list of the top 100 US companies. Now you will look in vain for the proud name of US Steel. Its assets are now only $6.5 billion – a fifth of what they were 80 years ago – and it employs a mere 20 800 people.[8]

But what are the main companies at the top of today's list? Quite simply they are companies that are specialists in intangibles. In the knowledge economy, products don't weigh a ton – they are, instead, the products of the human mind rather than of the production line. We have moved from the heavyweight society, to the weightless society.

Negroponte, the author of *Being Digital,* and columnist of nicholas@media.mit.edu wrote, 'One thing common to multinational corporations is bigness. In part this is because of the need to manage the world of atoms, to ship them, to store them, to disseminate them – something you and I cannot do easily as small-business players. We lack the capital, the

The new logic of organizing	
Old style	**New style**
Stable	Dynamic, learning
Information scarce	Information rich
Local	Global
Large	Small and large
Functional	Product/customer oriented
Job oriented	Skills oriented
Individual oriented	Team oriented
Common/control oriented	Involvement oriented
Hierarchical	Lateral/networked
Job requirement oriented	Customer oriented[9]

THE KNOWLEDGE DIVIDEND

economies of scale. But the world of bits is different. You and I can ship them at the speed of light at almost no cost, to anywhere on the planet. No big capital costs. No warehouse. No heavy distribution costs.'[10]

So why do we live under the glaring misconception that what worked in the past – in the industrial economy – will work in the new knowledge economy?

New style of organizing

In the new knowledge economy, 'management will be confronted with the re-everything bias'[11]: reorganization, reengineering, restyling, reexamining, repurposing, rearranging, refocus, reassessment, redefinition, revitalization and revision.

'However, in the world of increasing returns, especially in high tech, re-everything has become necessary because every time the quest changes, the company needs to change. It needs to reinvent its purpose, its goals, its way of doing things. In short, it needs to adapt and adaptation never stops.'[12]

One of the slogans frequently heard in business today is, 'Work smarter, not harder', and indeed we may very well be facing the attack of the 'smarts'. Everything is smart. This is perhaps why the magazine *Fast Company* lists the three most important rules in business: 'The first rule of business today: the smartest company wins. The second rule of business today: to be the smartest company, have the smartest people. The third rule of business today: to have the smartest people, keep learning.'[13]

If we are to put knowledge to work, working smarter rather than working harder is the key to the organization. Unstructured knowledge may be difficult to manage; but you can manage the process of creating and enhancing integrated knowledge environments that positively impact decisions both inside and outside the organization.

In other words, managing the smart knowledge process within smart organizations is where the real pay-off is.

All brains, no body

Organizations are in flux, constantly, but now that a new paradigm has presented itself as we move from the industrial economy into the knowledge economy, we see that it is no

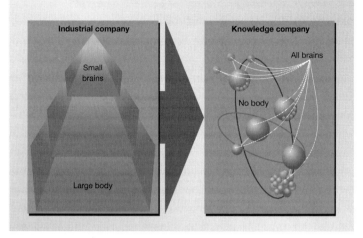

They are all brains, no body

longer simply a matter of fine-tuning; it is, quite simply, a new game, and every company is back to the starting-line.

Today, the most successful companies are becoming brain-rich and asset-poor. An 'all brains, no body' organization which is in diametric contrast to the traditional 'small brain, large body' organization of the Industrial Age.

As we move into the knowledge economy, so information and knowledge have replaced physical products – bits have replaced atoms – and this is causing the body to shrink. And shrink fast. The result is an 'all brains, no body' organization. The 'all brain' processes add value to the company – and they are the ones which have to be nurtured. All other processes and/or functions are outsourced or eliminated entirely. And the result is that the 'non-brain body weight is kept to an absolute minimum'.[14] What's more, 'no body' can also mean 'nobody'. How many people will be employed in the organization of the future?

Creating such an organization is certainly not easy. It requires a significant change of behaviour from everybody in the company. We have already seen how knowledge needs to be shared within the new economy. And this means that people will be expected to cooperate, to be open, to participate. Resistance can be expected. Particularly from those people who cannot or will not adapt to the new situation.

Key question	Industrial organization	Smart organization	Quantum organization
Economic principle	Diminishing returns	Both increasing and diminishing returns	Increasing returns
What is used to accumulate wealth?	Land, labour, capital	Knowledge as intellectual value	Wisdom, intuition, emotion, consciousness
What is our wealth?	Things, tangible assets, heavy material	Intelligence, knowledge, experience, brains, talent	Wisdom, human values, vitality
What creates value?	Volume	Speed	De-complexing complexity
For whom do we produce?	Mass market	Mass customization	Positive societal impact
What is our orientation?	Shareholder value	Shareholder value, market value	Societal value
What do we trade?	Money-based. Output of heavy goods	Usable, focused knowledge. Globally developed, traded and managed	Meaningful knowledge: synthesis of integrity, wisdom and conduct
How is information technology used?	Mechanization, automating the present	Enabling and supporting current and innovative business processes. Connectivity. Collaborative technologies.	IT forms a sustainable source of wealth itself. Part of human competencies are performed by smart machines. It is used to simplify business processes.
Skills?	Manual, single loop, for specific task	Mental, double loop, multi-tasking	Artificial, creative, interactive loop, competencies/capabilities
Dominant organizing principle	Hierarchical	Network	Virtual
Education	State-provided one-time education	Education permanent by several providers: schools, companies, interactive systems	Education is part of everyday life.

Adapted from: Arthur (1996), Bunc (1992), Despres and Hiltrop (1996), Lampel and Mintzberg (1996), Sveiby (1997)[15]

'Why on earth would a brewery need to become a knowledge company?' 'Well, it understands that it has to be ready to launch itself into the twenty-first century. That's why it has been preparing scenarios.' 'Give me an example.' 'Well, one scenario involved structuring the company to become a value-adding knowledge organization. From the core, the executive board directs and focuses company knowledge that relates to overall performance and strategic and operational decisions. Activities of the operating companies – the OPCOs – and their smaller production families called clusters are now process-based as are corporate functions and executive activities. Smart networks connect all functions to each other.'

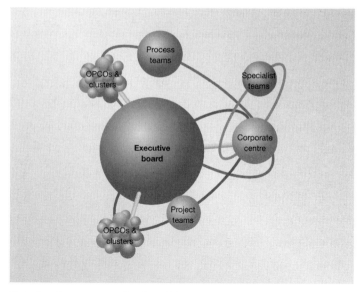

Heineken becomes a value-based knowledge company

Brewing up knowledge

Traditionally a pyramid has been used to show a functional organization. That, however, is now a thing of the past. Because a knowledge company is organized not like a static pyramid but rather like an atom. Key processes are interconnected around a nucleus, ensuring that everything is maintained in balance and is kept moving continuously.

Heineken is one of the world's leading breweries. Recently it has developed scenarios to restructure itself in a way particularly appropriate to a value-adding knowledge company. For it takes as its starting point the various processes which are needed to keep it in business. The strategic tasks are process-based and connected to each other by smart networks. The executive board gathers and manages all of the company's knowledge relevant to the overall performance of the company, including strategic and operational decisions, giving direction, and focusing knowledge. These company-wide issues are dealt with in the strategic sub-processes and processes of the organization. Major strategic activities of the operating companies – the OPCOs – as well as production families – called clusters – are gradually becoming process-based. Project teams work on projects for innovation and renewal. Whenever there is a major technical problem at one of the breweries, specialist teams are sent out to fix it.

Heineken is an excellent example of the fact that smart organizations are primarily process based. In fact, one of the basic aims of the company was to design an organization where functions are complemented by processes.

Form follows function

Whatever we might have to say about an organization, one fact remains: an organization is essential if people are to work together. But this also highlights one of the facts about any organization: it is only as good as the people who work in it.

One of the dictates of architecture, first suggested by the American architect Louis Sullivan in 1896 is that 'form follows function'. Gellerman suggests that he meant that a building's design should reflect, above all, the uses to which it would be put.[18]

Robbins maintains that organizations are like fingerprints.[19] Each has its unique form, its own identity. Yet we must state that no form is truly unique. Organizations have common aspects. True, they may all be different, yet they have ideas and other elements in common. This in turn means that no matter how well an organization may have been designed, this is no guarantee for future success. Some organizations flourish and others wither and die, even though they seem to share the same logic which resulted in their design.

Why study organizational design?

To a great extent, the design of an organization determines the distribution of resources, authority, information and knowledge. As a consequence, it directly impacts the ability of individual managers to make and implement timely, technically and economically sound and organizationally acceptable decisions. The ability to make and implement such decisions in turn affects a manager's ability to enhance organizational effectiveness. The design of an organization directly affects a manager's ability to coordinate and control the activities of subordinates in order to improve organizational performance. Organizational environments are changing more rapidly than ever. Because the effectiveness of organizational design erodes over time as the environment changes, the organization must be designed to fit current and future environments, not the environments of the past. The most interesting aspects of organizations are not the ways in which they repeat the past but the ways in which they revitalize their energy.
G.P. Huber and W.H. Glick[17]

NovaCare

NovaCare, the largest provider of rehabilitation care, is one of the fastest growing health companies in the US. NovaCare uses 'NovaNet', a software system that captures most of the organization's systems knowledge, such as the rules with which therapists must comply and the information they need to operate effectively. The corporate centre (support organization) uses the system to efficiently distribute logistics, analysis and administrative support to the professional therapists and provides the therapists with information about customers, schedules and billing. It does not, however, give them orders. Rather, it offers background information such as highlights from executive trends and problem areas most pertinent to future operations, collects information from therapists about their costs and services, techniques that have worked well, and changing care patterns in different areas.[16]

Most organizations – particularly those of well-established companies – seem solid, orderly, permanent. Yet closer inspection may reveal that they have become 'museums of history'.[20] Such an inspection will often show that the way they operate is totally different to the way they are organized. Yet even the most solid constructions may actually do little more than hide a situation verging on internal chaos when information systems break down, tribal warfare breaks out, or power games are played, and they certainly obscure the human effort which goes into making an organization work.

An organization is never static. Which is why the comparison with a building is less appropriate. Perhaps it is better to compare an organization to a river. 'Like a river, an organization may appear static, especially if viewed on a map or from a helicopter. But this says little about those who are actually in the moving rivers, swimming, drowning, or safely ensconced in boats.'[21]

Seeking a critical mass

A functional organization is typically an up and down affair: knowledge flows up and down, while instructions are issued from the top. Such organizations need a high critical mass of people and a low critical mass of talent. In a process-based organization, this vertical flow becomes horizontal. Communication is horizontal, the decision process is decentralized, and management is process oriented. And because of this, the organization needs to be less people-intensive but much higher on talented professionals.

Functional organizations flourish in a stable environment and are particularly effective in the production of tangible goods. Process organizations develop a market orientation and focus directly on their ultimate customers.

Knowledge companies shape a new organization architecture

Developing alternative ways of organizing work, and then structuring business processes accordingly, are rapidly becoming essential core managerial competencies for the twenty-first century. But many managers, who at first glance see the new organization graphically depicted, wonder if it is truly a different organizational structure or just a new way of portraying one.

Rest assured, modern knowledge-intensive organizations, built on a firm ICT foundation, have three distinctive features. They are entirely:

1. Process-based
2. Team-based
3. Virtual Community-based.

1. Process redesign is not enough

Various processes operate within an organization. There are situational processes which largely handle problems which arise, which are dealt with, and then discarded. Strategic processes deal with company-wide issues. Operational processes concentrate on day-to-day practices.

Some years ago, business process reengineering was heralded as a major step forward in helping organizations redesign their operations into processes. But while those activities, which were directly involved with customers, were carried out, however, the executive boards and the corporate centres were largely left as functional entities and the way they are organized is largely the legacy of the Industrial Age.

One of the aims of business process reengineering was to have decision making at a lower level in the organization. People often turned to a business unit structure as a first step to help move the company towards a process-based organization. Self-managed teams were introduced and this, it was hoped, would eventually evolve into a process organization. Unfortunately, this approach can take such a long time that the organization simply relapses into its old functional habits. Or companies don't dare take the consequences of a full process-based organization. And so the longer totally powerful at the top and no more functional empires. The effort comes to nothing. And the lesson we must learn is that business process reengineering is not enough to create a process organization.

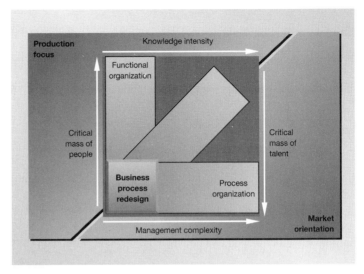

Value-creating knowledge companies focus on talent

Focus on talent

'Embracing an old paradigm, 'the functional organization produces tangible goods and services and has an overall production focus. Information flows up and down, utilizing a management style that controls and commands.' 'Workers just weren't supposed to be smarter than the boss.' 'Exactly. Generally speaking, the functional organization needs a large mass of people with little talent. When organizations cast off the mantle of this vertical structure and replace it with functional units they transform themselves into a total – process organization. Now the company is characterized by its horizontal flow of information and communication, its decentralized authority over decisions, and its process-oriented management.

These organizations may tend to be less people-intensive, but the professionals working in them score high on the talent scale.' 'Managers in knowledge organizations like this must cope with increasing complexity in order to develop process- and team-based organizations that are market and society driven...customer focused.' 'Business process

redesign was once seen as the solution.' 'True. Some years ago, BPR helped organizations reduce complexity by reengineering their operational and customer-directed activities into processes. Unfortunately, the executive board and corporate headquarters often remained functional, reflecting the old paradigm way of thinking.'

Committed to total process management

Instead, companies have to commit themselves to becoming totally process-oriented companies. This means a total transformation from the vertical structure of a functional organization to the horizontal structure of strategic and operational, cross-functional, empowered teams. Most importantly, these teams have to be held accountable for the work flow. Responsibility, authority and accountability have to go hand in hand.

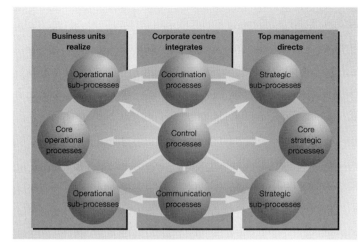

Commit to total process management

Business units are re-organized according to core operational processes and sub-processes. Each business unit realizes and delivers one or more products to a defined market. The corporate centre is redesigned to perform coordination, control and communication processes. Their key competence is to integrate the operational and strategic processes within one process organization. Top management concerned with company-wide issues directs core strategic processes to focus the company according to its mission and vision. These tasks can also be assigned to teams.

Staying ahead the Heineken way

Heineken NV designed a number of scenarios to see whether its corporate office could become more process oriented. This can be done once you think of the strategic activities a corporate office performs during the strategic process. Three questions need to be answered:

– What is the added value of the corporate office?
– What strategic processes apply?
– How can the corporate office be organized around these processes?

The main purpose of the corporate office was defined as providing effective support to the executive board in formulating and realizing the strategy of the company as a whole. The added value of the corporate office therefore makes the strate-

Commit to total process management

'Total-process organizations are horizontally structured, strategically and operationally oriented, with teams that are responsible for their own work flow. Three process groups are key. Business units, organized around day-to-day operational processes, realize products and services for defined markets. Executive management, concerned with company-wide issues, directs core strategic processes to focus the company according to its mission and vision. These tasks can also be assigned to teams.'
'And what about the corporate centre?'
'With its key competencies in integrating operational and strategic knowledge throughout the organization, it plays a pivotal role in coordination, control and communication processes.'

'When Heineken NV decided to become a process organization, the scenario it followed was to create a smart corporate centre. This translates the company's long-term business objectives into strategic processes. Heineken defined strategic and operational processes critical for its success. It continuously needs to strengthen its worldwide market presence, stimulate production facilities to further enhance their operational excellence …to maximize its financial leverage…and to optimize senior management performance.'

'So the company discarded functional specialization?'

'No, but it formed business teams for the purpose of identifying every strategic process and sub-process. Now, Heineken NV's professionals can work as both leaders and members of several different teams, adding focused value to the overall company performance.'

*In the further development of this scenario this strategic process was incorporated in the other three and in the tasks of the office of the executive board.

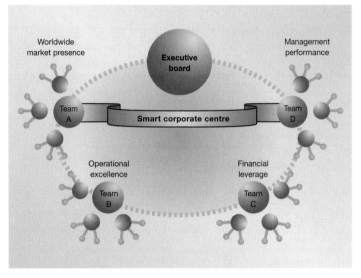

Staying ahead the Heineken way

gic and the operational knowledge which exists above the business units accessible and to use and gives value which it uses to achieve a competitive advantage.

The next step was to define the company strategic processes of the corporate office. Company strategic processes:

- those which are directly relate to the strategy of the company;
- those which are semi-permanent in character, only changing when the strategy of the entire company changes;
- those that make a multifunctional contribution to the company as a whole which goes beyond that of the business units;
- and those which can be divided into separate strategic processes.

In one of the scenarios the following strategic processes were identified:

- strengthening worldwide market presence;
- stimulating operational excellence;
- optimizing (senior) management performance;
- maximizing company financial leverage.*

In this scenario the corporate office will no longer be organized only in functional disciplines. Instead many people will also be organized in teams around the company strategic processes. Corporate office professionals can work in several teams both as team member and team leader. So one day a financial controller can work in a team on the acquisition of an Asian brewery and contribute to strengthening Heineken's worldwide market presence. The next day the same specialist can work in a team giving advice on the budget of a specific operating company.

A board member will no longer be responsible only for a specific function such as legal, tax or finance. In addition to their 'business responsibilities' they will also be responsible for one of the strategic processes ('corporate process responsibility'). The exercise of this responsibility and therefore the added value and accountability also become much clearer.

An office of the executive board will be created to handle those tasks that are essential but that are not related to a specific process. These tasks will include consolidation, office management and corporate communication. Multifunctional company matters which arise spontaneously, which require an immediate solution and which have a clear prescribed duration, are handled by 'corporate taskforces'.

The teams are connected together using smart networks. Professionals work together in soft networks of people and knowledge. They are supported by hard networks forming an electronic performance system: personal productivity tools, communication tools and knowledge tools.

A shift in focus
As managing knowledge and focusing efforts to ensure that it adds value becomes increasingly a core task of top management, so it will become increasingly more important to distinguish between content providers, content organizers, and content directors. It is essential that companies understand the significance of each of these activities and ensure that they are carried out by the appropriate parts of the company. The business units – those nearest the market and responsible for operational matters – are the basic content providers. This is also the area of operational knowledge management. The corporate centre acts as the content organizer, often using IT. Top management ensures that content is directed and strategically

Company processes focus on content

'There are three knowledge management processes that need to take place in all the units of the company.'

'All the same?'

'No – each with a difference in focus. The corporate centre primarily combines and connects knowledge to both strategy and operations in a powerful manner. The executive management senses and responds to both internal and external developments affecting the company. Business units interact directly with customers, teams and each other to create and produce products and services and relevant know-how for top managers and the corporate centre.'

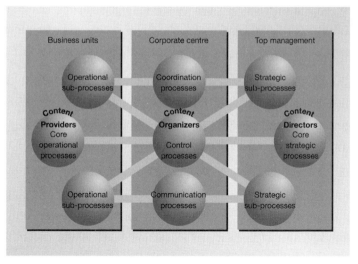

Company processes focus on content

focused on the value it needs to add to the company. The expansion of IT throughout the organization will probably mean that the role of the corporate centre will diminish in the future. Already many IT networks are directly connecting operational processes and strategic processes. All this implies that, as content becomes of increasing importance, units will need to play different roles to the ones they have become accustomed to playing in the industrial age.

2. Teams rule

Teams are the watchword in the new knowledge economy, for they are the force which can break the tyranny of the functional organization. Team-based management will give your company the competitive edge by helping you move away, once and for all, from the functional mind-set.

Teams, however, working in isolation, are not the complete solution. Because in the new knowledge economy, it is essential that the teams are tied together by knowledge management. Only then can the company really move into the new age.

In a team-based organization, executive management senses and responds to developments both inside and outside the company. The corporate centre has the task of combining and connecting value added know-how to both strategic and

Teams tackle three competencies with one being the core

'When value is the main focus of company processes, can management continue in the same old roles?'

'Of course not. They must assume new roles. In linking knowledge to value, the value-adding knowledge company distinguishes between three key responsibilities. Business units generally serve as content

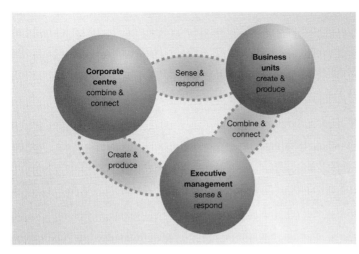

Teams tackle three competencies with one being the core

operational levels. And the business units – those nearest the customer – have the task of creating and producing relevant know-how for both markets and customers and for executive management and the corporate centre.

Thus we see teams at each level – business units, corporate centre, and executive management – which are responsible for all three knowledge management processes, but only have a core competency in one of those processes.

Similarly, each of the three knowledge management processes mentioned above serve a different purpose. Sense and respond deals with unstructured tacit knowledge. Create and produce deals with structured knowledge. While combine and connect keeps the wheels turning, combining and connecting knowledge from every part of the organization for a dual purpose: to realize improvements in the operational area and to create new ideas in the strategic area.

Managing teams

There is a simple definition of a team: people doing something together. Robbins and Finley point out,[23] it is not the something that is important, it is the together which is important.

The idea, however, that everything will be solved when smart professionals are formed into teams is an illusion. Because a team is a group of individuals, there is always the possibility of

providers regarding what happens within the markets in which companies operate. The executive board, as content directors, focus on what knowledge is of strategic value to the company and how best to create it. The corporate centre acts as a knowledge overseer…as the content organizer.'

'But doesn't that mean the corporate centre may become less important?' 'Indeed. As information technology continues to advance and brings strategic and operational processes closer together, the corporate centre may become less important than it is today.'

Teams are a fad

'Teams are surely a fad, judging by the many books and seminars out there competing for mindshare these days. And yet, it is a fateful fad. All the hoopla about it being the wave of the future is true. Individual teams may disband, or remix, or get shuffled into some new entity. But the idea of teams isn't going away, because it's simply not possible – it's simply not affordable – to return to the days of multiple supervisory levels.'
Robbins and Finley[22]

the individuals influencing each other, both positively and negatively. Forming a team does not do away with those age-old corporate enemies such as tribal warfare, bottlenecks, and the inability or refusal to cooperate. And these effects can emerge even in the knowledge economy. It is important that we recognize the symptoms and take action to rectify the problem.

But we shouldn't be too negative. Working in a team can also have positive, synergetic effects. It helps people to combine their energy. To share and work towards mutual goals, to share knowledge and ideas, to offer peer support and training. These are some of the very positive benefits which can be obtained with teams.

Teams can be very different in nature: some goals can only be achieved by a team with the individual contribution obscured. At other times, work is assigned to a team, taking into consideration the experience and competencies of the individuals within the team (or any variation of this theme).

So how, when teams differ so radically, can a solution be found for a team which is functioning less well than it should? A team which is underperforming and which needs to boost activities to achieve its potential?

Problem	Symptom
Not enough variety in members' backgrounds and experiences	Groupthink and lack of innovation
Too much variety	Output is confusing and no shared goals
Lack of sufficient senior management support and commitment	No sponsorship from top management
Lack of focus or direction	Hard to keep the team on track
Unresolved roles	Team members are uncertain what their jobs are
Lack of team trust	The team is not a team because members are unable to commit to it
Failure to recognize and reward group efforts	Lack of incentives to go the extra mile
The team is threatening the 'larger' organization	The team works unconventionally and therefore challenges conventional rules

Sources of failure: why teams don't work[24]

Despite differences in teams, the solution is always the same: we have to work on the individuals within the team. For teams are always made up of individuals. It is vital that we find a link between the individual and the output of the team as a whole.

Teamwork involves behaviours that coincide with the inter-action of team members to achieve desired goals and adapt to circumstances in order to do so. Each team member has differ-ent strengths and weaknesses, competency profiles, blind spots, humour, and 'hot buttons'. If such a 'melting pot' of behaviours is to be focused, a shared purpose and a sense of urgency is necessary to mobilize and direct the energy. To be able to measure the performance of a team, specific targets are required and performance indicators must be defined. Effective teams are characterized by their changing and developing behaviours and skills. Styles of performance may vary from team to team, or within some teams, depending on the circum-stance. Teamwork – and therefore overall team performance indicators and individual performance indicators – can change and develop over time.[25]

A necessary evil?

For many companies teams are still an unwanted intrusion into standard operating practice. Replacing a functional organi-zation with a team-based one requires a drastic change for any company. Management structures are often too inflexible to allow this to happen without a struggle. There is little support for the necessary transformation process. Companies are, they say, not ready for the radical departure from the past which the creation of teams will demand.

If this is the attitude, the only possible outcome is the slow death of the company. 'Slow death begins when someone, con-fronting the dilemma of having to make deep organizational change or accepting the status quo, regrets the option for deep change. This decision results in gradual (or occasionally not so gradual) disintegration of an organization, business or indus-try.'[27] Functionally based companies simply do not have the flexibility and speed to respond to the market, to get products and services faster to market than the competitors. It is these practical demands which are forcing companies to adopt a team organization, whether they like it or not.

A team consists of a small number of people – generally six to eight – with complementary skills who are committed to a common purpose, common performance goals and to an approach for which they hold themselves mutually accountable. And this underlines the difference between a team and a work group. For the latter is generally just a group of individuals who do little more than share information and help each other handle their area of responsibility more effectively. Work groups, moreover, generally focus on a specific task or function, while a team involves the organization of the work around a process.

Some teams can develop into high performance teams. Teams where members become committed to one another's personal growth and success.[28] In today's business world this is more complicated; in team-based organizations employees are increasingly forced to depend on others who have competencies and resources which they formally cannot control and often do not even understand. But on the positive side, each individual working in a team-based organization is encouraged to use his or her special competencies to the good of the whole.

The rise of virtual knowledge teams (VKT):

Virtual knowledge teams have three characteristics that distinguish them from other knowledge teams. First, their members are always in multiple locations. Second, they are often considerably more diverse than other teams (different cultures, languages). And third, these teams do not typically have constant membership. Some members may participate in all team activities, while others may only work on some. A successful example of a VKT is the Oklahoma City disaster task force (remember April 1995, when disaster struck Oklahoma City as domestic terrorists bombed the Murrah federal building?). 'As individuals, the members of the Oklahoma City disaster task force responded with courage and skill. They were smart people. But their individual effectiveness was amplified because they also had a smart organization, a special organization established just for this emergency. As a virtual knowledge team, they coordinated multiple dangerous tasks – no small accomplishment when you consider the number of agencies and specialists involved and the fact that they were operating under the pressure of the intense spotlight created by the international media. The diverse emergency team had a clear purpose: to rescue victims and catch the bombers. It succeeded to a large degree because the team members operated as though they had a common mind – a distributed mind – that shared information, clues, and ideas seamlessly.'
K. Fisher and M.D. Fisher[26]

Managing knowledge through teams of smart professionals

In the knowledge economy, it will simply not be possible to compete and be successful unless a company transforms itself into a team-based, process-driven organization. An excellent model for such an organization – and a way of defining the role the smart professionals will play in that organization – is called the double helix of teamwork. This is a double corkscrew which shows the various roles and functions of smart professionals in strategic processes – those which deal with the company as a whole – operational processes – those which deal with the products and services of the company – and as an individual – those factors which enhance the value of the smart professional through personal and professional development.

As we have already seen, team performance can only be improved by starting with the individual. A smart professional can participate in a team as team leader or team member, or adopt both functions by operating in two teams simultaneously. As a team leader in one team – team A in the example – a smart professional will need to show the core competence of sensing and responding while dealing with unstructured knowledge. After a few years in this team he can leave to refresh and refocus. Then as a team member in team B, he can use the core competence of direct and guide.

For knowledge professionals, the double helix contains four areas which are of particular importance to them. First is the area of knowledge management in which they will be expected to sense and respond, combine and connect, and create and produce unstructured knowledge. Second is the area of team management in which they must direct and guide, coordinate and control, and participate and develop (high) potential in colleague team members. Third, they must involve themselves in talent management to detect and develop. And fourth, they will have to become involved in self management by applying refresh and refocus at regular intervals in their career.

The double helix also illustrates three important truths about teamwork. First, that talent is abundant, if we know how to detect and develop it. Second, that people cannot constantly work 'in the firing line'; even management needs time to refresh itself and refocus its efforts. Third, the team has to be responsible for its own performance.

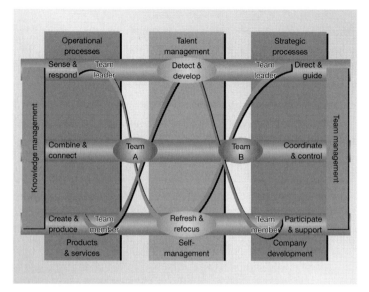

Follow the double helix of teamwork

The double helix of teamwork

'Four aspects of teamwork are essential to bring company processes to value…knowledge management…team management…talent management and self-management.'

'Explain, please.'

'Knowledge management involves the team's ability to sense and respond… combine and connect…and create and produce results. Team management's role on the other hand is to direct and guide…coordinate and control…and participate in and support team performance. To identify the roles and functions of smart professionals, we must follow the double helix of teamwork. Operational processes focus on the development of products and services… strategic processes head company development… talent management and self-management enhance the individual's professional and personal growth, increasing his or her competencies and value to the company at the same time.'

'And what does that mean in knowledge management terms?'

'Well, the team leader of process team A predominately senses and responds, and in team management she mainly directs and guides. After a few years, she might leave the team to refresh and refocus and become a member of a different team.

Then there's the member of team A who, in the area of knowledge management, focuses on creating and producing products and services while participating in and supporting the team. After completing this project, he may be identified as someone to develop as a team leader. He now has the job of directing and guiding the team.'

'So smart professionals can participate as either team leaders or members, or both at the same time.'

'Exactly. The double helix of team work acknowledges three important truths. Hidden talent is abundant, we just need to recognize and develop it. People cannot work on the 'firing line' without relief. And the team is responsible for achieving its business goals.'

Team leader

Making a team responsible and accountable for its own perform-ance obviously has repercussions for the team leader. They must avoid 'knowing what is best' for the team. They are facilitators, not old-style managers who are still trapped in the 'order and obey' environment which reigned for so long in the industrial age. Some team leaders are so smart, that their personal competency may actually exceed their ability to coach. They are in danger of taking control and rushing ahead, leaving others trailing behind.

A good team leader is one who realizes that his or her main task is to assign professionals to projects and processes that will develop individuals by providing learning opportunities in undiscovered areas.

Shadow teams: envisioning and creating your own competitor

A new phenomenon which is being introduced into knowledge management is the shadow team – a special team which has as its task 'shadowing' a competitor and learning everything there is to know about it. A team which can think, reason and react like the competitor is an invaluable source of information for any manager. Such teams must operate outside any structural confines of the company so that they can report unfiltered analyses directly to the strategic players. Early team development must be carefully monitored and ample technical training must be given. Measurable goals are essential. Ideally, the shadow team should be very small – perhaps made up of company 'champions' – and have access to a network of experts within the company. A variety of dispositions not such a long period with the company so that they are absorbed by it are obvious advantages.[32]

Affinity teams

Another specific type of team is the 'Affinity Team'. 'An affinity group is a collegial association of peers that meets on a regular basis to share information, capture opportunities, and solve problems that affect the group and the overall organization. Affinity groups are a horizontal, cross-cutting mechanism.'[34]

The key characteristics of an affinity group are:

– group members have the same job position or title;
– the specific role of each group member is formalized;

Talking about teams...

At a job interview, a man was asked if he was a 'team player'. 'Yes,' he replied, 'team captain.'[29]

Members of 'hot' teams feel that they are stretching themselves, surpassing themselves, moving beyond their own limits.[30]

'You are the problem. You prevent people from really doing their jobs. You dominate meetings. You give your own solutions – sometimes even before the problem is raised. You finish other people's sentences. You state your opinions first. Who's going to argue with you? You cut people off. You change agendas during the meeting, raising issues no one else is prepared to discuss. People leave meetings feeling discouraged rather than energized. You insist on making every decision. No wonder people don't take responsibility. You won't let them.'[31]

- group meetings are held at regular, frequent intervals;
- there is a charter which states the mission and domain of the specific group;
- the group is self-managing and is responsible for managing its processes and output.

Create the smart corporate centre

As teams become the central focus of many companies, the question arises whether, in a team-based organization, headquarters staff are really necessary. Indeed this is a question frequently asked during any reengineering process. As companies begin to abandon the hierarchical functional structure and move towards a process organization, so the position, task, and manpower required has been held up to close scrutiny. Accordingly, reducing headquarters staff is often seen as a first step in the right direction and is grasped by many executive boards to show they mean business. John Browne, the CEO of British Petroleum, acknowledges that a large staff at corporate headquarters is often the result of traditionally complicated structures. In a recent interview he underlined that the new BP corporate structure 'is a far cry from the complicated structure we used to have, which included enormous regional organizations, matrix management, and huge staffs in the headquarters of the company and of the business groups. Excluding the people in the financial and oil-trading organizations, the headquarters of the company and of the business groups now employ only 350 people – an incredibly small number for a company with revenues of $70 billion. In 1989, that total was about 4000.'[35] This reduction in headquarters personnel is being reflected by other major companies. KLM has reduced its HQ staff from 900 to 740.[36] At Philips, the reorganization has started by reducing the headquarters' staff from 730 to around 400.[37] Similar reductions have taken place at Shell.

This does not, of course, mean that all the functions undertaken by the corporate centre are by definition superfluous. There are many essential services which must be carried out, all aimed at supporting either the executive board (strategy, infrastructure, public relations, legal advice, mergers and acquisitions) or operations (personnel, purchasing, outsourcing contracts, accounting).

In accountancy terms, these 'overhead' functions are considered a 'burden'. And so, while many companies recognize the importance of the individual functions, they frequently take steps to reduce the costs involved in them and at the same time try to make them more productive and build up a base of competence around the corporate centre which is vital for success. The question asked by many large companies is how much the corporate centre, contributing to the success of the business?'

All too often, however, the 'reduction' of headquarters staff is little more than a 'displacement' exercise – the functions are shifted from head office down to the business unit or somewhere else in the organization. 'Today the guys from corporate are gone, scraped out like so much fatty arterial plaque. (Instead of clipboard-toting staff we have laptop-toting consultants.) But most companies still labour under a costly burden of staff work that adds little value. The fat's harder to find because it's less likely to clump around the corporate heart, but it's still there.'[39]

automatic right to exist. It can only be justified economically if it adds more value than it subtracts. In many cases, the net is negative for at least a major part of the portfolio. In other words, value destruction often exceeds value creation.'
Sadtler, Campbell and Koch[38]

The 'chaordic' organization

Dee Ward Hock, the founder of the VISA organization, uses a favourite trick to put his idea of a shining synthesis of chaos and order into practice: 'How many of you recognize this', he asks, holding up his own Visa card. Every hand in the room goes up.

'Now,' Hock continues, 'how many of you can tell me who owns it, where it is headquartered, how it is governed, or where to buy its shares?' Confused silence. No one has the slightest idea, because no one has ever thought about it.'[41]

– Business units fail to focus because they are preoccupied with the present or the past.
– Business units fail to refocus because they misunderstand the future. Future doesn't mean futuristic. Some companies lose their way when their strategies get so far ahead of reality that it becomes impossible for managers to evaluate intelligently strategic importance, significance and profitability.
– Companies fail to refocus because they have no formal procedure for pruning, only for planting. The scarcest resources in any enterprise are people who are knowledgeable, experienced, forward-looking and able to lead. What a shame when these resources are wasted on customers, products, services, and employees that are not strategically important, significant, or profitable. *Whitney*[42]

Expected value	Potential cost
Reduced size of corporate centre	Increased staffing in the divisions and business units
Reduced payroll	Increased capital expenses (investments in IT and insourcing)
Faster decisions and competitive response	Danger of 'corporate whiplash' unless rapid responses are anchored to a well-articulated corporate vision/mission statement
Higher management morale (greater degrees of freedom to act independently)	Necessity of adapting the profile and competencies of general managers according to the new requirements
Less 'analysis/paralysis'	Great danger of shooting from the hip and decisions based on *ad hoc* data and insufficient analysis
Delayering of management levels	Unavailability of 'organizational slack' for innovation and creativity and few management development opportunities
Fewer administrative procedures and policy manuals/rules	Increasing transaction and communication costs

Cost/benefit trade-offs in corporate centre staff reductions[40]

Multi-business companies have a variety of cutting back on their corporate centre staff. The table cost/benefit trade-offs in corporate centre staff reductions summarizes the traditional cost/benefits trade-offs in corporate centre staff reduction.

The end of business units?

At the end of the Industrial Age, many traditional corporate centres lost their strategic focus. Today, as Hans Strikwerda points out,[43] the same fate is threatening business units. It is perhaps strange that this should be happening: after all, business units are close to the market-place and should be carefully tuned to the needs and changing wishes of the customer.

The danger lies in the fact that the operational nature of many business units leads them to concentrate far too closely on what the organization does best. Whitney[42] may call this a 'bit of a popular business platitude'. Yet this does not detract from the truth of the situation. It is the same situation we have referred to in smart strategies: a too focused idea of a company's business can be restricting, for it prohibits a company from liberating resources which allow innovation and growth. It is a matter of whether you see yourself as a manufacturer of better carts – or a company that provides transport solutions.

Corporate centres: the pros and cons

The role of the corporate centre is changing. That is certain, and through IT, it could become even less important in the future than it is today. Many IT systems already allow for less involvement of the corporate centre by connecting strategic processes with operational processes. What's more, many corporate centres are being 'sandwiched' between operational business units and the executive board. Certainly the past has taught us that the corporate centre's influence over a business unit has caused business unit managers to make the wrong decisions – or at least to make poorer decisions than they would have if left to their own devices.

What is the smart solution?

Many 'old guard' corporate centres maintain authority over devising strategy, implementing financial controls and managing operations. In the knowledge economy, this 'old guard' can easily act as value destroyers as they become (too) bureaucratic and (too) expensive. When rethinking the role of the corporate centre, many managers fall into the 'industrial economy' trap of believing that they have to make an 'either/or' decision: should they become a strategic holding, with no operational influence or an operational holding, leaving the strategy to others.

The dangers of these two approaches is that a strategic holding can all too easily develop into an 'ivory tower', divorced from the reality of business. And an operational holding can fill up with 'know-it-alls' who quickly become a burden and easily duplicate the responsibilities of the other operational units within the company.

A third option is that the corporate centre should act as a financial holding, setting and plotting company-wide finan-

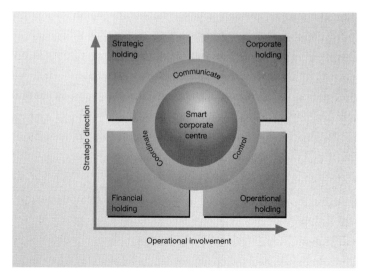

Smart corporate centres tie it all together

'In repurposing the role and responsibilities of the corporate office, more often than not, management believes it has only "either/or" choices. Some think their corporate office should become a strategic holding with no operational influence. They run the risk of falling into the "ivory tower syndrome". Other managers prefer that their office becomes an operational holding, leaving the strategy to others.

'When this happens, those "know-it-alls" at headquarters quickly become a burden and easily duplicate responsibilities of the business units, managers or functional specialists.'

'There are also managers who believe the Corporate Office should function as a Financial Holding...trailing illusive, company-wide financial targets. In essence, companies become banks, sometimes forgetting the heart of the business.'

'Gearing for the knowledge economy, the smart corporate centre is the best solution. It adds value to the future of the entire company because it knows all without trying to do all. It leaves decisions and the execution of strategies to knowledge professionals at all levels of the organization. The smart corporate centre proves its value by coordinating critical strategies and operational activities... by communicating this meaningful knowledge to all concerned, anytime, anywhere, anyway...and by controlling legal and financial knowledge that is required for effective company management.'

cial targets. With this option, companies can easily become banks, sometimes even forgetting the business they are in.

The smart corporate centre is the best solution in the knowledge economy – mainly because it is an 'and/and' solution. It adds value to the future of the entire company because it knows all without trying to do all. It leaves decisions and the execution of strategies to knowledge professionals at all levels of the organization. It coordinates critical strategies and operational activities by communicating this meaningful knowledge to all concerned, and by controlling the legal and financial knowledge that is required for effective company management.

And so we see that the knowledge holding combines all the advantages of the strategic holding, the financial holding and the operational holding. The emerging knowledge holding blurs the traditional differences between these various holdings.

3. Virtual communities provide the glue

Virtual communities are not just a concept that executives can choose to ignore, they represent a change that has already transformed the business landscape. A virtual community is an ICT-enabled network of people with a common (professional) discipline or interest. It enables its members to share information and innovation. Benjamin defines it clearly, 'In the end, communities are tools through which members can experience themselves – who they are and what they might become. Virtual communities must be established and managed with the fundamental requirements of trust and commitment.'[44]

The true killer approach of tomorrow's digital economy will be communities that allow us to work easily, universally, inexpensively and – most importantly – on our own terms.

We all know the informal networks that exist within organizations, they are in fact a rudimentary form of communities. Members of a network often use e-mail with the purpose of keeping each other informed. Communities of interest are built

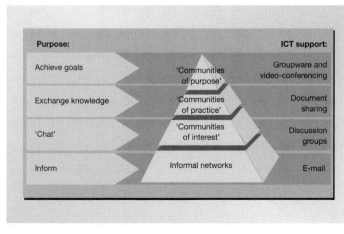

The rise of virtual knowledge communities

around a common interest like tasting fine wines, or listening to Motown oldies but goodies. These 'chat' communities are extremely popular on the Internet where the number of discussion groups and other chat-boxes is enormous.

Even more sophisticated are communities of practice. The purpose of this type of community is to exchange practice knowledge around, e.g. how to operate specific software or how to sell products to specific clients. Here knowledge sharing often takes place through document sharing. To prevent communities from becoming time-consuming chat-groups, companies can form communities of purpose and set specific targets for the communities, such as, cutting delivery times to customers by 20 per cent. In this type of community ICT support may include groupware and video-conferencing.

Communities can become very powerful tools when they are used to bind customers to the organization. Through these external communities employees and customers can discuss client problems and company solutions. Clients can share their experiences with the company; information the company uses to improve its products and services. Once again, this emphasizes the importance of connecting people.

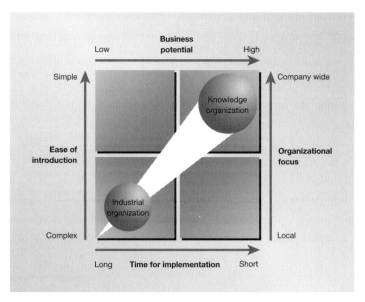

Communities offer four levels of intangible benefits

Virtual communities themselves can deliver four levels of intangible benefits. First of all, they have been known to have an enormous potential for success and unexpected profits. Second, for global-oriented companies, their focus – company wide – is ideal. Third, communities require a relatively short time to initiate and fourth, there is a comforting ease of introduction that prevails.

The successful introduction of virtual knowledge communities within such companies as Montell Polyolefins often raises issues around determining the 'true' value of the company (i.e. the value that is contained in its intangible, off-balance-sheet knowledge assets). In order to mine this 'hidden gold', companies have to recognize that their 'old' industrial ways of organizing and managing have become inadequate. Overall, companies take the significant step of introducing virtual communities to enhance business performance. It has proven to be a favourable decision, not only in terms of performance, but also by providing a solid basis for introducing new methods of working in the next century.

Virtualization holds exceptional business benefits

Forget about 'following', now it's either 'lead', or 'just get out of the way'. A major challenge for management, when deciding whether to start a virtual community is thinking and acting from a virtual perspective. In essence, 'virtual communities' can provide a good first step in transforming companies into 'virtual corporations'. A clear, generic organizational structure that encompasses all of these guiding principles, however, is not readily available off the shelf. It must be tailor-made with the particulars of your company in mind.

Experience in helping organizations go virtual revealed that business value can be created by adopting four guiding principles: 1) focus on business strengths by outsourcing non-core competencies, 2) minimize physical presence and infrastructure by organizing in virtual teams, 3) nurture intellectual capital by establishing a network of innovative business and knowledge alliances and 4) invest substantially in effective ICT.

Communities offer four levels of intangible benefits

'The reason why I like the concept of communities so much is that they enable companies to become true knowledge organizations without having to reorganize. The strength of a virtual community rests in its ability to fulfil multiple needs simultaneously. Through communities, management can stimulate and facilitate business expansion in new markets, global co-operation and coordination, and knowledge sharing. Communities allow for knowledge sharing, collaboration and coordination within the existing organizational structure without requiring a reorganization. The community structure is simply an overlay to your existing structure.'

Virtual plastics

Montell Polyolefins, a global leader in polyolefin materials and technology, created knowledge-sharing communities to reduce operating costs. Each community was given the target to improve extruder performance and therefore reliability by 1 per cent at all sites. Doesn't sound like much – until you understand that this community effort saved the company $15 million.

The three Cs to exploiting new market opportunities through communities relies on combining content, customers and communication. This seems to be the guaranteed way to unleash the creativity and innovation required to explore and exploit the enormous potential embedded in a virtual community. We believe that direct contact with the customer (marketing and sales) will be completely transformed within a community structure.

CHAPTER 9

'Smart professionals'

How companies and professionals
create an upward value spiral

In 1982 the editors of *Fortune* published a book entitled *Working Smarter*. At that time, the US economy was in a bad shape. The Chairman of the American Productivity Center, C. Jackson Grayson Jr., stated that 'The alarm bells are finally beginning to ring'.[2] He was talking about the deterioration of American productivity. Productivity performance was perhaps the best single indicator of an economy's vitality, and its decline was considered by many as the most basic sickness of the US economy. 'Rising productivity, after all, is where the gains in standard of living come from'.[3] And this productivity can primarily be produced by the diffusion of knowledge. 'This diffusion of knowledge is where the leverage comes from'.[4]

Bowen's ideas about knowledge were exceptional in his time. In the 1970s and 1980s, knowledge was considered a scarce commodity, inflexible in its supply, not a consideration for productivity. Not surprising because, for many economists and business people, the production of intangibles (goods and services) is based on ideas rather than material matters. Although many companies are moving away from being in the 'thing' business to being in the 'thinking' business, management problems are still found. And serious ones at that. Mainly because people have a burning desire to measure the knowledge content of economic activities. Early attempts at managing and measuring intangible assets – the talents of people, the ideas embedded in systems and humans, the software, the relationship to customers, the knowledge content of tangible products – have all been confronted with a mixture of enthusiasm and primarily scepticism. But mainly the latter.

Pricing knowledge

P.M. Romer, economist at Stanford University: 'The lesson is that as soon as you start to price knowledge, you get into awkward situations where your knowledge is not being used as it could be. This is just a fact of life.'
Kurzman[1]

In the Industrial Age, people turned up for work and did their jobs. It was a time when productivity was ensured by routinization of work and the elimination of any deviation from the norm. Creativity was frowned upon. Jobs were increasingly prescribed within ever narrower limits. And narrow jobs led to narrow people.

In today's hypercompetitive market space, narrow-mindedness is the last thing smart organizations can afford.

When people start working in a smart way, it is as if a breath of fresh air sweeps through their working environment. Almost every company agrees that we have entered the knowledge economy – and this means the age of the knowledge professional. Human capital is recognized as the driving force for innovation and sustainable competitive advantage.

Or is it? Much of our thinking about organizations was coined before or during the Industrial Age. We think in terms of functions, when we should be thinking in terms of individuals. For in smart organizations, individuals become the vessels of knowledge rather than the position they might hold. Coordination is not the result of a chain of command, but the result of collaboration between the various members of a team. The more smart knowledge is shared, the more the hierarchy as a coordinating mechanism is undermined, and the more management's source of legitimacy is eroded.

Professional work

The birth of assembly on-line workers

'Laptops, cellular phones, wireless modems and fax machines may change the work environment for many professionals, but they don't alter the thought process that ultimately leads to breakthroughs. What those tools have done, however, is to help extend the working day. In effect they have created a portable assembly line for the 1990s that allows white collar workers to remain on-line in planes, trains, cars and at home.'

Failing to reflect 'knowledge economy reality'

'Consider the financial services industry. According to the US Department of Labor, the average worker in finance currently toils 35.5 hours a week (a figure that has dropped more than a full hour from the 36.6 hours recorded a decade ago). Try finding a professional in that industry whose work schedule conforms to those numbers.'
S.S. Roach[5]

The value of information in the economy of ideas

'Value is highly subjective and conditional. Yesterday's papers are quite valuable to the historian. In fact, the older they are, the more valuable they become. On the other hand, a commodities broker might consider news of an event that occurred more than an hour ago to have lost any relevance.'
J.P. Barlow[6]

The knowledge worker's 'smart head' contains a share of the company's intellectual capital and this makes him or her both stakeholder and shareholder of the most valuable asset a company owns. The result is that the knowledge worker gradually moves into the role of manager, because developing and mining the new organizational wealth has traditionally been the work of managers and CEOs.

Companies depend on people for knowledge. But knowledge systems will challenge that position and will become more powerful. Indeed, this is already happening in a number of areas. Take, for example, the cockpit of an aircraft, which has almost become a smart machine in itself. The stock exchange is run almost purely on the basis of sophisticated IT. As this trend continues, a shift occurs away from machines that support people to people who are supporting systems. So the real value of knowledge systems will be to increase the professional performance of the individual. In addition, they will take care of creating and embedding knowledge in the organization.

The hard and soft parts of smart networks

All this presupposes an on-going integration of hard and soft networks. The hard network – knowledge systems, intelligent agents, quantum computers – will work together to distribute data, information and knowledge. And they will do it more quickly, more usefully and to a greater area than ever before.

Soft systems, on the other hand, will be the formal and informal networks developed between people. These will play an important part in decision making, making trade-offs, power politics, and the like.

The important task is to prevent people from becoming dependent on systems and at the same time prevent systems from becoming dependent on people.

And yet that has already happened. Take the electronic workplace. Thirty years ago, a power failure would have been irritating, but not totally disruptive. Work could have continued, albeit at less than full potential. Today? Everything grinds to a halt.

A smart network integrates hard networks and soft networks. It is made up of people who work with people, people who work with systems, and systems that work with systems to add value to both people and systems.

'The machine right now could be as smart as a person – if we knew how to program them.'
Minsky, quoted in Crever, 1997[7]

Malaysia: Prime Minister Mahathir says knowledge workers will drive the new economy
'Current global trends require that we switch our economic base again, from an economy reliant on cheap labour to one that is driven by knowledge workers. Current projections indicate that, through an information and knowledge–based economy, we can increase our Gross Domestic Product levels by fourfold within 20 to 25 years…'[8]

The nail in the functional coffin

The days of the functional way of working are numbered. And smart professionals are playing a vital role in bringing about the demise of this phenomenon that has outlived its usefulness.

Knowledge professionals use their unique competencies – often esoteric and well guarded – to tackle semi-structured/ unstructured problems and opportunities. Their work consists largely of converting data and information – and other intangible factors (feelings, ideas) – into meaningful knowledge. This knowledge is shared and focused on smart strategies and is usually highly contextual, acquired through practice and unique relationships, difficult to verbalize, much less to codify.[9]

Smart professionals, for example, act together to free a company from the tyranny of a functional organization in which managers are supposed to think and guide, while employees are supposed to work and do what they are told. This traditional separation of replaceable and irreplaceable employees – the haves and the have-nots – completely disappears.

In functional organizations, there is a distinct difference between line and staff managers in knowledge, orientation, and result-orientation. Staff managers tend to possess a great deal of knowledge about a limited number of things, while line

Smart professionals act together

'Connecting everyone throughout the company directly to our business strategy can be an organizational challenge. In old-style industrial organizations, managers were paid to think, employees were paid to do. Authority and knowledge went hand in hand. At the upper level, managers enjoyed an irreplaceable status. They were there to guide employees who executed directives…and once the work was done, oftentimes the workers were, too.'
'How many times have we heard people say they worked themselves out of a job?'
'Smart professionals no longer tolerate the separation between the "information haves" and the "information have-nots".'
'Smart organizations don't either.'

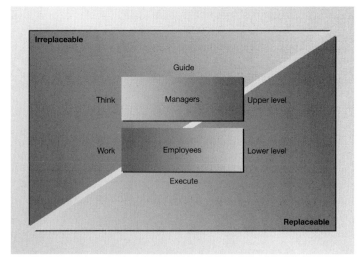

Smart professionals act together

managers have a smattering of knowledge about a whole range of things. Staff managers keep themselves up-to-date in their individual professions, thinking of themselves as specialists. Line managers make direct decisions and take personal responsibility for results, while staff managers advise, consult, and are only indirectly accountable.

The end of the functional specialist

In this discussion about smart professionals, it is tempting to assume that we are simply discussing highly trained people with a specialist background and a particular aptitude for knowledge. That we are talking about people with specialized knowledge or knowledge based on experience. This is not the case. Knowledge requirements change very quickly. Often in-house knowledge is rapidly depleted and this takes place randomly, without any logic.

The core business of professionals is to process real-time, up-to-date high-level know-how about business issues. This is what must occupy them. Specialized knowledge is not necessary – it can always be insourced from external specialists.

So what does the knowledge professional really look like in today's changing business environment? Consultants talk

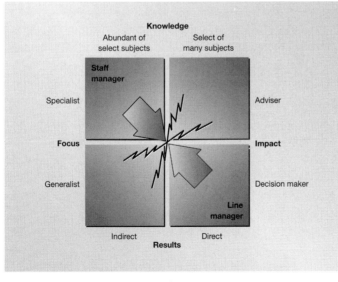

Smart professionals break through

Smart professionals break through

'In industrial organizations, there is a known clash between staff and line managers as a result of four critical differences. Most staff managers possess a great deal of knowledge about a limited number of subjects.'

'Sounds like a professor – somebody who knows so much about so little; they know everything about nothing.'

'Anyway...staff managers keep pace with changing expertise and technology in their respective fields, defining themselves as specialists who advise and consult. In contrast, line managers have some knowledge about many subjects. They make decisions and take direct responsibility for business results. Present day professionals break through the divide between staff and line, combining both perspectives into one generalist team player – the smart professional.'

'In the knowledge economy, the A-shaped knowledge professional is the person companies depend on. Someone who can sense and respond to unstructured knowledge, create and produce structured knowledge, and combine and connect the two, adding value to the organization. Smart professionals possess an individual knowledge perspective – how they view the world – that is mainly a result of their education and training. They build reliable networks of other professionals along the way. They apply any specialized education and work experience they possess in a general way. That's because we need specialized knowledge on a random basis and our requirements change rapidly over time.'

'Tell me then…how does a smart professional acquire new or different knowledge if he or she no longer accumulates know-how as a functional specialist?'

'The answer is simple – they buy experience from outside consultants.'

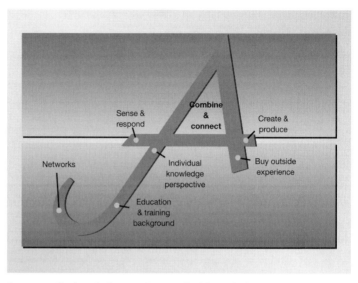

Smart professionals know where to find knowledge

about the T-shaped or π-shaped professional, indicating the need for generalism with one or two specialties.

The answer is that he or she should be A-shaped.

The A-shaped professional is able to sense and respond to unstructured knowledge, create and produce structured knowledge, and connect the two in order to enhance the value of the organization. An A-shaped professional must continuously update their individual knowledge base with specialized education and training. They should also create and maintain connections with other people who are both interesting and interested. And finally, as for in-depth expertise, they should buy it from outside experts.

Building new knowledge competencies

For many years training revolved around teaching people to operate machines. But during the last 20 years, a shift has taken place, and a start was made in training people to work with people. We gave them management courses, leadership training, team-building. We stressed how important it was to adopt an attitude of continuous learning. We impressed on people the need to 'keep up' with the latest developments in specific areas.

But there is one thing we don't do: we never train people in those competencies which are required if we are to use knowledge as a means of production.

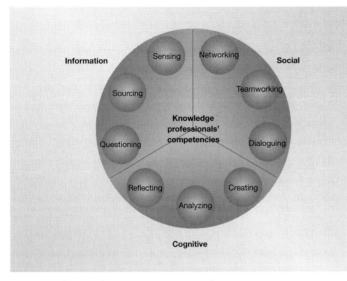

T-shaped skill sets

'People possessing these skills are able to shape their knowledge to fit a problem at hand rather than insist that the problem appear in a particular, recognizable form.'

D. Leonard-Barton[10]

Smart professionals own new competencies

Smart Professionals own new competencies

'Smart professionals possess a new combination of competencies.'

'How?'

'Because they work with knowledge instead of tangible assets. With information competencies, they know where to look for information and how to assess its value...and, they sense which questions to ask.

Smart professionals skilled in social competencies are receptive and without prejudice, welcoming new information they learn from networking with others. They work in teams, taking advantage of the synergistic effects of building on each other's capabilities. They also learn by listening and talking to colleagues and do both with an open mind. And with strong cognitive skills, smart professionals enhance their mental power by exercising their "right brain" abilities – creating, discovering new applications and solutions, analyzing and organizing information and concepts into systems and models. Reflecting, playing back and thinking about the lessons learned each day.'

Nonetheless, it is people that make knowledge smart. That is a fact which explains why it is vital that our knowledge professionals possess competencies which allow them to work with knowledge. These competencies support their learning and like most competencies, they themselves can be learned.

So what are these competencies? We can divide them into three main groups: competencies that help us learn from information; competencies that help us improve our thinking; and social competencies, which help us interact better with our colleagues and the world around us.

Learn from information

− Sourcing is a competence for knowing where to look for the information you are after. It also deals with how to find particular information.

− Questioning is all about turning data into information by making sure it gives an answer to a specific question. Knowing what question to ask is half of the battle.

− Sensing means being responsive and open to new information. It means postponing judgement on any matter until full information is available. It means listening with an open mind, observing, and perceiving.

Improving thinking

− Analyzing means developing a competency which is based on logic, systems thinking, reasoning and mental modelling. It is a rational approach to thinking.

− Creating requires an emotional approach, as we move outside the constrictive box of orthodox thinking. It means allowing our minds to move laterally, creatively.

− Reflecting is the ability to ponder the lessons which have been learned and developing the art of self reflection.

Social competencies

− Networking is vital, for it helps us build up a close circle where we can often find the information we are seeking. Or at least get pointers in the right direction.

− Team-working assists in developing the ability to collaborate and share knowledge.

− Dialoguing is the ability to rid your minds of any preconceptions and listen to all the arguments with full attention and without trying to interject views or ideas which may occur.

Instill a knowledge attitude

In February 1997, the major oil companies all gathered in London to discuss the use of knowledge management in their business. Formal meetings focused on IT, but in the informal sessions – the ones which took place in the corridors – there was only one topic on everybody's minds: how do we get people to share their knowledge. The last 10 years has seen industry-wide downsizing programmes, and people working in the industry now were wondering when it would be their turn. The result was that people no longer trusted the company they were working for. And they were asking: can I trust my company with my knowledge? Or will I get the chop once I've shared all I know?

And so companies are being faced with a seemingly insoluble problem: how to gain the trust of their employees to share knowledge against an on-going background of downsizing and reengineering programmes. Without trust there can be no sharing of knowledge. It is a situation which becomes even clearer when there is a drive to implement a new knowledge system such as Lotus Notes: everybody wants to get knowledge out, but nobody wants to put knowledge in.

True knowledge workers will only be willing to share their knowledge with their company when there is a solid basis of trust. This trust will lead to the belief that the company, and thereby the knowledge workers themselves, will benefit from the knowledge. The result is that they will try to fill the company's knowledge carriers, such as a lessons-learned database, with their knowledge. With the right knowledge competencies, a knowledge worker will be able and willing to externalize newly acquired insights.

But to do this requires a knowledge attitude. An attitude which makes knowledge workers convinced that they are working on their own knowledge careers. That it is their sole responsibility to learn and to keep on learning. And that, when it comes to sharing, the main value is respect for somebody else's knowledge, ideas and thoughts. Respect for the other person's context, culture and view of the world. This respect leads to the belief that knowledge is just like love: it grows when it flows. When knowledge is shared in dialogue, the sharer knows it will only get richer. It will be readjusted and supplemented by others. The result is a natural knowledge sharing behaviour.

Learn to listen

'I do not know if you have ever examined how to listen.

It doesn't matter to what – whether to a bird, to the wind in the leaves, to the rushing waters, or how you listen in a dialogue with yourself, to your conversation in various relationships with your intimate friends, your wife or husband. If we try to listen we find it extraordinarily difficult, because we are always projecting our opinions and ideas, our prejudices, our background, our inclinations, our impulses; when they dominate we hardly listen at all to what is being said. In that state there is no value at all. One listens and therefore learns, only in a state of attention, a state of silence, in which this whole background is in abeyance, is quiet; then, it seems to me, it is possible to communicate.

Real communication can only take place where there is silence.'
Krishnamurti[12]

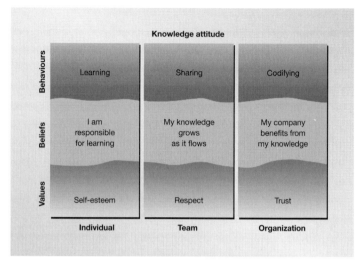

	Knowledge attitude		
Behaviours	Learning	Sharing	Codifying
Beliefs	I am responsible for learning	My knowledge grows as it flows	My company benefits from my knowledge
Values	Self-esteem	Respect	Trust
	Individual	**Team**	**Organization**

Smart professionals have an attitude

Smart professionals have an attitude

'Individuals tend to keep knowledge to themselves as they would any other prized possession.'

'The solution is to instil a knowledge attitude that regards knowledge as a valuable investment that only matures when communicated by the individual, shared by the team, and systematized by the organization. A knowledge attitude starts with values – esteem for one's self, respect for others and trust in the organization. Knowledge professionals should be encouraged to develop fundamental beliefs like, "I am responsible for my own competencies", "My knowledge increases when I share it", and "I contribute by putting my knowledge into systems". The combination of values and beliefs leads to a knowledge attitude and behaviour that is essential for value-adding knowledge companies.'

'Now our professionals can learn by keeping up to date. They can give, share and take knowledge, and we benefit by acquiring codified knowledge!'

Unfortunately, for many people such knowledge sharing behaviour is far from natural. And the biggest question many companies now face is how to instil a knowledge attitude in which such sharing is natural. That frequently requires a surgical operation aimed at changing beliefs and behaviour. Three methods can be used!

– Force & control: this is based on supervision, procedures, reporting and workflow management systems. Merrill Lynch, for example, has introduced a system whereby every employee is required to submit a confidential evaluation on everyone with whom they have worked closely. People are willing to share knowledge and cooperate because their compensation is attached to this mosaic of peer relationships. According to one vice president, 'In addition to profits generated, people are evaluated on how well they throw themselves into various projects, work with different groups to meet priorities and meet clients' needs. The culture penalizes those who fail to be team players or to meet clients' needs.'[13]

- Appraisal & reward: use appraisal and reward systems to encourage knowledge sharing.
- Fun, satisfaction & fulfilment: recognition can be serious – but it can also be fun. And inexpensive. One branch manager uses candy bars to thank people, actually throwing them to people in meetings. If, say, Tim has done an especially good job in an installation, the manager yells, 'Tim gets a Mr Goodbar for the installation' and throws him a candy bar. The funny thing is, nobody eats those bars: instead they are displayed on desks and in the workplace as proof of 'a job well done'. Another manager gives an employee a toy firefighter's helmet when he has 'successfully fought a fire' for the company. Again, these helmets are displayed with pride.[14] And at Cap Gemini they accompanied the introduction of their intranet reverse communication with a CD-ROM called 'You're on CapCom'. A cartoon character called Ronny Reverse, shows the viewer around all the features of the intranet and interviews all the general managers.[15]

All this brings to light a changing world of motivation: knowledge workers are seldom motivated by traditional tools. They react stubbornly to force & control methods; appraisal & reward becomes less effective as the level of professionalism increases. The only thing that really makes them run is the pleasure they have in their work. One manager cashed in on this by giving her employees a chance to 'bid' for projects they want. The better they did on the last project, the more chance they had of receiving one they wanted next time. The result: a happier, self-motivated employee. Both manager and employee win.[16]

You can lead a consultant to water...

A moderately large consultancy firm in the Netherlands installed a database on their intranet for the curricula vitae (CV) of the consultants. The consultants were asked to fill in the details in both Dutch and English and to make sure they were kept up-to-date. The chair of the board sent them a directive saying they were required to give information about educational background, work experience and so on. The chair pointed out that the board would be regularly informed about the results of each individual consultant's participation. Despite this top-down force & control model – the chair sent out a harshly worded memo after just one month, demanding co-operation – after three months, only 20 per cent of the consultants had filled in their details. Which proves you can lead a consultant to water – but don't expect him or her to drink without a struggle.

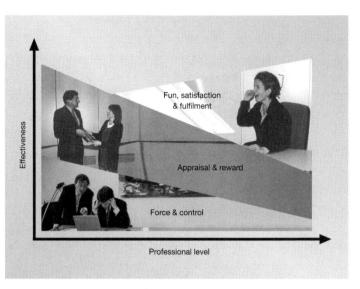

Smart professionals run on fun

Seeking the KiKo balance

A good way of creating pleasure in a knowledge worker's life is to ensure that there is a perfect balance between knowledge in and knowledge out. This KiKo balance addresses the concern many knowledge workers have in turning their knowledge into value for the company. If a knowledge professional only puts a little knowledge into the work but also only a little comes out, then both the company and the individual will consider this a waste of time, and allows frustration to take hold. Knowledge professionals will feel that their personal value is not being sufficiently enhanced.

If, however, knowledge professionals put in a lot of knowledge but only get a little knowledge out, they feel their work is a waste of effort. If, on the other hand, they put in only a small degree of knowledge but get a whole lot of knowledge out, then they know it is too good to be true and even if they feel pampered, it will be an empty, unfulfilled feeling.

If the KiKo balance is right, then knowledge professionals enjoy the best of both worlds: they will have job satisfaction and will be willing to create value through knowledge.

Motivating smart professionals

Smart professionals are committed professionals. They are hard working and, in many ways, ideal partners. For many employers, they are the ultimate in motivation and performance.

But there is a debit side. Knowledge workers are well aware of their own value. While they may not expect lifelong employment, they do expect lifelong employability. And so they can be demanding about compensation, incentives, and rewards. Managers can be uncomfortably aware of the damage a knowledge worker can inflict on a company by leaving. If a key knowledge worker leaves, the company loses more than just that employee; it loses the informal network that employee has constructed around himself or herself and is in danger of losing clients who see their relationship not necessarily with the company but rather with the individual concerned. The ultimate danger, of course, is that a whole group of key knowledge workers leave and take the cream of the customers with them, thus laying the foundation for a competitive operation, as is so often the case with small, privately owned and managed consultancies.

Knowledge-intensive companies must obtain the key competence of retaining their knowledge workers by increasing the significance of motivation, rewards and compensation, and performance appraisal.

Smart professionals go for KiKo

'An even exchange of knowledge in, knowledge out – what we call the "KiKo balance" – addresses the concern professionals have when asked to turn their knowledge into value for the company.'

'In the first scenario, a knowledge professional puts little knowledge in and also receives little knowledge out. KiKo is out of balance since the professional considers this a waste of time and frustration results.'

'When professionals put a lot of knowledge in but get little out…they view their work as a waste of effort and feel angry about it.'

'If a professional puts little knowledge in and receives great value in return, it's too good to be true, and even the most pampered professional will feel unfulfilled.'

'The KiKo balance is actually the best of both worlds where knowledge professionals enjoy job satisfaction.'

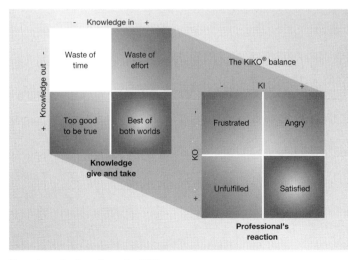

Smart professionals go for KiKo

Over the years, our ideas about motivation have moved from the simplistic to the diverse. We now realize the superficiality of expecting high motivation using the carrot and the stick method preferred in times gone by. Similarly, we have come to doubt the old maxim that a happy worker is a good worker. For most ideas about motivation seemed designed for 'partial people'[18] who were working in narrow, routinized jobs at the bottom and specialized functions at the top. Neither of these theories, however, give us any clue about how to motivate people to become more involved in self-management of their own line of business and to work in a collaborative manner with their colleagues for the good of the company.

The danger is that CEOs of smart companies will be misguided into thinking that established motivation theories, such as those of Maslow and Herzberg, which were successful for industrial bureaucracies will also work in new smart organizations. The new generation of knowledge professionals will be motivated by opportunities for self-expression and career development, combined with a fair share of the profits.[20] The name of the game now is motivating people to do more than their jobs.

People today recognize the importance of motivation. Yet strangely enough 'no integrated theoretical framework has thus far been developed. In practice, many different approaches have been used to optimize motivation with varying degrees of success'.[21]

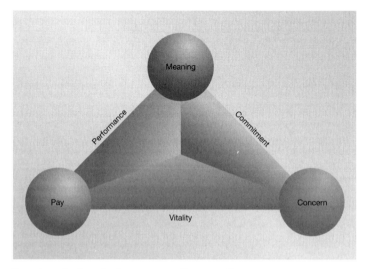

Smart professionals deserve more than merit pay

Nevertheless, we can say that basically there are two forms of motivation: one is 'extrinsic' – that is, motivation due to external incentives such as pay, promotion, or recognition; the other is 'intrinsic' – that is, motivation due to internal drives such as commitment and work values. Motivation, therefore, is looking at why people do the things they do. It is about people's drives, wants, needs, values, goals, emotions, accomplishments and actions.

Individual motivation is highest when the following circumstances are met:

- when an individual believes that what he or she is doing will lead to a certain outcome (performance-outcome expectancy);
- when an individual feels that the outcome is attractive;
- when an individual believes that the desired level of performance is possible (effort-performance expectancy).[22]

This need to motivate the individual is still valid today, even though we are moving into a time when teams are essential. And this concentration on the individual is vital, because there is no such thing as team motivation. At best, a team can become motivated by the individuals who form it, who create a synergy and motivation that combine to provide spirit or drive the team.[24]

People can be motivated by three basic types of drive:

- Personal forces: these come from within people themselves (i.e. strong political views);
- Push forces: these come from other people (i.e. family, colleagues); and
- Pull forces which come from external factors (i.e. second house, a new car).

In a team these drives can be highly relevant, and it may be necessary to an individual in satisfying his or her drives in such a way that they tie in with the organizational or team goals. The two must be brought into line for synergy to arise. 'Such a situation, where team and individual goals are optimized, might best be described as "integrated". This is more likely to lead to a high level of cohesion in carrying out tasks.'[25]

A new look at motivation

It is obvious that, within the context of smart organizations, it is vital that we take a new look at the motivational and environmental needs of today's breed of knowledge professionals. A

Smart professionals deserve more than merit pay

'Knowledge professionals crave opportunities to do meaningful work, appreciate it when concern for their well-being is demonstrated, and celebrate each time they fairly share in company profits.'
'When our company addresses these three areas, knowledge professionals become motivated and have the feeling that our company is genuinely concerned with their energy level and their professional development and feel a sense of commitment. Showing concern and providing equitable pay is like a shot of vitality to knowledge professionals.'
'Their performance goals continue to be surpassed as they are refreshed and re-energized in the anticipation of new opportunities, as their newly acquired competencies are rewarded and as more value is added to the organization.'

good guideline can be found in the four key motivators which have been identified by Tampoe:[26]

1. Personal growth: the opportunity for individuals to realize their full potential.
2. Operational autonomy: a work environment in which knowledge workers can achieve the task assigned to them within the constraints of strategic direction and self-measurement indices.
3. Task achievement: the possibility of producing work to a standard and quality of which the individual can be proud.
4. Money: earning an income which is just reward for the contribution made and which enables employees to share in the wealth they have created. Incentive schemes geared to the company's success can be useful, but these must be related to personal performance.

Smart professionals deserve more than merit pay

All the above has resulted in a new motivational theory for smart professionals in smart organizations. It acknowledges the drives and motivators listed above and also recognizes the changing perspective in which pay and even merit pay are not the primary driving force for today's emerging breed of knowledge professionals. They are motivated by opportunities for meaningful work and concern from the company, combined with a fair share of the profits.

Using a combination of these three areas, companies can successfully motivate knowledge professionals to:

- Show commitment to the organization. Such commitment can cover three broad themes: commitment can underline an effective orientation towards the organization; commitment can recognize the costs associated with leaving the organization – human capital losses; and commitment can endorse a moral obligation to remain with the organization.[27]
- Add vitality to their efforts. This distinguishes the strong from the weak. Nobody can renew a company without revitalizing its people and its systems. Exploring new opportunities can help create vitality.
- Surpass their performance goals. Performance = ability × motivation. High motivation but low ability will not lead to

high performance. But performance goals can be surpassed by adding more value to the organization; effective use of available resources; enhancing team synergy.

The three areas are:

- Meaning helps integrate the other drivers. We give meaning to all our experiences, whether we are aware of this or not. Even when we are asleep, the drive toward meaning continues in our dreams. A healthy person finds shared meanings that contribute to growth. Meaning must give hope; without that, there can be no motivation.[29]
- Pay is the financial reward which reflects that the 'partners' who contribute most to the performance of the organization get the most of what the organization has to share. Knowledge professionals will generally not be satisfied with pay which reflects a position in the company, nor will they find such a remuneration system stimulating enough to make them contribute to the current organization. Alternatives have to be found.
- Concern is an activity of management, and its importance and effectiveness cannot be overestimated. People who have received loving care as children and teenagers respond positively to caring managers, co-workers and partners. What's more, real concern generates a feeling of reciprocity:

The call of meaning

'I became aware of the call of meaning in our organizational lives when I worked with a number of incoherent companies that had been tipped into chaos by reorganizations and leveraged buyouts. They had lost any purpose beyond the basic struggle to survive...Most employees had, more predictably, checked out psychologically, just putting in their time. Waiting for the inevitable. But others stayed creative and focused on creating new services, even with the great uncertainty of the future. This puzzled me greatly. I assumed at first that they were simply denying reality. But when I talked to these employees, it became evident that something else much more important was going on. They were staying creative, making sense out of nonsense, because they had taken the time to create meaning for their work, one that transcended present organizational circumstance. They wanted to hold onto motivation and direction in the midst of turbulence, and the only way they could do this was by investing the current situation with meaning. In some ways, the future of the organization became irrelevant. Maybe the organization didn't make sense, but their lives did.'
M.J. Wheatley[28]

Who really cares?

'About any behaviour that is thought to be desirable by an organization, it's useful to ask: Is this behaviour rewarded, punished, or ignored? The answer to these questions tells you what an organization really cares about, not what it says it cares about.'
Warren Bennis[30]

people who receive care want to give care. This feeling is an essential ingredient in the knowledge organization. For there is a very real danger that in the electronic work place, care and concern are neglected and this can contribute to an uneasy feeling. 'If they don't care, why should I?'[31]

All this shows that rewarding a knowledge professional needs to be a combination of factors, many of which a company controls. Knowledge professionals are motivated by opportunities for meaningful work. They expect care and concern from a company that is truly interested in their performance and their well-being. And they expect a fair share of the profits – one which reflects their own contribution and shows that the company acknowledges and respects that contribution.

Appraising smart professionals

'The only purpose of performance appraisals is to remind you on a yearly basis that somebody owns you,' wrote Peter Block[32] in 1991. And indeed when asked nobody likes performance appraisals, but everybody does them and few are confident about the results. So why do we keep doing them?

We have certain expectations about performance appraisals. We expect the results to be of significant help in our efforts to improve the performance of employees in the short term and in the long term, and contribute to their own development. In addition, we expect them to serve as an effective and efficient administration system for the personnel department and give us something on which to base compensation.

The drawback of many systems is that they reflect a single moment, once a year, recorded by just one person – generally the manager. This is quite simply insufficient data on which to base any findings. And so we should develop a system in which we can record what a boss, peers, customers, and subordinates really think about a professional's work. As we have mentioned, Hewlett Packard has adopted such an approach, to ensure that everybody who comes into contact with an employee can make an appraisal of his or her functioning. Such a broad input is obviously of wider benefit than a very narrow input. What's more, competencies should become the basis for the development, monitoring and coaching process of performance management.

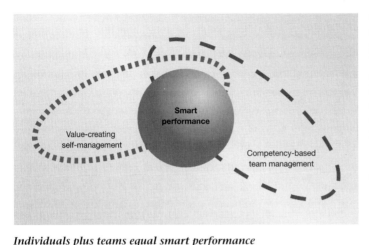

Individuals plus teams equal smart performance

Individuals plus teams equal smart performance

'Smart performance occurs through synergy between value-creating self-management and competency-based team management.'

'That's all there is to it?'

'Yes – but it's easier said than done.'

Individuals plus teams equal smart performance

Avoiding dysfunctionality

Today's smart professionals regard traditional appraisal systems as dysfunctional. The job they do is so diverse, so changing, and requires them to adopt so many different functions, that an objective appraisal is inappropriate. Instead, smart professionals prefer a system of self-measurement and multiple types of rewards and compensation. And this means that different aspects need to be appraised than in the past – certainly now that we also have to take into account the team and the functioning of the team as a whole and the functioning of the individual within that team. In other words,

Smart professionals manage themselves

'Smart professionals gain peer support by networking in an informal manner. These relationships are based on mutual trust and respect and through them professionals receive valuable informal feedback on their performance.'

'Professional career development depends to a large extent on proper assessment of current and future training and work requirements.'

'Electronic performance systems capture and store personal and corporate knowledge, work samples, examples of best practices and performance assessments, and they distribute this knowledge throughout the company.'

'Through a 360 degree performance appraisal, smart professionals

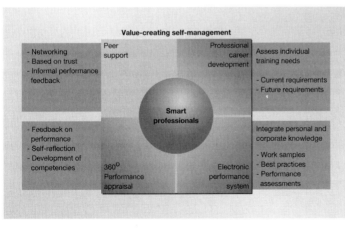

Smart professionals manage themselves

regularly invite mentors, team leaders, peers and customers to appraise their performance. This feedback is followed by a period of self-reflection so that professionals can rethink present levels of proficiency and set goals to develop further competencies.'

the focus should no longer be on assessing individual performance, but on supporting both individual and team performance. We should work on improving value-creating self-management and competency based team management. For when these combine, we can enjoy smart performance from our smart professionals and their teams.

Value-creating self-management

The more complicated a job, the less clear the performance measures become. And this is why peer appraisal, and techniques such as the 360-degree appraisal, are of use. Certainly the 360-degree appraisal makes people realize what their manager, peers, mentor and subordinates, really think of them. Applying this system can provide motivation by balancing individual and team-based rewards. It also provides the framework for a programme of self-assessment.

IT-based solutions include the Electronic Performance Support System (EPSS). At the heart of an EPSS is a belief that most organizations today face a performance crisis that training alone cannot solve. This is an electronic infrastructure that captures, stores and distributes individual and corporate knowledge throughout an organization in order to enable workers to achieve the required level of performance in the fastest possible time and with the minimum support from people.[36] It allows a professional's work to be appraised in context and delivers high-performance support, such as work samples, best practices and performance assessments.

Rethinking the concept of careers
'A career could be a portfolio of different projects that provide new skills, gain new expertise, develop new competencies, create innovative activities (part-time jobs, setting up your own business, two-year team projects, virtual knowledge team periods, sabbaticals and so on) that may not and most probably will not come neatly packaged and defined as a "job" in one organization but can provide lifelong employability, provide adequate compensation, rewards, and satisfaction to the individual.'[34]

Peer support can be gained through the formal and informal network which a professional builds up throughout a company. Such relationships are vital not only to the well-being of the professional, but also to the company. They are based on trust, and through them professionals can receive valuable informal feedback about their performance.

Professional career development is something which every smart professional expects. It largely depends on proper assessment of current and future training and work requirements. It should also provide a challenge to the professional, which in turn can be of importance for motivation.

Providing a supportive environment

Not everything about motivation deals with rewards. For today's smart professionals the environment in which they work is very important indeed. And a team needs to have a supportive environment if it is to function at its best.

To provide a supporting environment, we need to review at regular intervals how well a team is suited to meet its objectives. Such reviews should also examine the composition of the team and the team competencies. We should ask questions such as, 'Do team members represent all the necessary competencies?' 'Do we need to make changes in the composition of the team?'

Regular assessment of career and future team training and development needs can be a positive stimulus to effective team performance. Input from the team can be valuable in defining future training needs.

An integrated knowledge environment (see Chapter 10 of this section) needs to be installed and must be designed so that it can electronically support communication and knowledge building processes that assist smart professionals in their efforts to create knowledge.

And finally, we must do both internal and external team appraisals. This can help provide us with an overall evaluation of the team from the double perspective of the team itself and its customers.

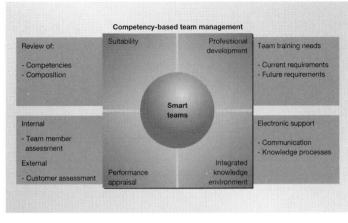

Smart teams win in supportive environments

effective team
performance.
"Are the current team
training requirements
sufficient?"
"Are future requirements
different?"
An integrated knowledge
environment provides
reliable electronic support
for communication and
knowledge-building
processes so
professionals can in fact
create value.
Team performance
appraisal provides an
overall evaluation of how
well the team is
functioning internally
through the eyes of the
team members and
externally from the
customer's point of view.'

The smart carrot

Motivation may be the result of a number of different factors; however, pay and the way in which smart professionals are compensated for their knowledge creation and sharing on behalf of the company, must be a fundamental part of any reward system. And this is why we have given it such an important place in our discussions about a new reward system for smart professionals.

Traditionally, salary and job function level went hand in hand: the longer you did a job, the more you got paid for doing it. Today, however, as the job which is done by smart professionals becomes increasingly diverse and complex, and requires a broader range of competencies than was traditionally required, such a simplistic salary concept is no longer acceptable. Instead, we must devise a remuneration system which is based on not only pay, but also on non-financial rewards such as recognition, responsibility, and growth.

In today's world smart professionals can be market makers and market shakers. Sometimes they imagine the future, at other times they actually make it happen. This means that pay can no longer be considered a standard, all for one amount. But the way pay is calculated should reflect the importance of the smart professional and his or her ever changing world. Pay is, after all, one of the strongest ways in which a company can show professionals how much they are appreciated.

Basic pay has traditionally been designed and implemented to attract and retain people. It is negotiated and therefore, once agreed, it becomes an entitlement over which there can be no further discussion.

Nowadays, individual performance is rarely linked to changes in entitlement. Instead, performance-related pay offers a tangible link of financial reward to individual, group, or company performance. Such performance-related pay includes merit pay, individual incentives, group/company performance bonuses and other variable payments which employees may earn. The single most important objective we should have in mind when designing a performance-related pay plan is that it must improve the performance by converting the pay bill from an indiscriminate machine to a more finely tuned mechanism. It should reward the achievement of specific goals rather than the expenditure of effort.

All this is further complicated by the fact that any reward system must acknowledge individual achievements as well as team effort. And current compensation systems often fail to balance individual and group contribution. Knowledge professionals are today expected to be thinkers, be creative to come up with innovative ideas and devise new services and to share their knowledge – all of which can be critical to a company's future success. But many feel that they are not rewarded appropriately.

All this might explain why at the British Deming Association Conference in May 1997, one of the key speakers, Alfie Kohn, claimed that 'performance based pay cannot work'. It is still being used extensively in the US, even though there is 'no evidence to support the belief that people will do a better job if they have been promised some sort of incentive'. In fact, he claimed, 'at least two dozen reports over the last three decades have conclusively shown that people who expect a reward for completing a task or for doing that task successfully simply do not perform as well as those who expect no reward at all'.[40]

Pay for knowledge schemes

All this implies that incentives must be offered if we are to retain smart professionals' knowledge and skill bases within our company and stimulate them to use them to the benefit of the company. These skill bases can in turn also form an intrinsic part of a pay system. In core process teams, members must rotate among jobs, accept changing and new responsibilities and be flexible and adaptable. This means that it is no longer possible to pay a professional for doing a single job. Rather they will have to be paid at a rate which is dictated by the repertory of jobs they are expected to do and the competencies they need to carry them out.

This is an attractive concept for many smart professionals. For it implies that individual employees can increase their level of pay by attaining and using an increasing number of skills. What's more, while it focuses on individual responsibility, it does not play one member of a team off against another as often happens in pay-for-performance systems.

Pay discussions

'It's unfair to reward cross-functional teams solely on the basis of results, because they are often put into positions to move organizations forward by taking risks. Sometimes the risks they take might not be successful.'
P. Pascarella[37]

'Even though merit pay has fundamentally failed, it is achieving other objectives. It's a way to retain people and avoid a lot of dissatisfaction around what people earn. It's avoiding anarchy.'
M. Budman[38]

'Pay-for-performance looks not for cost-drivers, but for contribution drivers that measure, in absolute terms, the amount of surplus that knowledge workers contribute to the overall surplus pool.'
R.L. Nolan and D.C. Crosan[39]

At McDonnell Douglas Helicopters, a new company-wide pay plan replaces a system of automatic pay increases with one which made pay increases depend on employees consistently learning and demonstrating new skills. The company defined 30 'job families' and within these the employees themselves defined the skill-based wage system. Under this new system, employees receive a wage increase only after demonstrating proficiency in a relevant skill block, which can include one or more skills relevant to the job concerned. Each job family determines when a potential increase can take place. Once a skill block has been successfully accomplished – and to do this employees must be monitored by a peer – employees agree with their supervisors what skills will be tackled in the next block. In this way managers are able not only to judge whether the skills suggested are relevant, but also to arrange training in them where necessary.[41]

Basically, these compensation systems can be grouped into two broad types:

– multi-skill based or breadth systems, where pay levels are linked to the number of different skills a worker learns and can perform in an organization;
– increased knowledge or depth systems, where pay levels are linked to increased knowledge and skill within the same general job category.[42]

Implementing knowledge-based pay systems

Knowledge-based pay systems certainly have advantages for both the employee and the employer. The company can enjoy increased flexibility and commitment, while the employee can enjoy increased satisfaction.

When implementing such systems, costs can be expected in the following areas:

– the pay rates produced by these systems tend to be higher than they would have been under a traditional pay system;
– they encourage employees to learn multiple skills. This obviously results in a greater investment by the company in training and education;
– they place extra demands on the appraisal system. Appraisals must take place at more frequent intervals. In

	Pay for skills	Pay for competencies
Examples	– equipment operation – equipment setup/changeover – elementary equipment trouble-shooting – team problem-solving skills	– customer service orientation – conceptual thinking – flexibility – team commitment
Emphasis	– developed	– selected for and developed
Organizational expectations	– fixed number of highest or multi-skill positions	– desire to have all employees strive for superior competencies
Impact	– short- to medium-term performance	– medium- to long-term performance

A comparison of the differences: skills vs competencies[44]

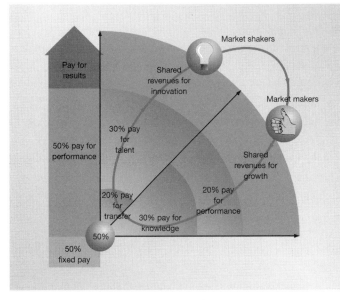

Smart professionals require new rewards

Smart professionals require new rewards

'Pay will be structured differently. Up to one half of a smart professional's pay will be fixed and based on performance. Market shakers will receive up to 20 per cent of their pay based on the ability to transfer knowledge to market makers and 30 per cent based on their individual talents. There is no ceiling on pay for results which rewards market shakers with shared revenues for innovation. Market makers, on the other hand, will be paid for their knowledge…and for their performance in bringing the right products and services to market in a timely fashion. They will also share revenues based on their contribution to company growth.'

'And what does that mean for the company?'

'The added value for our company is derived from the feedback given to market shakers by market makers on their own initiatives.'

Pay-for-skills vs pay-for-competence

'The key difference is that the skills approach focuses on demonstrations of certain knowledge, while a competencies approach pays for attributes that predict successful performance.'

S.E. Gross[43]

addition, they must take into account the multi-functional aspects of a professional's tasks. They must look at performance in multiple jobs, and this implies that their performance be evaluated by several assessors;

– multi-skilled employees are of greater value to a company than single-skilled workers. This means that a simple market comparison is inappropriate;

– the burden of administering such a system is greater than that of a more traditional system.[45]

Market shakers and market makers

But how can we reward those market shakers and market makers? For it is almost certain that, in the life of a smart professional, there will be times when they are one or both of these. Both will expect to share in the profits of their work along with the company. The pay structure for each group, however, will be different.

Market shakers will have to be rewarded for innovating the business. Their pay will have to be based on their individual talent and their ability to transfer knowledge to the market makers. Market makers, on the other hand, will have to be compensated for the way they help the company to grow, based on their individual knowledge and performance.

Smart professionals are a new breed of workers – people who need to be motivated and inspired to create and share knowledge. And because they are so different, we must not allow ourselves to harness them or our thinking in old-fashioned ways. If they are to be creative in their work, we must be creative in the way in which we find work which challenges them and compensation systems which make them feel that their contribution to the value of the company is appreciated and rewarded.

Market makers' status increases

Talent is essential in those unique individuals, of which there are only a few, that have the unique ability to make a significant difference in our companies – we call them market shakers. In the new economy, they will become the most sought after type of employee and companies will be willing to reward them handsomely. According to a survey of 300 executives in medium to large companies, more than half of the respondents said they expected skills shortages to be their industries' greatest challenge in the next four years. Interestingly enough, technical skills ranked lower than the 'soft' skills, such as, the ability to listen, solve problems, and interact with co-workers and they are in short supply. These shortages are undermining sales in US businesses by as much as a third according to the companies surveyed.[46]

We redefine talent as those hidden resources that employees possess, the ones employees were not allowed to use in the industrial economy. These resources are now first and foremost in the personnel search. In fact, human resources management obtains a completely different meaning, it is now about stimulating and managing the value-adding potential of people.

Already in the US, companies are using a vastly different approach to paying market shakers – they are seen as being similar to the successful, yet equally-scarce, sports professionals. For US football and basketball, it is accepted that most pro-players can only score in their prime years between 18 and 30. If they endure the physical torture and keep their game, they stand a chance of earning their life-time income in about 15 years, versus the typical 40 that it takes most employees. Although as our physical world becomes virtual, companies are prepared to pay truly talented ones just as much.

Want to find out what you are really worth? Why not auction yourself on the Internet? In the summer of 1999, 16 engineers, managers and administrative staff working for an unnamed Silicon Valley Internet services provider put themselves on the eBay.com block, with an opening price of $3.14 million for a year of their services. The auction was withdrawn three days before the bids were due, but nevertheless, this has started a trend on the personal trading community website.[47]

CHAPTER 10

'Smart knowledge'

How companies create
valuable content and context

W hat is knowledge? People have been trying to answer that question for thousands of years. The most celebrated and respected philosophers have tried to find the answer and have generally failed. So to continue the argument in this book would be presumptuous.

In the context of value-based knowledge management, however, there is one question about knowledge which is much more relevant, and that is 'How do I gain valuable knowledge?'[1]

Everyday information about our company's performance, passes over our desks. Information about turnover, market share, profits. You then use all this information to make decisions and the results of those decisions – whether good or bad – show up on the balance sheet. It is a continuous learning process based on information and is referred to as feedback learning. But with the on-going improvement and expansion of technology, the amount of information which bombards us is growing rapidly and achieving almost gargantuan amounts. It drains us mentally and emotionally.

Real decision making depends on the decision maker's point of view. We have all constructed our own idea of how this world and business runs. It is a view which is purely personal, and based on our personal experiences during our own lifetime. Yet it is this experience, this personal view which allows us to make split-second decisions. Decisions which are intended to guide our company through the present turbulent times.

But some decision making causes us to pause for a moment. To sit back and reflect on the results of our decisions. To rearrange our thoughts, gather new ideas, and work out a new

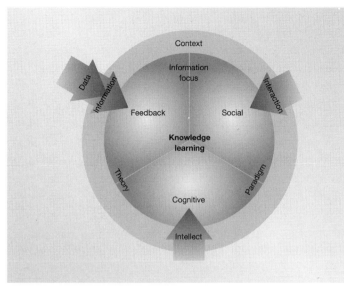

Discover the hidden sources of knowledge

Discover the hidden sources of knowledge

'When asked, "what is knowledge?" people usually think of information, and it's true, information creates the basis for the continuous process of learning through feedback.'

'One of the forgotten sources of knowledge, however, is just plain thinking. Relating our own experiences to information results in cognitive learning, on the basis of which we develop new concepts and theories.'

'Another source of knowledge people often overlook is interaction with other people. Social learning involves getting other opinions and points of view which help us to interpret our own thoughts, reshape someone else's thinking and select the information that is beneficial to the issue at hand.'

understanding of reality. To do this, we enter the world of intellect, where mental models shape our view of the world and help us keep things under tight control. This process of shifting paradigms and creating new ideas is called cognitive learning.

Everybody knows, however, that much of our learning is done in practice. When we talk to our managers in the morning, when we sit on a task force set up to develop our company's strategy. When we solved the problem of a production lead time by working in a multidisciplinary team. That's when we learned many valuable lessons. And we learned them by building on other people's knowledge, which we used with our own knowledge, to create something new. It was a process of sharing, exchanging ideas and experience, combining thoughts and concepts, using language to its fullest potential. This process of human interaction is known as social learning.

The I³ factor

The Three 'I's– information, intellect, and interaction – are the building blocks of knowledge and join forces in the knowledge circle.

Another important requirement for accurate use of information is to know the context. Recently one of us was listening to the radio and we heard that Air Force One had been hijacked. An event, one would have thought, of world-shattering importance. But the context made it less significant: it was a radio commercial for a new film starring Harrison Ford and it reminded us of the chaos caused in 1945 by the Orson Welles radio broadcast of H.G. Wells' 'War of the Worlds'.

It is the context which gives the message its meaning to the data and turns it into information.

When we share our knowledge using IT, we often forget the importance of context. Many companies have built up an enormous bank of information which is totally incomprehensible because of the lack of context information.

A metaphor is a wonderful mechanism for helping us put information into context without having to go into detailed explanations. The right half of the brain is particularly fond of metaphors because they are about structures and images – exactly what this half of the brain likes to work with most. What's more, a metaphor is often enjoyable, and conveys information in an amusing and memorable way.

The knowledge circle in different cultures; a hypothesis

– US: mainly information based. In the US, facts and figures are the most important factor in company decision making.
– Japan: interaction based. In Japan, consensus is the most important factor in corporate decision making.
– Western Europe: intellect based. In Europe, managers eagerly seek out concepts, theories and methodology to improve their performance.

Here's one such metaphor: A machine broke down in the factory, bringing production to a halt. A mechanic was called in, who spent a few minutes talking to the machine's operator and listening to the grating sounds coming from some of the machine's pipes. After a moment's thought, he walked over to the machine and hit it at a point where three pipes merged into one. The machine immediately sprung into operation.

Two day's later, the manager received an invoice from the mechanic for $500. He was surprised at the high cost for less than 10 minutes' work and phoned the mechanic to ask for a detailed specification of the invoice. He received that promptly the next day. It read, 'One hammer blow: 0.50 ct. Knowing where to hit: $499.50. Total $500'.[3]

Information, intellect, and interaction also interact with each other. Science exists by virtue of theory in which we confront our minds with reality. What Thomas Kuhn calls paradigms[4] can be described as mutually accepted views of the world which have been reached by interaction. Then there is one other factor: organizations suffer from 'information windows'. Experience is not only an expanding possibility but also a limiting one. Filters may have grown over the years in our information gathering systems which result in us having a limited view of reality. In our attempts to filter out 'noise', we often filter out the music as well.

Different types of knowledge

Some of the knowledge we acquire remains applicable for much of our lives; other knowledge ceases to be of use to us. One of the authors of this book remembers a lesson from one of his first consultancy assignments. The government had asked him to give his opinion on the efficiency of a museum. The first meeting with the director of the museum turned out to be a disaster. She was very unhappy that the government had wanted this review, but this was aggravated by the awareness that the person carrying out the assignment knew nothing whatsoever about the running of a museum. It was a hard way of learning a very important lesson: you have to know the customer's business if you are to be taken seriously. That lesson, learned nearly twenty years ago, is one which is still relevant today. Other knowledge which the same author acquired could be forgotten after just a few years. After all, who needs to be able to programme in Pascal or even DOS these days?

All this leads to an important conclusion: the value of knowledge depends on the stability of the environment.

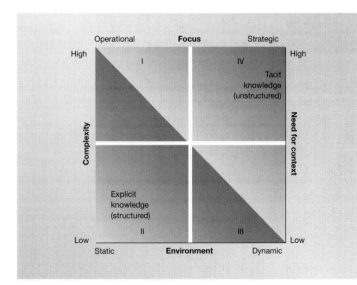

Companies cannot touch value-creating knowledge

Companies cannot touch value-creating knowledge

'Knowledge comes to us in different forms. Type I is of a structured nature. It is usually found in a static environment. It has an operational focus. It's quite difficult and requires a lot of contextual information. This is the kind of knowledge a judge uses.'

'Type II is also operational within a static environment but is less complicated and requires less contextual information to understand. The operator in a chemical plant uses this kind of knowledge.'

'Type III is also not very complicated but is needed in a very turbulent environment and has much more of a strategic focus. Stock dealers use this knowledge.'

'However, the most interesting and value-adding type is type IV. As explicit knowledge remains valuable for years, dynamic tacit knowledge can be obsolete within the hour. This highly complex knowledge requires extensive analysis to understand – or it may require complete and lengthy explanations. Tacit knowledge usually focuses on strategic issues, helping companies stay ahead of the game.'

Get to know your own personal I³ score

What is your personal learning style? Do you learn most from information, interaction, or intellect? Fill in this test and plot the results in the knowledge circle. Read each question, then decide which answer most suits you. Place a 3 in the box next to this answer. Place a 2 in the box next to the answer which comes second for you, and 1 in the box next to the answer which least reflects your way of learning. Add up each of the columns and colour in your score in the bull's eye. This bull's eye gives a weighted score. 25 per cent of the replies score in the first quadrant, 50 per cent in the first two, and 75 per cent in the first three quadrants. Now you can see what your dominant learning style is. You can then read the explanation about each style.

If you can't find the answer to something do you:	look up the answer		analyze the problem		ask for advice	
My strength is:	observation		reflection		communication	
My favourite occupation is:	reading		daydreaming		talking	
I learn from my mistakes by:	gathering information about the consequences		thinking about them		asking other people's opinions	
I prefer working:	in a duo		alone		in a team	
When making decisions I use:	management information		my intuition		consensus	
I solve problems at work by:	copying others		finding out myself		thinking up solutions together	
Solutions for management must:	be proven		be original		be supported by those who have to execute them	
I am particularly:	experimental	+	reflective	+	social	+
Total	**Information**		**Intellect**		**Interaction**	

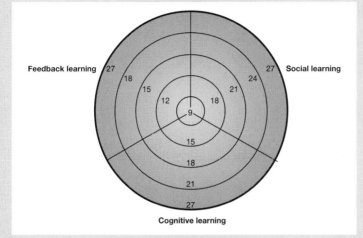

Your personal I³ score

Feedback learning as dominant learning style

You are particularly interested in figures. Before you reach a decision you gather data and analyze it. You try to learn as much as possible from your decisions by analyzing the results. When you read newspapers or magazines, your attention is attracted to graphs and statistics. You use figures to compare the most important parts of your company with other companies and with benchmarks. You get very annoyed if the figures are inaccurate. You regularly use sources of information such as the Internet and make use of the services of data suppliers such as the Gartner Group.

Cognitive learning as dominant learning style

You think mainly in concepts, models and theories. Before you reach a decision, you take time to weigh the pros and cons. You mainly learn by observing and translating what you see into general applicable rules. You are always on the lookout for new ideas and visions about the world. When you read newspapers and magazines your attention is attracted to pictures and models. You regularly read (management) books and are interested in examples of lessons learned and best practices from other companies.

Social learning as dominant learning style

You spend a lot of time listening to others. Before you reach a decision you categorize the opinions of all those involved. You try to find a consensus. You enjoy working in teams with people of various abilities and backgrounds. You largely learn by observing others and by attacking a problem together. When you read newspapers and magazines your attention is attracted to interviews and stories about other people. You often walk into somebody's office to ask for their advice and you ask questions via e-mail or via discussion groups on the Internet or on your company's intranet.

The knowledge circle in practice

Molecules with sunglasses

How could we have missed something like this? Chemistry has by and large been the subject of studying carbon. Now, at the end of the twentieth century, we've discovered yet another form of carbon, resulting in a new chemistry, new materials and new engineering on a molecular scale. This is the story of how two independent research teams created a fundamental shift in chemistry.

The data

In their lab in Heidelberg, Germany, Professor Wolfgang Kratschmer and Professor Don Hoffman shot light through vaporized graphite. The resulting absorption spectrum had an abnormal bump and was therefore named the camel spectrum. Both scientists agreed it was worthless.

The information

But to a third professor, Harry Kroto, this data was worth a Nobel Prize. In his laboratory in Houston, Texas, Kroto simulated atmospheres of dying stars by pumping out carbon atoms. He was the first to see the as yet unidentified long chain of carbon molecules and he was able to identify the number of clusters and atoms in each. Furthermore, he saw evidence of the existence of stable clusters of 60 carbon atoms. This left his research team wondering about what kind of structure the C60 could possibly have since carbon-based molecules are normally considered flat. They could not imagine the shape of a structure which had made 60 carbon atoms form such a stable cluster.

The interaction

Next, Harry Kroto came up with the idea of hexagons, like in Buckminster Fuller's geodesic dome, and the team set about visualizing the structure. After paper hexagons didn't work, they even tried 60 jellybeans joined by toothpicks. This too was fruitless, the jellybean structure collapsed. One of the team members, Nobel Prize winner Rick Smalley, that night recalled Harry saying that the geodesic dome also had pentagons, and that the structure had to consist of 12 pentagons and 20 hexagons. He called Bill Veetch because, if somebody had already discovered this structure, he was sure to know about it. Without hesitation Veetch simply said, 'Well, I could explain it to you in a number of ways, but what you've got there boys is a soccer ball!'

The intellect

This simple mental model gave the idea, the information and the interaction meaning, and from then on it could be explained and not only to intellectuals. The news spread like wildfire and a whole new area of science was born.

This knowledge gave meaning to old data

'It was so beautiful that it just had to be right, but how could we set about proving that it had this structure?' later explained Harry Kroto. But, the scientists continued to struggle with this puzzle. How do you prove the shape of something measured in electrical fields, held for only milliseconds in a laser beam, and existing only as long as the experiment?

To get a fingerprint of C60, they could shine light through the molecule, but couldn't extract C60 from the laser soot. Meanwhile C60 had already become a hot topic in the scientific community. Arizona professor Don Hoffman realized that the camel spectrum he discovered years earlier corresponded to the theoretical spectrum values of the illusive C60. The next batch of sooty specimens he produced he sent to Kratschmer who bathed them in an infrared spectrometer and got the same absorption bands that were predicted for C60. In addition, they found a way to produce C60 in solid form which can be dissolved and then dried into a solid of pure C60 crystals.

The purpose

Now everybody wants to use C60. It has been found to take on super-conducting qualities when doping with alkali metals and undergoes a transition to super-magnetism when doped with TDAE. AT&T has already used C60 as a chemical electric conductor with no resistance to electricity, and possibilities are being explored in nanometre architecture. Chemistry has turned into a 3-D world with 'Buckminsterfullerene' and this shift in thinking paved the way to the discovery of bigger carbon molecules of 70 and 76 atoms with the shapes of rugby balls.[2]

Know the context

The lesson learned at the museum is about the importance of business expertise. This may seem obvious, without information about the whole context in which the lesson was learned, but in the context of the person involved who, at that time still was a rookie, this lesson was vitally important. This shows how important the context is to give meaning to knowledge. Let us give another example: recently a colleague tried to explain what he had learned from his job as consultant to a government agency that was implementing a merger. To understand it all, he had to give us a whole lot of information about the organization, the merger, his role in the assignment, and even the temper of the CEO. He had to give us the context.

Know the complexity

The 'museum lesson' can be stated as follows: if you want to be taken seriously as a consultant, you have to know the client's business.

If you analyze that statement, you could say that the knowledge it contains is not particularly complex. In fact it is formulated as an 'if...then...' statement. This is the way a lot of knowledge can be formulated. This can vary from the knowledge an operator has in a chemical plant ('if that red light goes on, then I have to shut that valve') or the knowledge a dealer has in the stock dealer room of a bank ('if the price of this stock drops below $10, then sell!'). 'if...then...' is becoming a standard tool for knowledge experts, and they are using it with increasing competence when formulating expert knowledge and when building expert systems.

But there is still a whole lot of knowledge which cannot be encapsulated in even highly complex 'if...then...' statements. Think for a moment, about the expertise Niké has in marketing. There is simply no way that can be reduced to even a highly complex 'if...then...' statement.

Know the focus

Knowledge can have either an operational or a strategic focus. Operational knowledge is the knowledge required to 'create & produce' – you could say this is the knowledge Heineken needs

---

The 20 per cent fallacy

Many articles about knowledge management state that experts agree that in most companies only 20 per cent of the available knowledge is being used. There are three reasons why this is nonsense.

1. It is natural that only a small portion of knowledge is used. If one of your employees loves to go fishing at the weekend, what's the use of his knowledge about trout fishing if you manufacture wheelchairs? It's not just any knowledge that is important to you: it's only the knowledge that adds value that's important.

2. Experts agree ... what experts? These people must be awfully clever to measure all the available knowledge in a company. Perhaps they went around with a questionnaire asking, 'Hi, Bob, how much knowledge do you have?'

3. 20 per cent of what? What's the unit of knowledge? Bytes? Number of potential problems solved? cm^3 of brain tissue?

Combine and connect to realize knowledge value

'Tacit, unstructured knowledge enables us to sense market opportunities and respond in a creative way. Structured, explicit knowledge is our springboard to creating and producing innovative products and services. Combining and connecting the two proves invaluable for knowledge professionals throughout the organization who formulate strategies and realize operational improvements.'

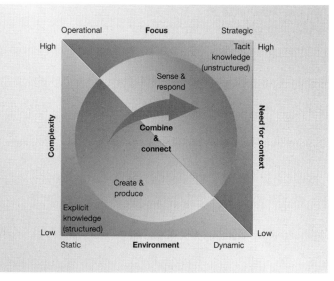

Combine and connect to realize knowledge value

and possesses to brew its beer. On the other hand, knowledge that is used to 'sense & respond' is vital for the direction a company takes. Knowledge about trends and discontinuities, competitors, core competencies and so on is therefore strategic knowledge.

Operational knowledge tends to be relatively uncomplicated. It is generally in a static environment and requires

The importance of reinventing the wheel

We all feel that one of the reasons we should do something with knowledge management is to make sure we don't keep on reinventing the wheel. We have all heard the horror stories about departments spending thousands of dollars on research for knowledge other departments already had on their shelves. But is it really a waste of time to reinvent the wheel? Here are three reasons that say it's not:

1. When someone invents the wheel, it becomes his wheel. He will fully understand its construction, function and context. Since the amount of context that is needed to give true meaning to knowledge is frequently very high, the process of reinventing the wheel can help give people that amount of context.

2. Most knowledge workers love to do innovating work. It's challenging, exciting and new. It creates a lot of energy and motivation. More energy than is created by somebody telling them they are not allowed to develop that knowledge and that they must follow somebody else's ideas. Again we see the ineffectiveness of force & control when dealing with professional knowledge workers.

3. In most cases, the reinvented wheel will look very different from the existing one. This in itself can be a very rich source of innovation. As Nonaka[21] showed us, at Honda they sometimes even create competing teams working on the same problem just to stimulate innovation.

relatively little context to make it understandable. This is largely due to its structured nature.

Complex knowledge with a strategic focus often exists in a much more dynamic environment. It also requires considerably more information about the context to give it meaning. It is generally tacit knowledge.

The following table gives you a framework with some examples in which you can plot your own work. Different job functions use different types of knowledge. Different knowledge carriers can provide different types of knowledge and offer transfer methods which are suitable for the different kinds of knowledge.

Type	Job function	Knowledge carrier	Knowledge transfer method
I	Judge	Legal publications	Library
II	Operator in a chemical plant	Process descriptions, manuals	Corporate Yellow Pages
III	Stock dealer	Company sales database	Internet discussion groups
IV	CEO	Strategy	Water cooler talks

Integrated knowledge environment

Increasing productivity still has overtones of the industrial economy. Yet it is also very relevant in the field of knowledge management. If knowledge workers are given the right tools, they can greatly enhance their productivity. Such tools should support their learning through information, interaction, and intellect.

Many companies are already involved to some extent in information technology. When this starts to support intellect and interaction it can slowly become knowledge technology. And many companies are taking the first steps in this direction by setting up an intranet to support their knowledge workers.

At the moment, however, most intranets are seen purely as a means of exchanging information and offering interaction. At the moment few support the intellect. It is important – as we have seen in our discussion of the knowledge circle – that we take into account all three 'I's – information, interaction, and intellect and a truly effective integrated knowledge environment must take this into account.

Integrated knowledge environment gives us the tools

'If we create an integrated knowledge environment, what kinds of knowledge tools are needed to best support learning from every source?'

'First, it should provide the tools which are used to learn from information. Known information is stored and retrieved from systems and databases. Workflow management systems access information as the flow of work demands. Data warehousing helps to find and organize new knowledge.'

'Interaction between knowledge professionals increases and improves when communication tools, groupware and discussion tools are utilized.'

'Analytical applications, like fishbone diagrams, data mining and mindmaps, improve our ability to comprehend information. Creativity stimulators help us to generate new ideas. Lessons learned and best practices databases tell us what we have learned from previous experiences. All three improve our cognitive way of learning.'

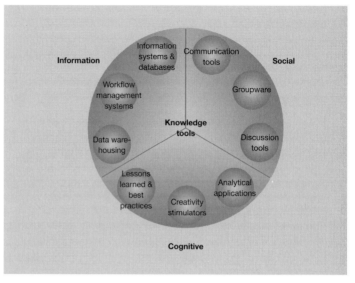

Integrated knowledge environment gives us the tools

For this reason, an ideal integrated knowledge environment
using the intranet should consist of the following tools:

Information tools:

– data warehousing and data mining
– information systems and databases
  These can include company databases, Corporate Yellow
  Pages, external databases, and a customized literature
  service
– workflow management systems
  These should be designed to both support the work flow
  and gather information.

Social tools:

– communication tools
  These should include e-mail, voice mail, news groups,
  bulletin boards, video-conferencing, fax
– groupware
  So that groups of people can work with the same document
– discussion tools
  discussions groups, chat groups, publish and subscribe
  systems.

Cognitive tools

– lessons learned and best practices
  computer-aided lessons learned, lessons learned examples,
  best practices examples
– creativity tools
– brain tools.

Analyzing tools

– fishbone diagrams
– mindmaps
– critical path analysis tools
– decision trees
– force field analysis
– SWOT analysis
– systems thinking tools
– black boards and white boards.

Brain tools

Royal Caribbean, one of America's largest cruise companies, uses a New Revenue Decision Support System to determine cruise fares, when and how to promote voyages, and whether there is a need to redeploy ships. A single screen provides data for deciding revenue status and deciding whether any action is required.[14]

There are many examples of companies turning to such tools on their intranets, and in fact Stewart, in *Intellectual Capital,* gives a whole list of the ways companies are designing branch-specific applications to meet their own requirements. Monsanto has developed knowledge management architecture which links hundreds of the company's sales people so that they can share news and gossip on a Lotus Notes database.[15] This is also used by major account managers and for in-house competitor intelligence. Advertising agency Young & Rubicam makes use of a Lotus Notes database with workflow software to cut out the physical movement of copy, sketches, and layouts and to improve its traffic management.[16]

But it is perhaps Hewlett Packard that has shown the most comprehensive use of an intranet. In fact it has several different systems which have been designed for specific applications.

First there is the customer response network which directs a customer call to one of four hubs around the world and zaps the file to one of twenty-seven centres where it is then picked up by a specialist team.[17] Then there is the work innovation network on which any business can set itself up as host for a series of presentations, conferences and seminars on a topic with which it is wrestling.[18] And there is knowledge links in

Data warehousing

Sears Roebuck and Co.'s credit department has been implementing a data warehouse which allows them access to the information about 500 million transactions made by 120 million Sears card holders in 80 million households throughout the US.[5]

Data mining

Accessing the information in a data warehouse needs to be fast and flexible. CUC International Inc. is in a wide range of business areas, from travel to time-sharing resorts. It uses a number of statistical software packages to find out which customers to target with which service and in which order to offer the services.[6]

Information systems and databases

Eli Lilly & Co.'s corporate intranet links more than 25 000 employees in 30 countries. It has more than 12 000 pages of information about job postings, handbooks, corporate news bulletins, stock prices, and a news feed about the pharmaceutical industry. Sales reps can access data through desktop or laptop on-line connections.[7]

Work flow management systems

The US Court of Appeals is undertaking an automation initiative to streamline the workflow. A customized application of groupware has been developed to replace the existing paper-based voting system.[8]

Communication tools

An audio-video intranet is being planned by Wall Street firm Bear Stearns & Co. to allow face-to-face discussions between traders and analysts without them having to leave their desks. The intranet will also be used for training.[9]

Groupware

Asea Brown Boveri has a Lotus Notes setup for 50 000 users. With 750 dedicated Lotus Notes servers linked to five main worldwide network hubs, it is the most sophisticated Notes system anywhere and is maintained by 300 dedicated administrators.[10]

Discussion tools

Since 1995, Hoffman-LaRoche's Bioscience intranet has grown from a simple telephone guide to a worldwide system connecting several company divisions on which Hoffman-LaRoche's scientists compare research results, discuss findings, and connect to on-line public information resources.[11]

which the staff product process organization acts as a go-between, collecting knowledge from one business unit and translating it to another. It identifies, edits, and formats the material, so that it is easier to access and use, thus increasing the returns on new organizational knowledge which is mined.[19]

Managing knowledge

Have you ever noticed how useful the verb 'to manage' is? How adaptable it is to a wide range of circumstances? As we have seen, the word 'knowledge' is equally adaptable. So does 'knowledge management' mean everything – and therefore does it deal with life, the universe and everything? Since Douglas Adams wrote *The Hitchhiker's Guide to the Galaxy*, we now know that the answer to life, the universe and everything is 42.[20] But what was the question exactly?

There is a growing store of literature about managing knowledge yet if we analyze it, we can say that most of everything written on the subject is about operational knowledge management and uses a management method directly derived from the world of industry and frequently makes use of the planning and control cycle. Some authors refer to this as the value chain – although it is evident, on closer investigation, that no value is added at any step in the process. People have assumed that knowledge management is all about control – knowledge is seen as a flow which has to be kept under strict control.

A closer investigation of the whole planning and control cycle shows that it is very difficult indeed to control the flow of knowledge. It can be done – but only if we are talking about the flow of operational knowledge in a very narrow and specified context which is highly stable and low in its complexity. Let's look at it stage by stage.

- The knowledge planning and control cycle starts with an inventory of available knowledge within the organization. Can one person actually handle such a task? Can you possibly give an answer to the question: 'What is the knowledge that you have available?' We can only start thinking about an answer if we narrow down the context, thus running the risk of excluding a whole lot of knowledge which we might otherwise have harvested.
- The second step of the planning and control cycle is to assess the received knowledge. Again this is an almost impossible task, unless we are talking about very specific knowledge – in line with a specific strategy we want to follow, or a specific product we want to produce. Only when we have narrowed things down can we roughly say what 'chunks of knowledge' are needed.
- The third step in the planning and control cycle is to develop the knowledge that is missing. This overlooks the fact that new knowledge is created every single day. In fact it is created every time people use and share their knowledge. What's more, you have to have an operational setting if you want to set out a research route that will bring in the knowledge you desire.

KPMG builds a knowledge factory

KPMG, the accountants and management consultancy organization, employs nearly 80 000 people worldwide. Open Access – an intranet-based information system – is being implemented worldwide to encourage the archiving of existing knowledge – often in the form of best practices – and its use in combination with new knowledge. Open Access also helps the exchange of knowledge between 'expertise centres'. Advanced software has been developed for navigation and distribution of the knowledge, thus ensuring that all the information needed – whether existing knowledge or communications with staff – can be easily accessed from any individual's PC. Individual intranets per location or country can be coupled together. KPMG employees now have at their fingertips the latest company news, information about KPMG, including names and telephone numbers, an index of all sources and a search engine. In this way, knowledge and information can be accessed whenever it is required without difficulty or loss of valuable time.

Only explicit knowledge can be managed

'The view that knowledge has to be controlled is true only insofar as it applies to structured knowledge. The planning and control cycle helps us manage our store of type II knowledge, demanding that current relative information is added to the inventory and its value judged and codified so that we can distribute it.'

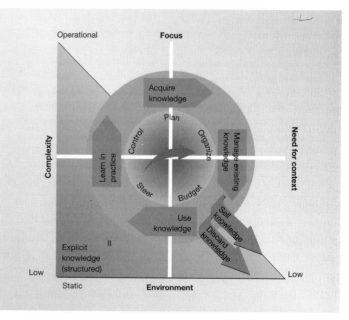

Only explicit knowledge can be managed

– The next steps in the planning and control cycle are to distribute and use the knowledge. This is something which happens all the time and takes place in an uncontrolled manner. There is absolutely no way you can control this. The only thing you can do is facilitate it and stimulate it. But these two attitudes are not part of the cycle.

– And the final step in such a planning and control cycle is to discard knowledge. We've already seen that knowledge is basically something held in the brain of a human being. So the only way to discard knowledge is to fire somebody. 'Thanks for doing a good job – now you can leave.' What we can do is to decide quite deliberately that we no longer wish to invest in knowledge in a particular knowledge domain. If we do that, the domain will gradually disappear as time goes on.

Our conclusion is that the planning and control cycle can be of use in knowledge management – but only for structured knowledge. For most companies, unstructured knowledge is where their future lies. It is this knowledge which is needed to guarantee future value creation, to create new opportunities

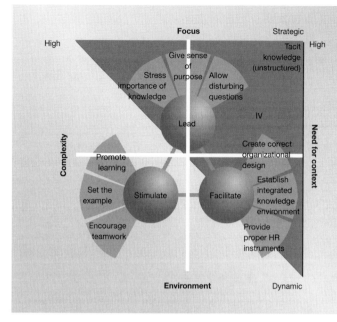

Controlling value-creating knowledge is an illusion

and to give a company a strategic advantage. Unfortunately it is exactly this area which cannot be helped by the planning and control cycle approach to knowledge management.

If we want to manage unstructured knowledge, we should stop thinking in terms of 'control'. Instead we should start thinking in terms of leading, facilitating and stimulating.

These are the three levels of the successful management of unstructured knowledge.

Lead

– Stress the importance of knowledge for your company. Mention it, underline it whenever you can. During a New Year's speech, in the annual report, in the mission statement.

– Give a sense of purpose. This means producing a vision, a mission, a strategy, and core values which reflect the importance of knowledge.

– Allow disturbing questions. Get your people to challenge orthodoxies. Get them to think out of the box – and then see if you are doing that as well. Play the devil's advocate and protect anyone else who shoulders that responsibility.

Facilitate

- Establish an integrated knowledge environment. Make sure everybody understands that you are doing it not because of any financial considerations, but because you have a clear vision of how ICT can benefit your company's sharing of knowledge.
- Provide the proper human resource instruments. Make sure these are fine-tuned to cater to the needs of knowledge professionals.
- Create the right architectural and organizational design.

Stimulate

- Set the right example. Make the lessons you have learned accessible to everybody, and encourage everybody else to do the same. Get them to contribute to a current CV, making sure that it is updated regularly. Stimulate people to make more use of the PC and e-mail.
- Encourage teamwork. Promote multidisciplinary teams for a whole range of activities. Use non-hierarchical teams. Give encouragement to young potentials.
- Promote learning. Make sure there is time for reflection. Stimulate the writing and publishing of articles on as wide a range of subjects as possible.

Orchestrate knowledge

So what is the best way to organize knowledge in our company? One approach which has proven successful is to manage knowledge by creating competence centres or centres of excellence around specific knowledge domains. It is then necessary to appoint a person to keep the knowledge in this area up to date. Such centres often create their own web sites on the intranet so that they can share their knowledge with others. A chief knowledge officer is often appointed to control the sharing of knowledge.

This approach could perhaps be called a 'supply-based approach'. The responsibility for making knowledge accessible is placed in the hands of the people who actually create the knowledge.

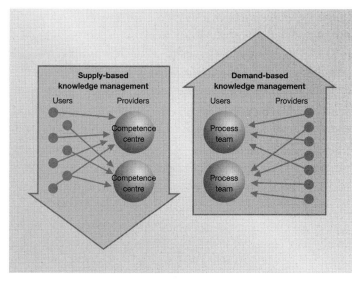

Supply or demand: which is better?

Supply or demand: which is better?

'In a supply-based knowledge management approach, knowledge providers are responsible for managing knowledge. As a result, intranets grow wild and professionals are lost, wandering aimlessly through a jungle of irrelevant information. Chief knowledge officers and competence centre leaders act like policemen and custodians, demanding workers to input their knowledge.'

'Therefore a demand-based approach is more productive. Knowledge users, working in process teams, are now responsible for codifying and dispersing knowledge. They have a proprietary interest in keeping it up to date and easy to locate.'

'So with demand-based knowledge management, no chief knowledge officer is needed.'

Unfortunately, early indications do not show particularly positive results from supply-based approaches. The creation of in-depth knowledge in specific domains is expensive and does not always add value to the company. Intranets can become chaotic jungles where the professionals cannot find the knowledge they are after or need. And chief knowledge officers and competence leaders can assume the role of knowledge policemen ordering people to input their knowledge – or else.

A demand-based approach, however, seems to be much more productive. Users of knowledge are encouraged to work in process teams which assume full responsibility for the codification and dispersion of knowledge. Because they are the users of knowledge they have a special interest in making sure it is available and up to date. A good example of how this works in practice has been given with the Heineken example in Chapter 8 – Smart organizations.

The smart approach to smart knowledge requires a varied use of tools, many of which can ensure that the knowledge gathered and stored in your company can be put to uses which you may never have considered before. Yet tools do not make a knowledge company. This requires, before anything else, understanding that the creation of valuable knowledge content and context is essential within the knowledge economy. Once this position has been fully endorsed by everybody in the company, the implementation of systems and networks to make things happen will be altogether easier.

PART FOUR

HOW DO WE IMPLEMENT VALUE-BASED KNOWLEDGE MANAGEMENT?

CHAPTER 11

'Three steps towards operational knowledge management'

How companies can improve the way they share and use meaningful knowledge

Operational knowledge management improves the way a company shares and uses its knowledge. It does this by linking people together using an IT system. But there are no quick solutions to implementing such a system in an organization. Certainly you can design and build a magnificent intranet, connecting everybody in your company to each other so that they can communicate with each other and access information they need for their work. You can include large-scale databases, even data warehouses and data mining.

The difficulties arise when you want this magnificent system

– to be used;
– to contain meaningful information; and
– to be easy to use and fully adapted to the company's processes.

The solutions to these needs are different in each situation. For Arthur Andersen, it was the development of ANet which facilitated sharing throughout the consultancy. Management designed major changes in incentives and compensation to ensure that the system worked. Not only was active participation in the ANet considered in all promotional and compensation reviews, senior management also made use of the system to send e-mail directives to employees which 'had to be answered by 10'.[1] At Coopers & Lybrand, on the other hand, they felt that creating a network and hoping people

Learning often cannot occur until after there has been unlearning. Unlearning is a process that shows people they should no longer rely on their current beliefs and methods. Because current beliefs and methods shape perceptions, they blind people to some potential interpretations of evidence. As long as current beliefs and methods seem to produce reasonable results, people do not discard their current beliefs and methods.
W.H. Starbuck[3]

We believe that to build smarter organizations, owners, managers, employees, and observers of organizations, all of us, must first concern ourselves with unlearning the organization. We all must set aside assumptions about business success that are captured in our attachment to knowing, understanding and thinking. We must clear our minds of where we have been and where we are in order to create for ourselves where we want to be.
M.E. McGill and J.W. Slocum[4]

would use it would be useless, so instead they set up the knowledge network with personal rewards rather than business payback. The network was designed using the model of television programming. Since its inception in 1988, the network has grown between 80 per cent and 100 per cent each year to more than 12 000 users. The chairman has used it for all his communications since 1992.[2]

The different ways companies have designed their internal networks, and the ways that have been employed to get people to use them, can help us when we design our own specific network. It requires a continuous learning style of working so that you can eventually achieve a system which best suits your company's style, culture, processes and IT environment.

Adopting a learning style of working implies that you constantly assess what you have done and achieved. It means reviewing exactly where you stand with the company and the implementation projects the company is handling. It also means setting up pilot projects so that you can gradually improve the situation in various parts of the company. This does not have to take place company-wide; it is often better to work with a project for a specific area of the company. It means asking yourself at the end of each day 'what have we learned today?'.

Such a learning style is something which needs to permeate the whole company. For this it is necessary to have a commitment from the top of the organization. As Peter Neff, CEO of Rhone-Poulenc, says, 'As leaders we have to accept that part of our job is to lead the way in learning.'[5]

A roadmap to implementing operational knowledge management

Implementing operational knowledge management is like undertaking a journey. You need a map to plan out your path and the possible alternative routes along the way. You will also need an understanding of the tools you have at your disposal and the resources you may need to reach your final destination and points in between. The operational knowledge management journey has five distinct stages spanning from knowledge-chaotic to knowledge-centric.[7]

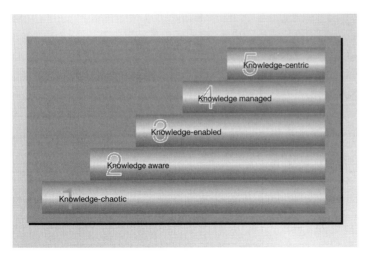

The knowledge journey

The five steps along the knowledge journey are:

1. Knowledge-chaotic

The organization is unaware of the importance of knowledge to the achievement of its goals. This stage is characterized by the storage and management of knowledge in an *ad hoc* manner across the organization. The accessing and retrieval of information is difficult and time-consuming because of the difficulty of identifying sources of knowledge. Systems may be incompatible. Processes for collecting information may be ineffectual or non-existent. People may be reluctant to share information or simply lack the time or incentive to do so.

2. Knowledge aware

The organization is aware of the need to husband its knowledge and some attempt has been made to do so. Knowledge processes and sources with the organization have been identified and documented. The retrieval of information is facilitated by a catalogue of the available knowledge sources and their use within established knowledge processes. Awareness and implementation across the organization, however, may not be uniform. Ownership and sharing of knowledge may be an issue.

3. Knowledge-enabled

Knowledge management is beginning to benefit the business. Standard procedures and tools are utilized across the

Cashing in on the relevant info

'Every company has a ton of information in its databases; the key to profitable underwriting isn't giving access to every bit of information that's important, it's how you determine which information is relevant and how you tailor it.'
Tom Valerio
Senior Vice President
CIGNA[6]

Knowledge management questions organizations should ask themselves:
1. Where are we today?
2. Where do we stand relative to our customers and competitors?
3. What are the barriers to moving to the next stage and achieving its benefits?
4. What are we doing and what should we be doing to make progress?
5. What is the cost or risk of doing nothing?

organization to access information stores. Knowledge resources have been inventoried, evaluated and classified, and procedures have been implemented to maintain this listing. A number of the cultural and technological barriers have still to be addressed.

4. Knowledge managed

The organization has an integrated framework of procedures and tools to discover, create, maintain and retrieve information. The technological and cultural issues have been overcome. The organization's knowledge strategy is reviewed and improved on a continuing basis.

5. Knowledge-centric

The organization's mission is the application and enhancement of its knowledge base, which is providing it with a demonstrable, sustainable competitive advantage in its markets. Knowledge management procedures are an integral part of organizational and individual processes. Knowledge management tools are highly integrated and reside on a robust technological backbone that allows knowledge to be mission-critical to the enterprise. The assessment and improvement of the knowledge environment are standard operating procedures. The value of knowledge to the organization is being measured and reported to stakeholders, is reflected in the organization's market value and is being managed as the organization's intellectual capital.

The knowledge journey is not only a journey – it is a race

The most innovative organizations have already started on the journey. Leading organizations in virtually every sector have shown, through an ever-growing number of case study examples, that more effective use of knowledge and insight gives *them* a competitive edge. Business success is not about amassing assets, it is about putting them to work. Now is the time for those who would be in the 'early majority' to take action, closing the narrow, but fast-growing, gap between themselves and the innovators, and seizing the remaining opportunity to reap competitive advantage.

Working simultaneously on motivation, knowledge content and systems

The major problem with knowledge-based systems – and this is something we have stated before – is that everybody wants to get knowledge out, but nobody wants to put knowledge in. And so the crucial aspect we have to attack is that of people & motivation.

As we have already seen in the chapter about smart professionals (Part 3, Chapter 9) there are no quick fixes for changing the knowledge attitude within your company. But there are steps you can take to make it work.

First, you have to assess the competencies your people possess which can help them work successfully with knowledge. How good are they at searching for knowledge? Do they follow well trodden paths, or are they creative in looking for new sources of knowledge? Do they know what questions they have to ask in order to get the knowledge they need? Do they have the capabilities to analyze the information and to reflect on the lessons they have learned? How well have they mastered the dialogue which is necessary to exchange knowledge without compromising it? Can they work with the knowledge without prejudice?

Such an approach is not new. As far back as 1966 Texas Instruments discovered that there was a lack of minimal job competence and the results of this caused failures in solving problems. A special orientation programme was designed by manufacturing managers at Texas Instruments to help reduce the anxiety of new employees so that they could reach the required competence level more quickly. The results of this programme were significant gains in learning time, quality production and job attendance.[8]

You must also ask yourself what the knowledge attitude is in your company. Do your people have enough self-esteem to realize that their own knowledge is invaluable? Do they respect each other sufficiently to be prepared to listen to each other's opinions? And do they have sufficient trust in the organization? Are they willing to put their knowledge into the system? To what extent is there a common belief about who is responsible for learning? Is there an understanding, an acceptance, of

Key questions to determine knowledge competencies

1. Identify the group of people you want to be in the operational knowledge pilot.

2. Score them on a scale from 1 to 10 on the following competencies:
   - the ability to gather information by observing, postponing judgement, etc. (sensing);
   - the ability to know where to look for information (sourcing);
   - the ability to ask the right questions (questioning);
   - the ability to analyze the information (analyzing);
   - the ability to be creative;
   - the ability to reflect on what was learned;
   - the ability to network;
   - the ability to work in teams; and
   - the ability to participate in a dialogue.

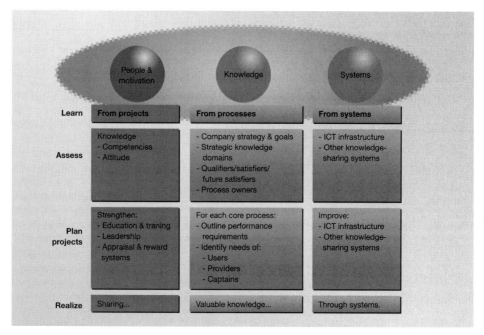

	People & motivation	Knowledge	Systems
Learn	From projects	From processes	From systems

Assess	Knowledge
	- Competencies
	- Attitude
		- Company strategy & goals
		- Strategic knowledge
		  domains
		- Qualifiers/satisfiers/
		  future satisfiers
		- Process owners
			- ICT infrastructure
			- Other knowledge-
			  sharing systems

Plan projects	Strengthen:
	- Education & traning
	- Leadership
	- Appraisal & reward
	  systems
		For each core process:
		- Outline performance
		  requirements
		- Identify needs of:
		  - Users
		  - Providers
		  - Captains
			Improve:
			- ICT infrastructure
			- Other knowledge-
			  sharing systems

Realize	Sharing...	Valuable knowledge...	Through systems.

Three steps toward operational knowledge management

'The three-step approach teaches us to build knowledge through projects, processes, and systems.'

'Does it allow us to learn what's best for us?'

'Of course. Now, we first have to assess our company's position, then plan learning projects for improving our current situation, and finally realize operational knowledge management.'

'Assess, plan, learn. Right.'

'We start by improving the way people work with knowledge and systems.'

'Start with people. Got you.'

'We can then decide whether we need to plan for their training, their leadership, and our appraisal and reward systems.'

'And that helps people share their knowledge better?'

'It's a start. We then have to make sure that we gather knowledge to support our operational processes. We choose one of our core operational processes as a pilot, and we outline the performance requirements and identify the critical knowledge necessary.'

'So then we know who needs the knowledge – and who can provide it.'

'Right. Then we have to decide who is responsible for the knowledge. Now some people appoint a knowledge officer – but smart professionals don't really like that approach. It's better to select a team member to become a sort of knowledge captain.'

'Aye, aye, sir.'

'Then the third thing we need is to get our systems in order – assess our IT position and our knowledge-sharing systems. Then we can implement projects to make these systems our right hand to transform personal knowledge into company knowledge.'

'And it only takes three steps.'

'Build, share, and renew.'

the importance of knowledge flow? Indeed what is the importance of knowledge for the company as a whole? Are these beliefs really translated into learning, knowledge sharing and knowledge codifying behaviour?

At 3M, the company's creativity and productivity is sustained by the institutional management of core competence technology and corporate values that honour the needs of the innovators. Centralized ownership of core technologies promotes knowledge transfer. On the cultural side, values captured in corporate maxims and stories express unusual support for individual creativity. A 15 per cent rule allows employees to set aside 15 per cent of their time to pursue personal research interests.[9]

As a second step you should define projects to improve competencies and attitudes. There are many training courses available for improving knowledge competencies, so that is not the problem. Changing an attitude, however, requires more thought and attention. The approach chosen depends on the severity of the situation. If, for example, you discover that there is a lack of self-esteem, respect and trust, then you can expect to face a very long process which will have to start at the very top. If there is no respect and trust with the management team, you need to start team-building there. From there you will have to give people responsibility, independence and trust. This is essential. You must also set people's minds on success rather than failure. You must work on team building, ensuring that there is room for different skills, styles and viewpoints.

If such beliefs are already well accepted within the organization, you should concentrate on reinforcing leadership qualities. Here you should set the example yourself and talk knowledge at every possible opportunity. You must be consistent and you must learn to lead, stimulate and facilitate.

A further important task is to look at your appraisal and reward system. These can work like Herzberg's dissatisfiers: if they stimulate good behaviour they will not necessarily add to the improvement of the knowledge attitude; but if they contain the wrong incentives, they will certainly frustrate knowledge behaviour.

While you are working on the motivation of your professionals, you also must make sure you are working on gathering

The wrong incentives

A large consultancy firm was very result oriented: individual business units set high targets for turnover, margins and profits. In addition, individual consultants were given high acquisition targets. And they were given very high billable hour targets. The result was a knowledge attitude which said, 'keep everything to yourself and let God look after the rest.'

'There exists, even among the best professionals and professional firms, a perverse belief that only billable time (chargeable time spent serving clients) really counts. Anything non-billable is viewed as either worthless or as not as valuable as "real" work … What you do with your billable time determines your current income, but what you do with your non-billable time determines your future.'
D.H. Maister[10]

valuable knowledge to support the operational processes. To do this, you first have to identify the core processes and the people who are responsible for them. From these processes you should choose one to act as a pilot project. The pilot must be carefully defined and the performance requirements must be clearly outlined. You should then identify the critical knowledge needed at every step of the way to fulfil those requirements. In this way you can obtain a very clear picture of who needs the knowledge and who can provide it.

Pfizer[11] has developed competency models for its treasury executives that call for more than basic financial skills. Knowledge building and knowledge sharing are considered critical for management as the company strives to create linkages across the organization. Managers are regularly evaluated against these models.[12] Similarly, Asea Brown Boveri evaluates its managers not only based on the results of their decisions but also on the knowledge and information applied during the decision-making process.[13]

The third thing you need to do is to get your systems in order. You have to assess very carefully your present IT position and any other knowledge sharing system you may have in place. When you have done that, you can implement projects to make these systems a really useful and effective tool in helping transform personal knowledge into company knowledge.

Sending a team (or more) into battle

All too often, projects for improving operational knowledge management take technology as their starting point. The impulse for improvement can arise in the IT department, which can affect the focus of the project.

In order to avoid an approach which is too technically biased, it is better to form a multidisciplinary team which contains both line and staff people. It should contain people responsible for the systems, such as IT and HR, but also people who are the (proposed) users of it. The team should also include people from both the management and the operational level.

Often it is a sound strategy to set up three separate teams who can work simultaneously on three separate projects:

motivation, knowledge content and systems. Such an approach ensures that all aspects of the proposed knowledge system are approached at the same time. This allows eventual implementation to be based on full details of the major aspects of the system.

Whatever teams you decide to send into battle, it is important to remember that when deciding who should be in a team, energy, enthusiasms, and diversity in skills are more important than knowledge of the content.

CHAPTER 12

'The Value Enhancer'

How your company can become a truly value-adding knowledge company

If you are to implement strategic knowledge management, you will need to adopt a balanced approach and work simultaneously on six core abilities in which your company will need to achieve success in the twenty-first century. These take into account the changing demands which will be placed on your company, and the new attitudes you will need to develop to be effective in the knowledge economy, while at the same time preparing yourself for the quantum economy.

These six abilities can be summed up as follows: You need the ability to **respond** swiftly to changes in the market, and at the same time **anticipate** future customer needs. You have to **produce** products and services while at the same time **learning** from your experiences. You need to develop the ability of your professionals to **create** knowledge while at the same time you need to **build** a company to last.

Decentralization of authority throughout your organization will not only make sure that units are closer to their customers, it will also ensure that they are better suited to respond to market changes. Unfortunately, decentralization will almost automatically lead to greater reluctance for units to share knowledge with each other. The spirit of cooperation has flown the corporate coop and few teams are eager to share their knowledge. When they haven't got an overview of what knowledge is available, many of these teams are, despite all good intentions, not really in a position to anticipate trends in changing (market) circumstances. And for this reason many companies are now recognizing the need to balance decentralizing authority with centralizing knowledge.

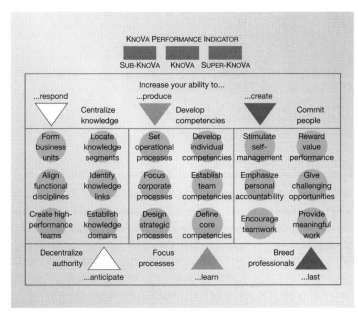

The value enhancer

'All six elements of strategic knowledge management are incorporated in The Value Enhancer – an extremely handy device on CD-ROM, and included with this book – which helps you determine your company's current KnoVa position and shows you how you can improve it.'

The Value Enhancer

To make full use of their knowledge-potential, companies are shifting from functional-based organizations to organizations that are entirely process- and team-based. Many companies are in the throes of changing to better meet the challenges of the future. And this change undoubtedly increases their ability to produce products and services much faster than before. It also contributes to getting products faster to market, thus adding a competitive edge to their operations. But to make a team-based process-organization really effective, you need to develop those competencies in your people that allow them to work in a non-functionally organized environment. The payback will be significant: it will increase value to both your company and the individuals working in it.

To achieve a more knowledge- and value-intensive company requires not only new competencies but also new professionals. In other words, it becomes essential to attract knowledge professionals and encourage them to develop themselves in such a way that they add value to both the company and themselves on a continuous basis. At the same time, however, the more value-adding a knowledge professional becomes, the greater will be his or her value on the labour market. It is for this very reason that it is vital

**Asea Brown Boveri:
business unit
champion**
When ASEA and Brown
Boveri merged, a
massive
reorganization took
place, turning the
company into a
confederation of
business units. Central
office staff was reduced
from 6000 to 150. Layers
of middle management
were stripped out. And
the company was split
up into 1300 smaller
companies and around
5000 profit centres. The
reorganization was
aimed at ensuring that
managers moved closer
to their customers so
they could become more
responsive to changing
market situations.[1]

you not only breed professionals, but also increase your efforts to get knowledge professionals to commit themselves to your company so that you can create a company that is built to last.

Decentralizing authority and centralizing knowledge

Decentralizing authority will increase your company's ability to respond to changes in local markets. The following three steps will make it happen.

1. Form business units. In the past decade many companies have decentralized authority into (business) units. Much of the reasoning behind this has been to segment the business to match the segments of the market. Business unit managers are given personal responsibility for achieving bottom-line results.

2. Align functional disciplines. Traditional functional specialists almost always have a very high level of expertise. Yet it is not always clear how these specialists add value to a company. Remember that your principle aim should always be to create value – not to accumulate knowledge for the sake of it. This implies that functional disciplines should be redesigned to give them a greater business and process orientation. By doing this you can ensure that functional expertise has a clearer and more direct impact on strategic and operational performance.

3. Create high-performance teams. Old-fashioned companies are still characterized by employees working in rigidly defined

**Shell creates a
separate functional
alignment company**
Shell is establishing a
separate company to
align functional disciplines.
The oil multinational is still
managed by strong
country organizations that
have considerable
freedom to follow their
own policies. With
competition squeezing out
the margins on the sales
of gas, a strong and
aligned European
organization is being set
up to focus staff
professionals and to
breed more
responsiveness among
employees. As Shell
President Herkströter
said: 'Nobody can permit
himself to occupy a room
and a desk knowing that
he is not adding value to
the group.'[2]

**Teams accept
responsibility**
'Change will bring
merriment to the brewery.'
That is the motto for a
process started by
Heineken for starting self-
managing teams in the
packaging and brewing
departments. Teams are
given an area of
responsibility – for
example, quality, safety
and so on – and, although
they have received
training, actually pointing
to responsibilities is more
difficult than envisaged.
Nevertheless, the result is
an increase in the
involvement of the
employees with the
company.[3]

functions and performing routine tasks to accomplish highly repetitive objectives. It is essential that these structures are replaced with new organizational forms which allow professionals to work individually and with a greater degree of autonomy. They should be given the feeling that they are truly adding value to the company, not simply performing a task.

Balance the decentralization of authority with centralizing your companies knowledge using these three steps.

1. Establish knowledge domains: Start by translating your business strategy into key knowledge areas which are essential for realizing your strategy in a value-creating way. The creation of knowledge domains helps you to focus more clearly on the building and sharing of your company's knowledge. It is essential to ensure that knowledge professionals do not start gathering knowledge in a disorganized and random way, but rather in a way which ensures that meaningful value-adding knowledge is harvested.

2. Identify knowledge links. The knowledge domains you have identified can now be divided into a number of specific knowledge topics or issues that provide a link between the work being done by individual professionals and teams to realize company objectives. Such knowledge links act as business enhancers, and strengthen and connect the separate flows of knowledge into knowledge domains.

3. Locate knowledge segments. Having created knowledge domains and knowledge links, the third step is to identify those segments of knowledge that together form the strategic body of knowledge that is of value to your company. These are called knowledge segments and their source can be either a person or a system. It can also be extremely useful to make use of a knowledge map. You can use it to reach a number of important conclusions for every individual in your company. First, you can determine to what knowledge segments an individual contributes to. Second, you can see in which knowledge segments an individual has growth potential, and this, in turn can be used as the basis for a competency profile and competency development. And third, it also becomes clear which people do not contribute to your company's strategic knowledge.

NEC's strategic architecture

NEC, originally a supplier of telecommunications systems, realized that the communication industry was converging with the computer industry. It set out a strategic architecture which specified the competencies the company needed to develop knowledge and to capitalize on the overlap which was starting between the computer, communication and components industry to become a leader in communication and computer technology.[4]

'A prescription for knowledge'

At pharmaceutical company Hoffman-LaRoche, a knowledge management initiative was started to help product teams prototype the knowledge required for new drug applications and to produce a comprehensive map of the knowledge sources in the company that might contribute to their completion. The result has been an enormous cut in the time needed to get a drug to market – a valuable exercise, since each day gained could earn the company around $1 million.[5]

Focusing processes and developing competencies

To make full use of your company's knowledge potential, organize your company around processes and teams using these three steps.

1. Set operational processes. These are the 'create & produce' processes that allow your company to produce products and services, and deliver them to your customers. By initiating and redesigning operational processes, you form the core of bottom-line business unit and team performance.

2. Focus corporate processes. It is vital that strategic processes and operational processes are carefully connected. In an effort to 'combine & connect', you should take a close look at those corporate processes that connect strategy to operations through coordination, communication and control. This is often very difficult in 'old-style' corporate headquarters, which are traditionally based on functions and hierarchies. Success will depend on your ability to also recreate the corporate office into a process-driven, team-based, corporate centre which is able to align operational issues with your company's strategy and vice versa.

3. Define strategic processes. Strategic processes are directly related to a company's long-term business objectives and should clearly reflect the main direction in which the company needs to develop. They should be used to focus your company's knowledge creation, so that meaningful knowledge is harvested – that is, knowledge which adds value to the company – rather than just knowledge for knowledge's sake.

Balance your new organization by providing your people with the right competencies to work in a team-based process environment.

1. Define core competencies. Core competencies accurately reflect your company's key strengths which allow you to add value to your customers, to society and to the company under changing market conditions. Once you have defined core competencies they become a stable part of your business. Core competencies tend to remain constant for a longer period of time.

2. Establish team competencies. When a professional team is required to build knowledge, the team will need a number of unique capabilities that allows it to work effectively. Team competencies serve as the framework for effective team performance. Teams combine and connect the individual competencies of a number of professionals in such a way that the team is not adversely affected when team members leave.

3. Develop individual competencies. It is essential to stimulate smart professionals to focus on high performance by

W.L. Gore Associates, manufacturers of Gore-tex waterproof fabric, operates 44 plants worldwide.

The company has no job titles, hierarchy, or other conventional structures, but works through associates that want to better themselves. Lines of communication are direct; there is no fixed or assigned authority; natural leadership is defined by fellowships; objectives are set by those who make it happen and tasks and functions are organized through commitment.[12]

continuously improving the individual learning abilities they need to build knowledge.

Breeding professionals and committing people

To become a fully fledged value-adding knowledge company you need more than skilled individuals, you need true knowledge professionals. The 'breeding' of these professionals takes the following three steps.

1. Stimulate self-management: Knowledge professionals constantly work in teams. In some teams they act as the team leader, in others as a team member. This takes its toll on even the most resilient professional, and it is important that you encourage them to 'refresh & refocus' at regular intervals. In this way they remain in shape and can continue to add value to both the company and themselves.

2. Emphasize personal accountability. Modern companies depend on the effective performance of individuals to achieve success. These individuals are motivated by the degree to which they can personally contribute to business results. As the emphasis on individual performance increases, personal accountability becomes the standard for setting and meeting targets and objectives.

3. Encourage teamwork. Once you have created a process-driven and team-oriented organization then effective team

IBM has 3000 business partners

At IBM employees are expected to commit themselves to decisions which are reached using their input. Each employee must address three concerns: 'how to win', describing how their contribution adds to the success of IBM; 'how to execute', describing how they are going to deliver the best; and 'how to team', showing who they need to complete the task. IBM employees are held accountable for their own personal plans and these are used for discussing salary increases and bonuses. A database offers over 11 000 skills, allowing employees to map current and future skills and work on any gap through education.[13]

Management DNA

At Minnesota Mining and Manufacturing Company, management talks about DNA: define (direction), nurture (support) and allocate (coordination). It is not management's job to run teams and projects, rather it has to decide what needs to be done (direct) so that projects don't run off in every direction. They then have to nourish the skills essential to the business (nurture), reward the results and ensure a beneficial environment. Finally they have to make a choice between the dozens of opportunities (allocate) and manage the use of the team's resources.[11]

management becomes one of the pillars on which successful business performance is built. Effective team management largely depends on your ability to direct and guide team efforts, coordinate and control individual team member performances and support team performance.

This should be balanced by a careful process of actually committing professionals to your company in an enduring way, using the following three steps.

1. Provide meaningful work. Knowledge professionals can be motivated to add value to the company and to themselves. But they must be able to relate to the company's overall purposes in such a way that these purposes also provide personal fulfilment. Many professionals constantly question the extent to which their performance makes sense to the company, to their careers and to their personal lives.

2. Give challenging opportunities. Challenging smart professionals to add value in a continuous learning situation is a great way to motivate them. They feel stretched and energized to go beyond 'business as usual' and fully commit themselves to what needs to be achieved.

3. Reward value performance: To recognize and reward value-enhancing performance are two essential elements in your company's strategy to ensure that knowledge professionals commit themselves to your company. Nonetheless, in the long run this may not be sufficient unless you make more tangible rewards available, i.e. have them share in the profits and

Motivation at Intel
Intel was able to motivate its R&D teams working on innovations in the processing speed of chips to such an extent that Intel is now the industry leader. The company does one thing that no competitor can match: builds state-of-the-art microprocessors in quantities of tens of millions. In 1996 Intel spent $5 billion on capital projects and R&D; every nine months or so it builds a new chip plant – two years before it is needed.[15]

'Internal competition'
At Canon, internal competition plays an important role.
A product development team is divided into competing groups that develop different approaches to the same project, then argue about the relative advantages and disadvantages of the proposals. Because of this, the team is encouraged to approach the problem from a variety of viewpoints, and the result is that a better understanding of the best approach to the problem can be achieved.[16]

Leading companies reward professionals
Many of today's leading companies are recognizing the importance of employees in their compensation systems. Microsoft has introduced virtual employee ownership. General Electric offers stock ownership. Owens Corning pays a large part of their wages in gain-sharing, in which employees are paid extra if the company meets certain targets.[17] And the Dutch Institute of Applied Research, TNO, stimulates its employees by naming 'TNO toppers', who are assigned extra budgets and freedom because of their results.[18]

success of your company in direct relation to their contribution both from a compensation and career point of view.

A long climb

Mount Everest was not conquered in a single day. It required careful planning, persistence, and an understanding that you have to move up in carefully gauged steps, moving from one camp to the next.

The same is true for implementing strategic knowledge management. Here, too, you must move from one clearly defined position to the next. Obviously the approach you take will depend on your present position on the mountain and on the amount of energy you can generate to get your people moving from one camp to the next.

Reaching a camp in company terms is the same as in mountaineering terms. You can celebrate the progress you have made. You can secure and imbed the things you have learned while climbing. And you can take a rest to regain your strength before moving on to the next leg of your climb.

Make a plan of each leg of your journey – a plan for each camp on the way up. In this way, you can focus your people on the ulti-

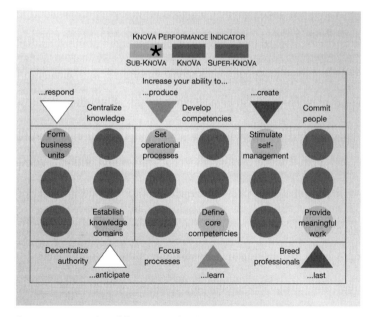

Base camp: market-driven organization

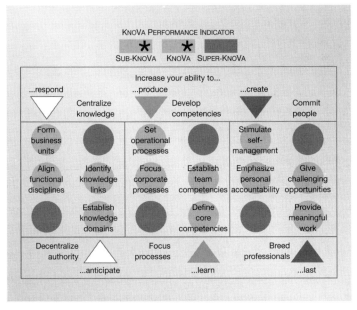

Camp 1: competency- and process-based

mate goal and on the way you are planning to get there. You will have to take time to reassure uncertain people in your team and explain to them that you will not be able to achieve everything in one leg of the journey. This informs impatient people of when the problem which worries them most will be attacked.

Climbing from camp to camp

Your first aim is to reach base camp where your company becomes truly market driven. This is the sort of organization which listens carefully to its customers and market and is able to react quickly and effectively to changing market circumstances and behaviour.

Of course base camp cannot be reached without effort. Success depends on carrying out the six actions indicated by The Value Enhancer.

The second camp on your climb to the top will be one in which you turn your company into a team-based process organ-ization, an organization which rests on competencies rather than on functions or hierarchies. Again, reaching this camp requires considerable effort, commitment and determination. To be successful you will once again need to carry out the six actions The Value Enhancer indicates.

The top is in sight. You and your company are increasingly ready to face the challenges of the knowledge economy. You need to turn your company into a continuous learning organization. To reach this ultimate goal, you again have to carry out the six actions as indicated by The Value Enhancer.

Becoming a value-adding knowledge company

Using The Value Enhancer you have step by step worked your company up to becoming a continuous learning organization. When you combine this with what you have been doing from an operational knowledge management point of view you rapidly can become a value-adding knowledge company. You will have built a stable company that is skilfully responsive to take advantage of a rapidly changing environment. Combining the strengths of both knowledge management perspectives results in the continuous creation of meaningful knowledge that adds value to your company. You will have strengthened the six abilities needed to be ready for the next century. You will have created smart knowledge that is available to your smart professionals that work in a smart organization on creating and realizing smart strategies. The result is a twenty-first century company: knowledge intensive, people rich.

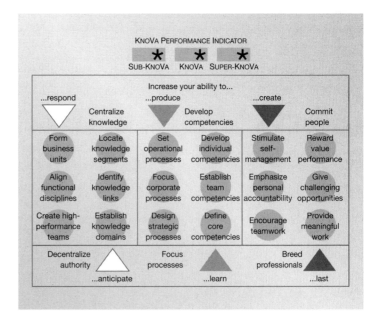

Camp 2: continuous learning organization

360 degree performance appraisal smart professionals regularly request mentors, team leaders, peers and customers to appraise their performance by completing a formal performance survey.

agricultural economy traditionally a land and labour intensive economy primarily aimed at the production of food.

align functional disciplines traditionally, functional specialists tend to have a high level of expertise although it is not always clear how this attribute adds value to the company. Since companies are not in the business of building knowledge but in the business of creating value, functional disciplines are increasingly redesigned to become more business and process oriented. In this way, functional expertise has a clearer and more direct impact on strategic and operational performance.

analytical applications help analyze information (e.g. fishbone diagrams, mind maps, critical path analysis tools, decision trees, force-field analysis, strengths, weaknesses, opportunities and threats [SWOT] analysis, system thinking tools, blackboards and whiteboards).

analyzing the ability to use logic, systems thinking, reasoning and mental modelling.

brain-level complexity traditional and alternative methods of computing in this respect focus on increasing storage capacity and processing speed to the level of the average brain storage capacity and 100 000 teraflops processing speed). It is expected that during the first quarter of the twenty first century computers with brain-level complexity will be commercially available.

browser a programme that allows users to access documents on the World-Wide Web (WWW). Browsers can either display text or graphics. They read HTML and interpret the code into what we see as web pages.

business process redesign (BPR) returns an organization to its prime principles. BPR concerns itself with detecting the core processes which make up the business and then reassembling them more efficiently in a way which is free of functional divides and which reduces complexity by reengineering operational and customer directed activities into processes.

communication processes information technology (IT) and cultural processes that enable people to share information in an efficient and effective manner (i.e. intranet, e-mail).

communication tools support electronic communication (e.g. electronic mail, voice mail, news groups, bulletin boards, audio and video conferences, faxes.

communities of interest are built around a common interest with a primary focus on the exchange of information. These 'chat' communities are extremely popular on the Internet.

communities of practice have the purpose to exchange knowledge within a specific professional expertise area usually through document sharing.

communities of purpose have been appointed specific business targets by management for the community as a whole. Its ICT support may include groupware and video conferencing.

competence centre team (virtual) of people organized around a specific knowledge domain.

competency-based team management characterized by four distinct team competencies:
1. the degree to which the team's competencies match with business goals and the level of team members' compatibility;
2. the training and work requirements of members (professional career development);
3. the appraisal of team members both internally and externally;
4. the electronic support systems available for building and communicating knowledge (integrated knowledge environment).

content directors executive management levels that design, set and execute strategies on issues for which they provide focus regarding the process of knowledge sharing and building value.

content organizers the organizational unit (usually the corporate office of a company) that coordinates, controls and communicates knowledge by combining and connecting strategy to operations.

content providers organizational units that work directly with customers through the delivery of products and services. They acquire knowledge that helps to shape company strategy and develop operations.

control processes enable a company to create and maintain stability regarding business performance and legal and financial requirements.

coordination processes are activities that link strategic and operational sub-processes in a timely, and value-adding manner.

core competence is a set of intangible assets that enables a company to provide a particular benefit to customers or to create a substantial cost benefit to the company. A core competence is a combination of:

- skills and implicit knowledge;
- culture and values;
- technology and explicit knowledge;
- (management) processes; and
- assets and endowments, e.g. image, customer relationships, networks.

core operational processes key operational activities, when grouped together in a clear and logical way, enable a company to make and deliver products and services to customers in an effective and efficient manner.

core strategic processes future-oriented business activities that, when logically grouped, contribute to designing, setting and realizing a company long-term business objectives (i.e. objectives concerned with the future direction of a company).

corporate holding most often recognized as 'the headquarters' of a company which claims and maintains authority over design and strategy, implementing financial controls and managing operations.

create high-performance teams old Tayloristic organizations are characterized by employees working in distinctly separate functions and performing routine tasks to accomplish highly-repetitive objectives. These structures are being replaced by new organizational forms that allow professionals to work with a high degree of authority for themselves and their team in order to create value for the company.

creating the ability to conceptualize, to conceive new ideas while mainly using the intuitive part of the brain, making nontraditional associations.

creativity stimulators creativity stimulators help to stimulate new concepts (e.g. creativity software that helps generate ideas).

data warehousing a collection of data designed to support management decisions. These warehouses contain a wide variety of data that present a coherent picture of business conditions at any given point in time.

define core competencies core competencies reflect the key strengths of companies to such an extent that they allow the company to sustain its competitive advantage in order to add value to customers, and to increase its overall value to society under changing market circumstances. Core competencies, semi-permanent in nature, are largely independent of individual performance.

design strategic processes directly related to a company's long-term business objectives, strategic processes must clearly reflect the main direction in which a company wishes to develop. These processes focus the knowledge behaviour of a company. Strategic processes are limited in number, highly visible and semi-permanent in nature. They only change when a company's overall business objectives change.

develop individual competencies when professionals develop learning abilities, they build and share knowledge essential for realizing strategic and operational objectives.

dialoguing the art of conversation that allows the free flow of meaningful information between a number of people.

discussion tools discussion tools make electronic discussion possible (e.g. group vision, discussion groups, chat groups, publication and subscription techniques).

E-commerce, electronic commerce is the commercial activity that is enabled by processes over an electronic infrastructure. Most business-to-business and business-to-consumer transactions are delivered via the Internet.

electronic performance support system electronic performance systems support professionals by capturing and storing individual contributions to corporate knowledge such as work samples, best practices and personal feedback on performance assessments.

emphasize personal accountability modern KnoVa-driven companies depend on the effective performance of professionals who are motivated by the degree to which they can personally influence and control business results. This allows executive managers to emphasize accountability based upon mutually agreed objectives.

encourage teamwork in entirely process-driven and team-oriented companies, effective team management is one of the keys to successful business performance. Team management involves three leadership issues:

1. Direction and guidance of team efforts.
2. Coordination and control of member performance.
3. Support of team performance.

establish knowledge domains start by translating your company's business strategy into a select number of key knowledge requirements. This identifies the knowledge areas the company needs in order to realize its strategy in a value-creating manner. Knowledge domains focus the building and sharing of a company's knowledge, preventing professionals from gathering knowledge in a random and inefficient manner.

establish team competencies unique capabilities of a professional team allow it to build knowledge in strategic and operational processes in a continually value-adding manner. Teams combine the competencies of professionals in such a way that team performance is not affected when individuals change teams.

extranets an extranet is an intranet which allows access both to and from the Internet. Some extranets allow portions of the company intranet to be accessed by the general Internet public; however, most allow select clients and employees access via password through a firewall to all or some of the information contained within the company intranet. As businesses grow and as employees have become more home based, extranets have also grown more popular, allowing employees to upload and download vital information in a timely and efficient manner from any remote location using a common Internet dial-up account.

financial holding a corporate office that acts as a bank with regard to the individual operating units. Financial targets are set and 'cheap' money is made available to focus and support operations on achieving business objectives. No strategic or operational activities take place.

firewall device that protects a private network from the public domain. A computer that monitors traffic between an Internet site and the Internet. It's designed to prevent unauthorized people from tampering with a computer system thereby increasing security.

focus corporate processes corporate processes are coordination, control and communication processes that allow companies to 'combine & connect' strategic processes to operational processes and vice versa. Whereas traditional corporate offices act as 'old style', functionally designed headquarters, smart corporate centres are entirely process-driven, using focus to add value to strategic planning and operations in a clear and direct manner.

form business units in the past decade, while operating in an increasingly changing environment, many companies have recognized the need to decentralize authority in order to increase their ability to respond. As a first step, they have segmented the company into market-driven business units with unit managers holding personal responsibility for the bottom line results.

functional organization the functional organization produces tangible goods and has an overall production focus, utilizing a management style that controls and commands. Traditional organizations are seen as vertical structures built on the basis of specialization and a division of labour. Different functions such as marketing, sales, R&D, and finance operate separately from each other.

genetic computing genetic computing uses DNA strings to perform computations. Its four basic materials adenine, guanine, thymine and cytosine are combined to form strings of information. Computing capacity is enormous. A test tube of 1 billion DNA strings has a capacity of 1 billion parallel computations per second. Mistakes, however, are made during the replication of DNA and the durability of DNA is limited, lasting only a few days.

give challenging opportunities when knowledge professionals are challenged to add value in continuous-learning situations, they are challenged and energized to go beyond business-as-usual performance and to commit themselves to the organization.

group vision software that enables electronic brainstorming between people.

groupware groupware tools allow people to work on the same document at the same time.

hard networks hard networks distribute data and information by connecting computers through a variety of information technology systems (network computing).

high-performance companies are e-commerce organizations that continuously deliver value for their customers and other relevant stakeholders through a team-based approach supported by committed (knowledge) professionals and enabled by state-of-the-art ICT.

HTML hypertext markup language is the coding method used to format documents for the World Wide Web. Web pages can be seen due, in part, to HTML codes or tags as they are commonly known. Tags are interpreted by a web browser which renders your web page.

human-level complexity experimental ways of computing – such as quantum computing – focus on trying to emulate human-level decision-making complexity. In addition to logic and brain-level complexity, other factors such as intuition and emotion affect decisions. Quantum computing specifically addresses the ability of people and machines to handle paradoxes.

identify knowledge links each knowledge domain should be segmented into a number of subsections – knowledge topics or areas – becoming knowledge links between the work of individual professionals and/or teams in order to realize business objectives. They serve in this respect as value enhancers, connecting and strengthening separate knowledge flows into knowledge domains.

industrial economy an economy dominated by the large scale, volume-driven manufacturing of products and related services through capital and labour intensive industries.

information systems and databases a collection of data organized in such a way that a computer program can quickly select desired segments. A database is best described as an electronic filing system.

integrated knowledge environment information technology that supports the flow of knowledge.

intranets intranet is a private organizational network that uses the same kinds of software you find on the public Internet, but it is only for internal use. As the Internet has become more popular, tools used on the Internet are being adapted for private networks. For example, many companies have web servers that are available only to employees. Note that an intranet may not be an Internet; it may simply be a network.

Java Java is a program language designed for writing programs that can be downloaded through the Internet and run without fear of viruses or other damage being caused to computers or files. Using small Java programs called applets, Web pages can include animations, calculators, and other enhancements. It is a simple, object-oriented, platform-independent, multi-threaded, dynamic general-purpose program environment. Java is best for creating applets and applications for the Internet, intranets and other complex, distribution networks.

the KiKo balance the fair exchange between knowledge in/knowledge out. The KiKo balance addresses the concern knowledge professionals have when asked to share knowledge and turn it into value for the company.

the KnoVa factor indicator for the value-adding potential of a company. This potential depends on both the service level and knowledge intensity of a company. Companies that score high on both will show super-KnoVa performance. Companies that score low will show sub-KnoVa performance.

knowledge connectivity relates to managing knowledge that is exchanged between business or service units that is mutually beneficial to share. This is the strength that holds a company together and improves its business performance.

knowledge dividend the proceeds that are created by initiating value-based knowledge management, the framework for linking company knowledge to business strategy, a knowledge-supportive organization and knowledge professionals, and utilizing ICT to organize and distribute information and knowledge among them.

knowledge domain a collection of related knowledge.

knowledge economy a value-driven economy in which companies provide knowledge-intensive products and services that enhance:
1. market value,
2. value to society; thereby enhancing
3. overall intangible value.

knowledge efficiency results from carefully codifying and storing already existing company knowledge in databases with the ultimate goal to (re)use it, resulting in knowledge at the fingertips of the company and its employees.

knowledge innovation is the process of creating new knowledge through improvisation, experimentation, creativity and one-on-

one contact. It results in the kind of knowledge that is closely tied to a person or (virtual) team. Novel and valuable ideas, solutions, services and products are identified through new combinations of existing knowledge and/or the creation of new knowledge.

knowledge journey is what leading organizations in virtually every sector have travelled in order to make more effective use of knowledge and insight, and gain a competitive edge.

knowledge link a collection of specific knowledge segments that, when combined, enhances the value of a knowledge domain.

knowledge map an overview of all the knowledge that is vital to attainment of strategic business goals.

knowledge professional competencies competencies that professionals possess and use for gathering, using and sharing knowledge.

knowledge segment everything a company's professionals and systems know about a specific topic.

lessons learned and best practices databases in which examples of previous experiences are stored, the reasons why they worked best (or failed) and the lessons that were learned.

linear computing a present day 'Von Neumann' computer is still much like an abacus. Sequences of instructions are processed one after the other. No matter how fast the processor is, the laws of physics – atom sizes and electron speeds – put an upper limit on the attainable capacity.

locate knowledge segments a source of knowledge can be a person or a system. Through knowledge segments the process of knowledge building begins by using three key areas of operational knowledge management:
- sense & respond
- combine & connect
- create & produce.

networking the process of establishing and/or contacting a number of people who can be called upon when expertise is required.

neural computing neural computing mirrors the working of the brain in terms of parallel spreading of activation patterns in densely interconnected networks of simple computational units. This way, a large number of soft or 'fuzzy' factors can be simultaneously optimized. However, because neural hardware is still in its infancy, applicability to large problems still remains a problem.

operational holding a corporate office that provides added value to the company by coordinating economies of scale that cannot be achieved by individual operations (i.e. coordination of purchasing contracts). It does not focus on strategy.

operational knowledge management use of information technology to organize and distribute information from and to employees.

operational subprocesses logically-grouped support activities that, together, form a core operational process.

optical computing executes parallel computations on both photons and electrons at very high speeds. Optical computers perform thousands of times faster than electronic computers. A reliable optical memory, however, has yet to be developed.

paradoxical change issues that are paradoxical and cannot be solved by simple 'either/or' approaches. They represent different and ever-changing interests of international stakeholders.

parallel computing parallel computing is based on a divide and conquer strategy. Many processors are put to work on sub-tasks of a problem. Each processor can be relatively simple, but the unit achieves unrivalled speed and capacity. High speed network connections make parallel computing possible even when multiple computers are located great distances from each other. The network is the computer, however, as with any subdivided task, relatively great effort is spent reintegrating the subresults.

peer support professional workers can rely on others as informal support systems. Professionals gain peer support by informal networking. These relationships are based on mutual trust and respect and, through them, professionals receive informal feedback on their performance.

performance appraisal performance appraisal provides an overall evaluation of how well a team is doing in the eyes of its members as well as its customers.

process organization a process organization is characterized by its horizontal flow of information and communication, its decentralized authority over decisions, and its process-oriented management.

process team a group of professionals responsible for a company's operational, corporate and/or strategic processes.

professional career development largely depends on proper assessment of training and work requirements.

professional development effective team performance by assessing training requirements for members and forecasting future competencies and individual training needs.

provide meaningful work knowledge professionals are driven to add value if they can relate to the company's overall purpose in such a way that it provides personal fulfilment as well. Many professionals are driven by the question, 'To what extent does my performance make sense for the company and for my working and personal life?'

quantum economy representing the far side of our knowledge economy, quantum computing allows us to resolve conflicting paradoxical business issues with meaningful knowledge. This results in 'the best of all worlds' for shareholders, stakeholders and society.

quantum paradox still experimental, quantum technology is expected to address a number of issues of equal importance by creating meaningful knowledge. This will enable companies and governments to add business and societal value in a globally domestic world.

questioning data becomes information when it gives an answer to a question. Therefore asking the right question is 50 per cent of the work.

reflecting the art of playing back and thinking about the lessons learned each day.

reward value performance recognizing and rewarding the value-enhancing performance of knowledge professionals forms one of the basic building blocks of a professional's willingness to continue to commit himself to the organization. In the future, knowledge professionals will increasingly want to share in the wealth created by their efforts, both from career and compensation points of view.

router hardware (or software) that connects local networks to the Internet. Routers screen destination addresses of packets passing through them and decide which route is best.

sensing the ability to observe and perceive without passing judgement.

set operational processes these 'create & produce' processes enable a company to deliver quality products and services to its customers. Operational processes form the core of bottom-line business unit and/or team performance.

smart corporate centre coordinates, communicates and controls core knowledge flowing within the company, adding value to performance by linking strategy and operations.

smart knowledge knowledge that adds real value to your company.

smart networks combine hard and soft networks, linking smart business strategies to everyone throughout the company. People work with systems; people work with people; and systems are connected to each other, ultimately supporting knowledge professionals who add value.

smart organizations entirely process- and team-based organizations that use knowledge as their primary asset.

smart professionals people that work in teams to skilfully build, share and harvest knowledge.

smart strategies the mission, vision and action plans that leverage company knowledge.

soft networks soft networks include the networked intelligence of individuals based on informal networks where people work together to create innovative ideas and innovations.

sourcing knowing how to find information.

stimulate self-management knowledge professionals work in teams, alternating as team leaders and team members. Performance requirements constantly change and it is essential for professionals to have the opportunity to 'refresh & refocus', helping them to continue adding value to the company and themselves.

strategic holding a corporate office acts as a strategic holding when its core purpose is to prepare, design and implement a long-term business strategy. It does not focus on operations.

strategic knowledge management process of linking your company's knowledge to your business strategy, designing knowledge-supportive organizational structures, and breeding knowledge professionals.

strategic subprocesses logically grouped support activities that form a core strategic process.

TCP/IP transmission control protocol/Internet protocol makes TELNET, FTP, e-mail, and other services possible between computers that belong to the different networks.

team suitability refers to providing all the competencies required to address every business goal.

teamworking the process of working together as a team that creates synergy by combining each member's unique knowledge.

value-based self-management creating self-management with the support of others where the organization will increasingly:

1. allow professional knowledge workers to rely on others as informal support systems (peer support);
2. provide training and development opportunities for professional and individual learning (professional career development);
3. implement formal appraisal systems (360 degree performance appraisal);
4. develop self-assessment tools (electronic performance systems).

Value Explorer© is an approach to determining a company's intangible assets. First, it measures a company's intrinsic strengths by analyzing the intangible assets hidden in the company's core competencies. Then, it rates and assigns them a monetary value based on their economic potential. The Value Explorer also provides the information needed to manage these assets.

virtual community an ICT-enabled network of people with a common (professional) discipline or interest that enables its members to share information and work effectively, universally, inexpensively and on their own terms.

virtual economy is an intangible economy driven by the rapidly accelerating rate of change and empowered by the Internet.

workflow management systems a series of tasks within an organization that produces a final outcome. Sophisticated workgroup computing applications support workflows. In a publishing setting, a document might be automatically routed from the writer via the editor and a proofreader to printing. Once the task is complete, the workflow software ensures that the individuals responsible for the next task are notified and receive the data they need to perform their part of the process.

REFERENCES

Adams, Douglas, *The Hitchhiker's Guide To The Galaxy*, Harmony Books, 1979

Albrecht, K., *The Northbound Train*, Amacom, 1994

Baardman, Paul, *Management With Metaphors*, Mingus, 1996

Barker, J.A., *Paradigms. The Business Of Discovering The Future*, Harper Business, 1993

Barley, S.R., *The New World of Work*, British North American Committee, Needhams Design & Print, 1996

Bennis, W., Biedermann, P.W. *Organizing Genius. The Secret of Creative Collaboration*, Addison Wesley, 1997

Birchall, D., Lyons, L., *Creating Tomorrow's Organization. Unlocking The Benefits Of Future Work*, Pitman Publishing, 1995, London

Blanchard, Ken, Waghorn, Terry, *Mission Possible*, Scriptum Books/ McGraw Hill, 1996

Breuker, J., van de Velde, W., *Common KADS Library For Expertise Modelling – Reusable problem solving components*, IOS Press, Amsterdam, 1994

Bridges, W. *Jobshift. How To Prosper In A Workplace Without Jobs*, Addison Wesley, 1994

Bunc, M., *Global Economy In The Age Of Science-Based Knowledge*, United Nations Institute For Training And Research, 1992

Collins, James C., Porras, Jerry I., *Built To Last: Successful Habits Of Visionary Companies*, Century Business, 1996

D'Aveni, R.A., *Hypercompetition: Managing The Dynamics Of Strategic Manoeuvering*, The Free Press, 1994

Denning, P.J., Metcalfe, R.M., *Beyond Calculation. The Next Fifty Years Of Computing*, Springer Verlag, 1997

Dunnette, M.D., Hough, L.M., *Handbook Of Industrial And Organizational Psychology*, Consulting Psychologists Press, 1992

Edvinsson, L., Malone, M.S., *Intellectual Capital, Realizing Your Company's True Value By Finding Its Hidden Roots*, HarperBusiness, 1997

Ellis, Jonathan, Overkleeft, Dick, *The Sum That Is Philips*, Corporate Bureau External Relations, Philips Electronics NV, 1983

Ellis, Jonathan, *Sound Investments – The Story of Philips Classics*, Internal Publication, Philips Classics, 1990

Fisher, K., Fisher, M.D.F., *The Distributed Mind: Achieving High Performance Through The Collective Intelligence Of Knowledge Work Teams*, Amacom, 1997

Fortune Magazine, *By The Editors Of Fortune,* Penguin Books, 1984

Galbraith, J.R., Lawler, E.E, and Assoc., *Organizing For The Future,* Jossey-Bass, 1993

Gross, S.E., *Compensation For Teams,* Amacom, 1995

Guzzo, R.A., Salas, E., and Associates, *Team Effectiveness and Decision Making In Organizations,* Jossey-Bass, 1995

Hall, D.T., et al., *The Career Is Dead – Long Live The Career; A Relational Approach To Careers,* Jossey-Bass, 1996

Hamel, Gary, Prahalad, C.K., *Competing For The Future,* Harvard Business School Press, 1994

Hammer, M., *Beyond Reengineering,* Harper Business, New York, 1996

Hesselbem, F., Goldsmith, M., Beckhard, R., *The Organization Of The Future,* Jossey-Bass, 1997

Huber, G.P., Glick, W.H., *Organizational Change And Redesign. Ideas And Insights For Improving Performance,* Oxford University Press, 1993

International Monetary Fund, *World Economic Outlook,* International Monetary Fund, 1996

Jacobs, R.W., *Real Time Strategic Change,* Berrett-Koelhler, 1994

Katzenback, Jon R., Smith, Douglas K., *The Wisdom of Teams. Creating the High Performance Organization,* Harvard Business School Press, 1994

Khalil, T.M., Bayraktar, B.A., *Management Of Technology IV,* Industrial Engineering and Management Press, Georgia, 1994

Knoke, William, *Bold New World: The Essential Roadmap To The Twenty-first Century* (Plaatsloze nieuwe wereld), Scriptum Books, 1996

Kuhn, Thomas, *The Structure of Scientific Revolutions,* 3rd Edition, University of Chicago Press, 1996

Larson, Richard W., Zimney, David J., *The White Collar Shuffle: Who Does What In Today's Computerized Workplace,* Amacom, 1990

Leonard-Barton, D., *Wellsprings Of Knowledge,* Harvard Business School Press, 1995

Lynch, Richard, *Corporate Strategy,* Pitman Publishing, 1997

Maccoby, M., *Why Work. Motivating And Leading The New Generation,* Touchstone / Simon & Schuster, 1988

Maister, D.H., *True Professionalism,* Free Press, New York, 1997

Manz, Charles C., Sims, Henry P. Jr., *Business Without Bosses,* John Wiley & Sons, 1995

Mazlish, Bruce, *The Fourth Discontinuity,* Yale University Press, 1993

McAdams, J.L., *The Reward Plan Advantage,* Jossey-Bass, 1996

McGill, M.E., Slocum, J.W., *The Smarter Organization: How To Build A Business That Learns And Adapts To Marketplace Needs,* John Wiley & Sons, 1994

Meyer, J.P., Allen, N.J., *Commitment In The Workplace. Theory, Research And Application,* Sage Publications, 1997

Mohrman, S.A., Cohen, S.G., Mohrman, A.M., *Designing Team-Based Organizations. New Forms For Knowledge Work,* Jossey-Bass, 1995

Murray, John A., *Strategy And Process In Marketing,* Prentice Hall Europe, 1996

Myers, P.S., *Knowledge Management And Organizational Design,* Butterworth-Heinemann, 1997

Nadler, D. A. C., Tushman, M. L., *Competing By Design, The Power Of Organizational Architecture,* Oxford University Press, 1997

Nolan, Richard L., Crosan, David C., *Creative Destruction: A Six Stage Process For Transforming The Organization,* Harvard Business School Press, 1995

Nonaka, Ikujiro, Takeuchi, Hirotaka, *The Knowledge Creating Company: How Japanese Companies Create The Dynamics Of Innovation,* Oxford University Press, 1995

Peters, T., *Crazy Times Call For Crazy Organizations,* Vintage Books, 1994

Philips Electronics NV, *Centurion: A Process Of Change,* 1996

Quinn, R. E., *Deep Change: Discovering The Leader Within,* Jossey-Bass, 1996

Rifkin, Jeremy, *The End Of Work: The Decline Of The Global Labor Force And The Dawn Of The Post-Market Era,* Putnam Publications, 1995

Robbins, H., Finley, M., *Why Teams Don't Work: What Went Wrong And How To Make It Right,* Peterson's/Pacesetter Books, 1995

Robbins, S.P., *Organizational Theory, Structure, Design, And Applications,* Prentice Hall, 1987

Ruggles III, R.L., *Knowledge Management Tools,* Butterworth-Heinemann, 1997

Sadtler, D., Campbell, A., Koch, R., *Break up! When Large Companies Are Worth More Dead Than Alive,* Capstone Publishing, 1997

Schrage, M., *No More Teams: Mastering The Dynamics Of Creative Collaboration,* Doubleday, 1995

Schumpeter, J., *Theorie Der Wirtschaftlichen Entwicklung,* zweite neubearbeitete Auflage, Ducker & Humbolt, 1926

Senge, Peter, *Transforming The Practice Of Management,* Paper Presented At The Systems Thinking In Action Conference, 14 November 1991

Sims, D., Finemena, S., Gabriel, Y., *Organizing & Organizations,* Sage Publications, 1993

Stewart, Thomas, *Intellectual Capital, The New Wealth Of Organizations,* Doubleday / Currency, 1997

Stott, K., Walker, A., *Teams, Teamwork & Teambuilding,* Prentice Hall, 1995

Sveiby, K.E., *The New Organizational Wealth. Managing & Measuring Knowledge-Based Assets,* Berrett-Koehler Publishers, 1997

Teije, A. ten, *Automated Configuration of Problem Solving Methods in Diagnosis*, PhD Thesis, University of Amsterdam, 1997

Tipler, Frank J., *The Physics of Immortality*, Doubleday, 1994

US Bureau of Labor Statistics, *Occupational Outlook Handbook*, 1994–2005

US Bureau of Labor Statistics, *Statistical Abstract of the United States*, 1992, 1996

US Bureau of the Census, *Historical Statistics Of The United States, Colonial Times To 1970*, 1976

Walden Publishing, *The World Business & Economic Review*, Walden Publishing, 1994

Wellins, R. S., Bynham, W. C., Dixon, G. R., *Inside Teams: How 20 world-class organizations are winning through teamwork*, Jossey-Bass, 1994

Wheatley, Margaret J., *Leadership And The New Science: Learning About Organization From An Orderly Universe*, Berrett-Koehler Publishers, 1994

NOTES

Chapter 1

1 'Downsizing Guru Admits Mistake' *(Guru downsizing heeft zich vergist), De Standaard,* 14 May 1996

2 Ibid.

3 Peter Scott-Morgan, author of *Unwritten Rules of the Game,* quoted in 'Change the Rules', M. May, *Information Strategy,* April 1997

4 *Hypercompetition: Managing The Dynamics Of Strategic Manoeuvering,* R.A. D'Aveni, The Free Press, 1994

5 'New Rules For The New Economy', Kevin Kelly, *Wired,* September 1997

6 'Are You As Good As You Think You Are?', Justin Martin, *Fortune,* 30 September 1996

7 *Competing For The Future,* Gary Hamel, C.K. Prahalad, Harvard Business School Press, 1994, page 94

8 'The Next Big Thing, Re-engineering Gurus Take Steps To Remodel Their Stalling Vehicles', *Wall Street Journal,* 27 November 1996

9 'Corporate Anorexia', D. Stamps, *Training,* vol. 33, 1996

10 'Sony To Enter Market For Telecom Services' *(Sony gooit zich op market telecom diensten), De Volkskrant,* 22 August 1997

11 Ibid.

12 'The Great Consultancy Cop-out', *Management Today,* March 1997

13 'Alliances And Networks: The Next Generation', KPMG Survey by KPMG Alliances, Networks and Virtual Organizations, 1996

14 'The Advice Business', *The Economist,* 22 March 1997

15 *Competing For The Future,* Gary Hamel, C.K. Prahalad, Harvard Business School Press, 1994, pages 216, 217, 229

16 'Galileo Offering Exceeds Expectations', *Financial Times,* 28 July 1997

17 'Dow's Journey To A Knowledge Value Management Culture', Gordon Petrash, *European Management Journal,* August 1996

18 *Competing For The Future,* Gary Hamel, C.K. Prahalad, Harvard Business School Press, 1994, page 251

19 Ibid., page 259

20 Ibid.

21 Quoted in: 'Dow's Journey To A Knowledge Value Management Culture', Gordon Petrash, *European Management Journal,* August 1996

22 'Dow's Journey To A Knowledge Value Management Culture', Gordon Petrash, *European Management Journal,* August 1996

23 'Benchmarking Knowledge Management', Robert J. Hiebeler, *Strategy & Leadership,* March/April 1996

24 'There's A Price On Your Head: Managing Intellectual Capital Strategically', Nick Bontis, *Business Quarterly,* Summer 1996

25 'Are You As Good As You Think You Are?', Justin Martin, *Fortune,* 30 September 1996

26 'Mr. Knowledge', *The Economist,* 31 May 1997

27 *Intellectual Capital, The New Wealth Of Organizations,* Thomas Stewart, Doubleday/Currency, 1997

28 'The Light From Amsterdam' *(Het Licht uit Amsterdam),* NRC *Handelsblad,* 29 May 1997

29 'Yes, Stork Is Still Building Machines' *(Jawel, Stork blijft ook machines bouwen),* Harmen Keiser, *Fem,* 21 June 1997

Chapter 2

1 'The New CIO/CEO Partnership', Harry M. Lasker & David P. Norton, *Computerworld,* 22 January 1996

2 'Intranets In A Knowledge Based Economy', Gerhard Schulmeyer, *Netscape Columns:* Intranet Executive, www.netscape.com

3 'Knowing The Drill: Virtual Teamwork At BP', Don Cohen, *Perspectives on Innovation,* Issue 1: Managing Organizational Knowledge, www.businessinnovation.ey.com

4 'AT&T See End Of Paper Trail', *Information Week,* 25 November 1996

5 'Intranets Reach The Factory Floor', Mary J. Cronin, *Fortune,* 18 August 1997

6 'If HP Only Knew What HP Knows', Thomas H. Davenport, *Perspectives on Innovation,* Issue 1: Managing Organizational Knowledge, www.businessinnovation.ey.com

7 Ibid.

8 'Do You Have The Knowledge?', *Information Strategy,* February 1997

9 Ibid.

10 'A Prescription For Knowledge Management: What Hoffman-LaRoche's Case Can Teach Others', Patricia Seemann, *Perspectives on Innovation,* Issue 1: Managing Organizational Knowledge, www.businessinnovation.ey.com

11 'Lead, Don't Manage', Michael A. Verespel, *Industry Week,* March 1996

12 Ibid.

13 Ibid.

14 'The Importance Of Unlearning', Allan J. Magraith, *Across the Board,* February 1997

15 'The New CIO/CEO Partnership', Harry M. Lasker, David P. Norton, *Computerworld,* 22 January 1996

16 'Some Principles Of Knowledge Management', Thomas H. Davenport, *McKinsey Quarterly,* Winter 1996

17 'Eastman Chemical's Spanish Composition', *Journal of Business Strategy,* September/October 1995

18 Article in *Wall Street Journal,* 1993, quoted in: 'Buckman Labs Focuses On Engaging The Customer', Daniel Tobin, *Knowledge Inc.,* June 1997

19 'Buckman Labs Focuses On Engaging The Customer', Daniel Tobin, *Knowledge Inc.,* June 1997

20 'TSC Guides Banks Through Their Own Data Maze' (TSC leidt banken door eigen datadoolhof), *Het Financieele Dagblad,* 26 September 1995

21 'ING Restricts Pleasure Mail', *Intermediair,* 16 October 1997

22 'The Real Problem With Computers', Michael Schrage, *Harvard Business Review,* September/October 1997

23 Ibid.

24 Ibid.

25 Ibid.

26 Ibid.

27 'Creating Fertile Ground For Knowledge At Monsanto', Bipin Junnarkar, *Perspectives on Innovation,* Issue 1: Managing Organizational Knowledge, www.businessinnovation.ey.com

28 Ibid.

29 'A Prescription For Knowledge Management: What Hoffman-LaRoche's Case Can Teach Others', Patricia Seemann, *Perspectives on Innovation,* Issue 1: Managing Organizational Knowledge, www.businessinnovation.ey.com

30 'The New CIO/CEO Partnership', Harry M. Lasker, David P. Norton, *Computerworld,* 22 January 1996

31 'Managing Professional Intellect: Making The Most Of The Best', James Brian Quinn, Philip Anderson, Sydney Finkelstein, *Harvard Business Review,* March–April 1996

32 Ibid.

33 Ibid.

34 'Benchmarking Knowledge Management', Robert J. Hiebeler, *Strategy and Leadership*, March/April 1996

35 Ibid.

36 Ibid.

37 'Knowledge Management: Key To Long-Term Organizational Success', *Long Range Planning*, August 1996

38 'Serve Each Customer Efficiently And Uniquely', B. Joseph Pine II, *Business Communications Review*, January 1996

39 Promotional material for new 300 series (BMW).

40 Adapted quotation from: *Strategy And Process In Marketing*, John A. Murray, Prentice Hall Europe, 1996; *Corporate Strategy*, Richard Lynch, Pitman Publishing, 1997; 'ABB: Model Merger For The New Europe', Carol Kennedy, *Long Range Planning*, October 1992

41 'Why Barnes & Noble May Crunch Amazon', Randall E. Stross, *Fortune*, 29 September 1997

42 'Profile Netscape' *(Profiel Netscape)*, *Het Financieele Dagblad*, 29 July 1996

43 'Why Barnes & Noble May Crunch Amazon', Randall E. Stross, *Fortune*, 29 September 1997

44 *Theorie Der Wirtschaftlichen Entwicklung*, J. Schumpeter, zweite neubearbeitete Auflage, Ducker & Humbolt, 1926

45 'Best Medicine: Data Warehouses', Jill Gambon, *Information Week*, 9 September 1996

46 'Benchmarking Knowledge Management', Robert J. Hiebeler, *Strategy and Leadership*, March/April 1996

47 '*Intellectual Capital, The New Wealth of Organizations*', Thomas Stewart, Doubleday/Currency, 1997, page 139

48 'The Learning Organization: A Review And Evaluation', T. Garavan, *The Learning Organization*, vol. 4, 1997

49 *Transforming The Practice Of Management*, Peter Senge, Paper Presented At The Systems Thinking In Action Conference, 14 November 1991

50 *Intellectual Capital, The New Wealth Of Organizations*, Thomas Stewart, Doubleday/Currency, 1997, pages 119/120

51 Ibid., page 99

52 'The New Job Mobility', *Training*, May 1997

53 'ING Barings: Surviving In The London's Lions' Den' (ING Barings: Overleven In Londonse Leeuwekuil), *Het Financieele Dagblad*, 17 July 1996

54 'Unleashing The Power Of Learning', Steven E. Prokesch, *Harvard Business Review*, September/October 1997

55 Ibid.

56 Ibid.

57 Ibid.

58 Ibid.

59 Ibid.

60 Ibid.

61 Ibid.

62 Ibid.

63 Ibid.

64 Ibid.

65 Ibid.

66 Ibid.

67 Ibid.

68 Ibid.

69 Ibid.

70 Ibid.

71 Ibid.

72 Ibid.

73 Ibid.

Chapter 3

1 *Internet Adoption Worldwide: Industrialized Countries,* A. Roussel, Gartner Group, March 1997

2 NRC Handelsblad, International Data Corporation, January 1999

3 *Oh, what a tangled web,* Barry Riley, *Financial Times,* 1 May 1999

4 *Business Week,* January 1997–January 1998

5 'The Next Net', Jeffrey S. Young, *Wired,* April 1999

6 'High-flying Amazon feels the pain as its losses mount up', John Auters, *Financial Times,* 1 May 1999; 'The Inner Bezos', Chip Bayers, *Wired,* March 1999; 'Interview with Jeff Bezos', *Worth,* May 1999

7 Second Annual E-Business Conference, The Economist Conferences, 27–28 October 1999; Case studies, http://www/eresources.com/presentations/mcginnis/tsld023.htm

8 'When companies connect', *The Economist,* 26 June 1999

9 'Customer Relationship Strategies Vital to Success', *Knowledge Inc.,* March 1999

10 *Op Weg naar Nederland Kennisland,* René Tissen, Nienke den Haan, Siemen Jonge-dijk, Nyenrode University Press, 1998; 'R.I.P. Yahoo', *The Volkskrant,* 25 February 1999

11 'Interview with Jeffrey Bezos', *Worth,* May 1999; 'High-flying Amazon feels the pain as its losses mount up', John Auters, *Financial Times,* 1 May 1999; 'Oh, what a tangled web', Barry Riley, *Financial Times,* 1 May 1999

12 'Do they have anything in common', *The Economist,* 13 February 1999

13 'America's Fastest Growing Companies', *Fortune,* 14 October 1996

14 'New Rules For The New Age', Kevin Kelly, *Wired,* 1997

15 *Beyond Reengineering,* M. Hammer, HarperBusiness, New York, 1996, page 33

16 *Intellectual Capital, The New Wealth of Organizations,* Thomas Stewart, Doubleday/Currency, 1997

17 *Historical Statistics Of The United States, Colonial Times To 1970,* Washington D.C., US Bureau of the Census 1976; *Statistical Abstract of the United States,* US Bureau of Labor Statistics, 1992, 1996

18 Ibid.

19 *Occupational Outlook Handbook,* 1994–2005, US Bureau of Labor Statistics

20 Statistics compiled from:
   1. Brian R. Mitchell, *International Historical Statistics Europe 1750–1988,* 1992, Stockton Press, pages 913–919
   2. Brian R. Mitchell, *International Historical Statistics The Americas 1750–1988,* 1993, Stockton Press, pages 775–781
   3. Brian R. Mitchell, *International Historical Statistics Africa, Asia & Oceania 1950–1988,* 1995, Stockton Press, pages 1022–1032

21 'Information Warfare', *Information Strategy,* June 1997, vol, 2, no. 5

22 'ING Barings Loses Team Of Exchange Dealers' (ING Barings raakt team effecten handelaren kwijt), *Het Financieele Dagblad,* 1 April 1996

23 The Value Explorer©, KPMG Knowledge Management, The Netherlands

24 Actual names have been withheld to protect non-disclosure agreements

25 'The price tag on you is what drives net stocks', Stewart Alsop, *Fortune,* 1 March 1999

26 'The Innovation Lethargy Cannot Last' (De innovatie-lethargie kan niet duren), Bram Pols, *NRC Handelsblad,* 17 January 1997

27 *Intellectual Capital, Realizing Your Company's True Value By Finding Its Hidden Roots,* L. Edvinsson, M.S. Malone, HarperBusiness, 1997

28 Ziff-Davis, 'The Next 20 Years', Series, http://www.next20years.com

Chapter 4

1 *The End Of Work: The Decline Of The Global Labor Force And The Dawn Of The Post-Market Era,* Jeremy Rifkin, Putnam Publications, 1995

2 'Electronic Banking Bad For Bank Jobs' (Elektronisch Bankieren slecht voor bankbanen), *NRC Handelsblad,* 15 October 1997

3 *Intellectual Capital, The New Wealth of Organizations,* Thomas Stewart, Doubleday/Currency, 1997, page 28

4 'Taking AI On-Line Is A Real No-Brainer', Chuck Williams, *San Francisco Examiner,* 23 June 1996

5 *Brain Builder Wants To Grow Silicon Brains Trillions Of Times As Complex As Human Ones,* Otis Port, New York

6 Ziff-Davis, 'The Next 20 Years', Series, http://www.next20years.com

7 'A World Without Jobs?', *The Economist,* 11 February 1995

8 'Computers That Think Are Almost Here', *Business Week,* 17 July 1995

9 *Bold New World: The Essential Roadmap To The Twenty-first Century* (Plaatsloze nieuwe wereld), William Knoke, Scriptum Books, 1996, page 88

10 *The White Collar Shuffle: Who Does What In Today's Computerized Workplace,* Richard W. Larson, David J. Zimney, Amacom, 1990

11 *Collective Mind In Organizations: Heedful Interrelating On Flight Decks,* Karl E. Weick, Karlene H. Roberts, *Administrative Science Quarterly,* September 1993

12 *Taking AI On-Line Is A Real No-Brainer,* Chuck Williams, *San Francisco Examiner,* 23 July 1996

13 'Computer Takes Psychiatric Diagnosis' (Computer stelt psychiatrische diagnose), *Intermediair,* 16 October 1997

14 'Computers That Think Are Almost Here', *Business Week,* 17 July 1995

15 *Common KADS Library For Expertise Modelling – Reusable problem solving components,* J. Breuker, W. van de Velde (editors), IOS Press, Amsterdam, 1994; *Automated Configuration of Problem Solving Methods in Diagnosis,* A. ten Teije, PhD Thesis, University of Amsterdam, 1997

16 'The Brand Called You', T. Peters, *Fast Company,* August/September 1997

17 'A Bright Light On The Horizon For Employees' (Voor werknemer gloort licht aan de horizon), *De Volkskrant,* 1997

18 'Office Without Hierarchy' (Kantoor zonder hiërachie), *Intermediair,* 16 October 1997

19 'A World Without Jobs?', *The Economist,* 11 February 1995

20 'A Bright Light On The Horizon For Employees' (Voor werknemer gloort licht aan de horizon), *De Volkskrant,* 22 October 1997

21 'Knowledge Workers Gain Power' (Kenniswerkers krijgen macht), *Intermediair,* 23 October 1997

Chapter 5

1 'The Fortune Global Five Hundred', www.Fortune.com

2 'Company Concentration Promotes Inequality' (Bedrijfsconcentratie bevordert ongelijkheid), Sarah Anderson, John Kavanagh, *NRC Handelsblad*, 26 October 1997

3 Statistics compiled from: 'Fortune's Global 500', *Fortune*, 5 August 1996, *The World Business & Economic Review*, 1994; *World Economic Outlook*, 1996

4 *Centurion: A Process Of Change*, Philips Electronics NV, 1996

5 'Herkströter: Shell, Despite Arrogance, Strong Hold Of Integrity' (Herkströter: Shell ondanks arrogantie bolwerk integriteit), *Het Financieele Dagblad*, 12 October 1996

6 *Built To Last: Successful Habits Of Visionary Companies*, James C. Collins, Jerry I. Porras, Century Business, 1996

7 'The Second Eco Wave Arrives In Silence', *NRC Handelsblad*, 13 June 1997

8 'The Living Company', Arie de Geus, *Harvard Business Review*, March–April 1997

9 *Built To Last: Successful Habits Of Visionary Companies*, James C. Collins, Jerry I. Porras, Century Business, 1996

10 'Information Technology And Accelerated Science: The Case Of The Pentium Flaw', *California Management Review*, Winter 1996

11 Statistics compiled from: 'The Fortune Global 500', *Fortune*, 5 August 1996; *The World Business & Economic Review*, 1994; *World Economic Outlook*, 1996

12 'Company Concentration Promotes Inequality' (Bedrijsfconcentratie bevordert ongelijkheid), Sarah Anderson, John Kavanagh, *NRC Handelsblad*, 26 October 1997

13 'The Fortune Global 500', *Fortune*, 5 August 1996

14 'Joblessness, Pain, Power, Pathology And Promise', *Journal Of Organizational Change Management*, vol. 10, no. 2, 1997

Chapter 6

1 *Built To Last: Successful Habits Of Visionary Companies*, James C. Collins, Jerry I. Porras, Century Business, 1996

2 Ibid.

3 'Growing Up In A Culture Of Simulation', S. Turkle; In: *Beyond Calculation. The next fifty years of computing*, P.J. Denning, R.M. Metcalfe, 1997, Springer Verlag, New York

4 *The Fourth Discontinuity*, Bruce Mazlish, Yale University Press, 1993

5 *The Physics of Immortality,* Frank J. Tipler, Doubleday, 1994, page 31

6 Ibid., page 22

7 Ibid., page 23

8 Ibid., page 24

9 'Cue The Qubits', *The Economist,* 6 March 1997

10 'Cat With Nine Lives: Quantum Mechanics Has No Paradoxes' (Kat met negen levens, De Quantum mechanica heeft helemaal geen paradox), Vincent Icke, *NRC Handelsblad,* 19 April 1997

11 'Cue The Qubits', *The Economist,* 6 March 1997

12 Ibid.

13 Ibid.

14 Ibid.

Chapter 7

1 *Competing For The Future,* Gary Hamel, C.K. Prahalad, Harvard Business School Press, 1994, page 34

2 Ibid., page 214

3 Ibid., pages 85, 233

4 'Are You As Good As You Think You Are?', Justin Martin, *Fortune,* 30 September 1996

5 'New Rules For The New Economy', Kevin Kelly, *Wired,* September 1997

6 *Competing By Design, The Power Of Organizational Architecture,* D. A. C., Nadler, M. L. Tushman, Oxford University Press, 1997, page 227

7 'Trendsmart – about trends and a new way of being clever' (Trendsmart: over trends en een nieuwe manier van slim zijn), D. Devos, S. Olthof, *Strategie,* vol. 1, 1997

8 *The Northbound Train,* K. Albrecht, Amacom, New York, 1994

9 'CNN No Longer Believes In Global Formula' (CNN, geen geloof meer in mondiale formule), *DeVolkskrant,* 4 March 1997

10 'ABB: Model Merger For The New Europe', Carol Kennedy, *Long Range Planning,* October 1992

11 *Mission Possible,* Ken Blanchard, Terry Waghorn, Scriptum Books/ McGraw Hill, 1996

12 'Trendsmart – about trends and a new way of being clever' (Trendsmart: over trends en een nieuwe manier van slim zijn,) D. Devos, S. Olthof, *Strategie,* vol. 1, 1997

13 *Sound Investments – The Story of Philips Classics,* Jonathan Ellis, Internal Publication, Philips Classics, 1990

14 'Benchmarking Knowledge Management', Robert J. Hiebeler, *Strategy and Leadership,* March/April 1996

15 *Competing For The Future,* Gary Hamel, C.K. Prahalad, Harvard Business School Press, 1994, page 90

16 Quoted in: 'The Future Is Up To You' (De Toekomst is aan U), KPMG Strategic Vision, Amstelveen

17 *Centurion: A Process Of Change,* Philips Electronics NV, 1996

18 'Shell's New Decision-Making Model' (Nieuw beslismodel Shell) *NRC Handelsblad,* 6 July 1997

19 *Real Time Strategic Change,* R.W. Jacobs, Berrett-Koelhler, San Francisco, 1994

20 'Group Vision: Constructive Dialogue In An Inspiring Environment', KPMG Strategic Vision, Amstelveen, 1997

21 'Dutch Prosperity' (Hollands Welvaren), *Source,* no. 1, 1996

22 'Organizational Vision And Visionary Organizations' (Organisatie-Visie en Visionaire Organisaties), James C. Collins, Jerry I. Porras, *Holland Management Review,* no. 30, 1992

23 'Built To Last: Successful Habits Of Visionary Companies', James C. Collins, Jerry I. Porras, Century Business, 1996

24 'Knowledge Creation In The Telework Context', S. Raghuram, *International Journal of Technology Management,* vol. 11, iss. 7/8, 1996

25 'New Rules For The New Economy', Kevin Kelly, *Wired,* September 1997

26 Ibid.

27 *Mission Possible,* Ken Blanchard, Terry Waghorn, Scriptum Books/ McGraw Hill, 1996

28 'Some Principles Of Knowledge Management', Thomas H. Davenport, *McKinsey Quarterly,* Winter 1996

Chapter 8

1 Based on Arthur, 1996, Edvinson & Malone, 1997, Stewart, 1997, Sveiby, 1997; 1997
'Increasing Returns and the New World of Business', W.B. Arthur, *Harvard Business Review,* July 1996
Intellectual Capital, Realizing Your Company's True Value By Finding Its Hidden Roots, L. Edvinsson, M.S. Malone, Harper Business, 1997
Intellectual Capital, The New Wealth of Organizations, Thomas Stewart, Doubleday/Currency, 1997
The New Organizational Wealth. Managing & Measuring Knowledge-Based Assets, K.E. Sveiby, Berrett-Koehler Publishers, 1997

2 'Musings On Management', H. Mintzberg, *Harvard Business Review,* July 1996

3 *Jobshift. How to prosper in a Workplace without jobs,* W. Bridges, Addison Wesley, 1994

4 'Looking Ahead: Implications of the Present', Peter F. Drucker, *Harvard Business Review,* September 1997

5 *The Sume That Is Philips,* Jonathan Ellis, Dick Overkleeft, Corporate Bureau External Relations, Philips Electronics NV, 1983

6 *Paradigms. The Business Of Discovering The Future,* J.A. Barker, Harper Business, 1993

7 Ibid.

8 'Steel Versus Silicon', *Forbes,* 7 July 1997

9 'Effective Organizations: Using The New Logic Of Organizing', page 298, In: *Organizing for the future,* J.R. Galbraith, E.E. Lawler and Associates, Jossey-Bass, 1993

10 'Psst! Transactions', *Forbes,* 7 July 1997

11 'Increasing Returns And The New World of Business', W.B. Arthur, *Harvard Business Review,* July 1996

12 Ibid.

13 'Fast Company', July 1997

14 'The Brain-Based Organization', O. Harari, *Management Review,* June 1994

15 'Increasing Returns And The New World Of Business', W.B. Arthur, *Harvard Business Review,* July 1996
Global Economy In The Age Of Science-Based Knowledge, M. Bunc, United Nations Institute For Training And Research, 1992
'Compensation For Technical Professions In The Knowledge Age', C. Despres, J. Hiltrop, *Research-Technology Management,* September/ October 1996
'Customizing Customization', J. Lampel, H. Mintzberg, *Sloan Management Review,* Autumn 1996
The New Organizational Wealth. Managing & Measuring Knowledge-Based Assets, K.E. Sveiby, Berrett-Koehler Publishers, 1997

16 'Managing Professional Intellect: Making The Most Of The Best', James Quinn, Philips Anderson, Sydney Finkelstein, *Harvard Business Review*, March–April 1996

17 'Sources And Forms Of Organizational Change', G.P. Huber, W.H. Glick, In: *Organizational Change And Redesign. Ideas And Insights For Improving Performance,* G.P. Huber, W.H. Glick, Oxford University Press, 1993

18 'In Organization As In Architecture, Forms Follow Functions', S.W. Gellerman, *Organizational Dynamics,* 1990

19 *Organizational Theory, Structure, Design, And Applications,* S.P. Robbins, Prentice Hall, 1987

20 'Maverick! An Alternative Approach To Leadership, Company Organization, And Management', B. Lloyd, *Leadership & Organization Development Journal,* vol. 15, iss. 2, 1994

21 *Organizing & Organizations,* D. Sims, S. Finemena, Y. Gabriel, Sage Publications, 1993

22 'Why Teams Don't Work: What Went Wrong And How To Make It Right', H. Robbins, M. Finley, Peterson's/Pacesetter Books, 1995

23 Ibid.

24 Table compiled using information from the following sources:
Why Teams Don't Work. What Went Wrong And How To Make It Right, H. Robbins, M. Finley, Peterson's/Pacesetter Books, 1995
Creating Tomorrow's Organization. Unlocking The Benefits Of Future Work, D. Birchall, L. Lyons, Pitman Publishing, 1995, London
'The Tyranny Of A Team Ideology', Amanda Sinclair, *Organization Studies,* vol. 13, iss. 4, 1992
'Moving Beyond Team Myths', J. Beck, N. Yeager, *Training & Development Journal,* March 1996
Designing Team-Based Organizations. New Forms For Knowledge Work, S.A. Mohrman, S.G. Cohen, A.M. Mohrman, Jossey-Bass, 1995

25 'Measuring And Managing For Team Performance: Lessons From Complex Environments', R.M. McIntyre, E. Salas, In: *Team Effectiveness and Decision Making In Organizations,* R.A. Guzzo, E. Salas and Associates, Jossey-Bass, 1995

26 *The Distributed Mind: Achieving High Performance Through The Collective Intelligence Of Knowledge Work Teams,* K. Fisher, M.D.F. Fisher, Amacom, 1997

27 *Deep Change: Discovering The Leader Within,* R. E. Quinn, Jossey-Bass, 1996

28 'The Wisdom of Teams. Creating the High Performance Organization', Jon R. Katzenback, Douglas K. Smith, Harvard Business School Press, 1994

29 *No More Teams: Mastering The Dynamics Of Creative Collaboration,* M. Schrage, Doubleday, 1995, page XI

30 'Hot Groups', Harold J. Leavitt, Jean Lipman-Blumen, *Harvard Business Review,* July–August 1995

31 'Why Empowerment Doesn't Empower: The Bankruptcy Of Current Paradigms', James A. Belasco, Ralph C. Stayer, *Business Horizons,* March/April 1994

32 'Shadow Teams: Envisioning And Creating Your Own Competitor', H.N. Rothberg, *Competitive Intelligence Review,* vol. 8, 1997

33 *Inside Teams: How 20 world-class organizations are winning through teamwork,* R.S. Wellins, W.C. Bynham, G.R. Dixon, Jossey-Bass, 1994, pages 308–309
Organizing Genius. The Secrets of Creative Collaboration, W. Bennis, P.W. Biederman, Addison Wesley, 1996

34 'Affinity Groups: The Missing Link In Employee Involvement', Eileen M. van Aken, Dominic J. Monetta, D. Scott Sink, *Organizational Dynamics,* vol. 22, iss. 4, Spring 1994

35 'Unleashing The Power Of Learning', Steven E. Prokesch, *Harvard Business Review,* September–October 1997

36 'KLM Cuts 160 Jobs At HQ' (KLM bezuinigt 160 banen weg uit het hoofdkantoor), *De Volkskrant,* 8 February 1997

37 'Philips cuts half jobs at HQ in white-collar reorganization' (Halvering hoofdkantoor Philips begin van witteboorden-sanering), *De Volkskrant,* 4 February 1997

38 *Break up! When Large Companies Are Worth More Dead Than Alive,* D. Sadtler, A. Campbell, R. Koch, Capstone Publishing, 1997

39 'Yikes! Deadwood Is Creeping Back', Thomas Stewart, *Fortune,* 18 August 1997

40 Based on 'Reducing The Girth Of Headquarters Staff', R.M. Tomasko, *Management Review,* vol. 73, 1984

41 *Fast Company,* Greatest Hits, vol. 1, 1997

42 'Strategic Renewal For Business Units', J.O. Whitney, *Harvard Business Review,* July 1996

43 'The End Of The Business Unit' (Het einde van de business unit), *Holland Management Review,* no. 41, 1994; 'The Pitfalls Of The Business Unit' (De valkuilen van de business unit), Hans Strikwerda, *Intermediair,* 22 November 1996

44 'Cybercommunities: better than being there?', Robba Benjamin, *Blueprint to the digital economy,* Don Tapscott, Alex Lowly, David Ticoli, 1998

45 deja.com

Chapter 9

1 'An Interview with Paul M. Romer', J. Kurzman, *Strategy & Business,* First Quarter 1997

2 'The Prospects For Productivity', W. Bowen, In: *By The Editors Of Fortune,* Penguin Books, 1984, page 1

3 Ibid., page 1

4 Ibid., page 18

5 'The Hollow Ring of Productivity Revival', S.S. Roach, *Harvard Business Review,* November/December 1996

6 'The Economy Of Ideas: A Framework For Rethinking Patents And Copyrights In The Digital Age', J.P. Barlow, 1993–94, *Wired Online,www.Wwu.edu/~market/idel.hmtl*

7 'How Many Bulldozers For An Ant Colony', D. Crever, In: *Knowledge Management Tools,* R.L. Ruggles III, Butterworth-Heinemann, 1997

8 *First Intranet,* 13 October 1997

9 Based on: 'Management Of Technology Issues In Research And Development Work Analysis', C.K. Koeling, M.G. Beruvides, In: *Management Of Technology IV,* T.M. Khalil, B.A. Bayraktar, Industrial Engineering and Management Press, Georgia, 1994; *The New Organizational Wealth. Managing & Measuring Knowledge-Based Assets,* K.E. Sveiby, Berrett-Koehler Publishers, 1997; *The New World of Work,* S.R. Barley, British-North American Committee, Needhams Design & Print, 1996

10 *Wellsprings of Knowledge,* D. Leonard-Barton, Harvard Business School Press, 1995, page 75

11 'Ten Rules for Better Networking', Charles F. Harding, *Journal of Management Consulting,* vol. 6, iss. 1, 1990

12 'Trendsmart – about trends and a new way of being clever' (Trendsmart: over trends en een nieuwe manier van slim zijn), D. Devos, S. Olthof, *Strategie,* vol. 1, 1997

13 'Managing Professional Intellect: Making Most Of The Best', James Quinn, Philips Anderson, Sydney Finkelstein, *Harvard Business Review,* March–April 1996

14 'Can You Give Good, Inexpensive Rewards? Some Real-Life Answers', Peter Meyer, *Business Horizons,* November–December 1994

15 'You're On CapCom', CapVolmac

16 'Can You Give Good, Inexpensive Rewards? Some Real-Life Answers', Peter Meyer, *Business Horizons,* November–December 1994

17 'Promotional letter', October 1997

18 *Why Work. Motivating And Leading The New Generation,* M. Maccoby, Touchstone/Simon & Schuster, 1988

19 'The Seven Deadly Demotivators', D.R. Spitzer, *Management Review,* November 1995

20 *Why Work. Motivating and Leading the New Generation,* M. Maccoby, Touchstone/Simon & Schuster, 1988

21 'Motivation, Work And Organizational Psychology' (Motivatie en Arbeids-en organisatiepsychologie', W. Van Breukelen, R. Van der Vlist, *De Psycholoog,* February 1997, page 70

22 'Strategic Reward Systems', E.E. Lawler, G.D. Jenkins, In: *Handbook Of Industrial And Organizational Psychology,* M.D. Dunnette, L.M. Hough, editors, Consulting Psychologists Press, California (second edition), 1992

23 *The Reward Plan Advantage,* J.L. McAdams, Jossey-Bass, 1996

24 *Teams, Teamwork & Teambuilding,* K. Stott, A. Walker, Prentice Hall, 1995

25 Ibid.

26 'Motivating Knowledge Workers: The Challenge For The 1990s', M. Tampoe, In: *Knowledge Management And Organizational Design,* P.S. Myers, Butterworth-Heinemann, Boston, 1997

27 *Commitment In The Workplace. Theory, Research And Application,* J.P. Meyer, N.J. Allen, Sage Publications, 1997

28 *Leadership And The New Science: Learning About Organization From An Orderly Universe,* Margaret J. Wheatley, Berrett-Koehler Publishers, 1994

29 *Why Work. Motivating And Leading The New Generation,* M. Maccoby, Touchstone/Simon & Schuster, 1988

30 Warren Bennis cited in Brenden, 'Esteem In The Information Age', N. Branden, In: *The Organization Of The Future,* F. Hesselbem, M. Goldsmith, R. Beckhard, Jossey-Bass, 1997

31 *Why Work. Motivating And Leading The New Generation,* M. Maccoby, Touchstone/Simon & Schuster, 1988

32 'Do Performance Appraisals Change Performance?' P. Block, *Training,* May 1991, page 34

33 *The Reward Plan Advantage,* J.L. McAdams, Jossey-Bass, 1996

34 Based on 'New Organizational Forms And The New Career', P.H. Mirvis, D.T. Hall, In: *The Career Is Dead – Long Live The Career; A Relational Approach To Careers,* D.T. Hall and associates, Jossey-Bass, 1996

35 'Performance Support Systems, A conversation with Gloria Gery', P.A. Galagan, *Technical & Skills Training,* vol. 5, 1994

36 B. Raybould, 1996, www.goparagon.com

37 'Compensating Teams', P. Pasceralla, *Across the Board,* February 1997

38 'Is There Merit in Merit Pay?', M. Budman, *Across the Board,* June 1997

39 *Creative Destruction: A Six Stage Process For Transforming The Organization,* Richard L. Nolan, David C. Crosan, Harvard Business School Press, 1995

40 ACAS, *QWL News Letter,* no. 131, Summer 1997

41 *Compensation For Teams,* S.E. Gross, Amacom, New York, 1995

42 'Strategic Reward Systems', E.E. Lawler, G.D. Jenkins, In: *Handbook Of Industrial And Organizational Psychology,* edited by M.D. Dunnette, L.M. Hough, Consulting Psychologists Press, 1992

43 *Compensation For Teams,* S.E. Gross, Amacom, 1995

44 Ibid.

45 'Strategic Reward Systems', E.E. Lawler, G.D. Jenkins, In: *Handbook of Industrial and Organizational Psychology,* edited by M.D. Dunnette, L.M. Hough, Consulting Psychologists Press, 1992

46 'Skills Gap Jeopardizing U.S Companies' Ability to Compete', Select Appointments, North America, 27 April 1999

47 'When women rule the web', Louise Kehoe, *Financial Times.*

Chapter 10

1 In developing the ideas about the components of knowledge we have been inspired by 'Learning From Company Evaluation: Correction, Reflection, Or Argument' (Leren van beleidsevaluatie: correctieve, reflectie of argumentatie), P. van der Knaap, *Beleidsanalyse,* no. 3, 1995

2 'Molecules With Sunglasses', John Lynch, Horizon, *BBC Television,* 9 December 1996 – programme transcript is available at http://www.bbc.co.uk/

3 *Management with Metaphors,* Paul Baardman, Mingus, 1996

4 *The Structure of Scientific Revolutions,* Thomas Kuhn, 3rd Edition, University of Chicago Press, 1996

5 'SP Serves The Software Side of Sears', Michele Rosen, *Midrange Systems,* 16 August 1996

6 'Digging For Consumer Gold In Buying Patterns', Linda Wilson, *Computerworld,* 21 July 1997

7 'Eli Lilly Links Global Staff With ELVIS Net', Len Strazewinski, *Advertising Age's Business Marketing, Marketing Supplement,* November 1996

8 'How The US Court Of Appeals Reengineered Its Paper-Bound Appeals Voting Process', *I/S Analyzer Case Studies,* February 1996

9 'Bear Stearns Stretches Its Net', Mary E. Thyfault, *Information Week,* 15 April 1996

10 'Hitting The Right Notes', Marc Ferranti, *Computerworld: The Network 25 Supplement,* 9 September 1996

11 'Bionet', Kin S. Nash, *Computerworld,* 29 July 1996

12 'Exchanging Best Practices Through Computer-Aided Systems', Paul S. Goodman, Eric D. Darr, *Academy of Management Executive,* May 1996

13 'An Empirical Examination Of The Value Of Creativity Support Systems On Idea Generation', Brenda Massetti, *MIS Quarterly,* March 1996

14 'Royal Caribbean Cruises For Profit In A Sea Of Data', Jaikumar Vijayan, *Computerworld,* 26 May 1997

15 *Intellectual Capital, The New Wealth of Organizations,* Thomas Stewart, Doubleday/Currency, 1997, page 116

16 Ibid., Page 121

17 Ibid., Page 119

18 Ibid., Page 139

19 Ibid., Page 139

20 *The Hitchhiker's Guide To The Galaxy*, Douglas Adams, Harmony Books, 1979

21 *Intellectual Capital, The New Wealth Of Organizations*, Thomas Stewart, Doubleday/Currency, 1997

Chapter 11

1 'Managing Professional Intellect: Making Most Of The Best', James Quinn, Philips Anderson, Sydney Finkelstein, *Harvard Business Review*, March–April 1996

2 'The Greater Good', *CIO*, 15 November 1994

3 'Unlearning Ineffective Or Obsolete Technologies', W.H. Starbuck, *International Journal of Technology Management*, vol. 11, 1996

4 *The Smarter Organization: How To Build A Business That Learns And Adapts To Marketplace Needs*, M.E. McGill, J.W. Slocum, John Wiley & Sons, 1994, pages 53–55

5 'Lead, Don't Manage', Michael. A. Verespel, *Industry Week*, March 1996

6 *Computerworld*, 22 January 1996

7 KPMG Knowledge Management, United Kingdom

8 'Breakthrough In On-The-Job Training', E.R. Gomersall, M.S. Myers, *Harvard Business Review*, 7 January 1966

9 'A Question Of Balance, Case Studies In Strategic Knowledge Management', A. Graham, V. Pizzo, *European Management Journal*, August 1996

10 *True Professionalism*, D.H. Maister, Free Press, New York, 1997, page 46

11 'Benchmarking Knowledge Management', Robert J. Hiebeler, *Strategy & Leadership*, March/April 1996

12 'GM's First IT Chief Seeks 300 CIOs', Robert L. Schreier, *Computerworld*, 22 January 1996

13 'Some Principles Of Knowledge Management', Thomas H. Davenport, *McKinsey Review*, Winter 1996

Chapter 12

1 *Corporate Strategy*, Richard Lynch, Pitman Publishing, 1997

2 'Three Thousand Jobs Scrapped By Shell' (Drieduizend banen weg bij Shell), *De Volkskrant*, 1 October 1997

3 'It's Better To Do It Yourself' (Liever zelf doen), Ted de Bruijn, *Management Team,* 22 September 1997

4 *Competing For The Future,* Gary Hamel, C.K. Prahalad, Harvard Business School Press, 1994, page 111

5 'A Prescription For Knowledge Management: What Hoffmann-LaRoche's Case Can Teach Others', Patricia Seeman, *Perspectives on Innovation,* Issue 1: Managing Organizational Knowledge, www.businessinnovation.ey.com

6 'Knowing The Drill: Virtual Teamwork At BP', *Perspectives on Innovation,* Issue 1: Managing Organizational Knowledge, www.business innovation.ey.com

7 'Chrysler Must Pay A Quarter Of A Billion' (Chrysler moet half miljard betalen), *NRC Handelsblad,* 9 October 1997: 'Quality revolution not over yet', *Purchasing,* 6 March 1997

8 *Break up! When Large Companies Are Worth More Dead Than Alive,* D. Sadtler, A. Campbell, R. Koch, Capstone Publishing, 1997

9 *Transforming The Practice Of Management,* Peter Senge, Paper Presented At The Systems Thinking In Action Conference, 14 November 1991

10 'Get The Most Out Of People' (Mensen maximaal inzetten), P. Droge, *Personeelsbeleid,* no. 2, 1997

11 *Intellectual Capital, The New Wealth of Organizations,* Thomas Stewart, Doubleday/Currency, 1997, pages 189–192

12 *Business Without Bosses,* Charles C. Manz, Henry P. Jr. Sims, John Wiley & Sons, 1995

13 '3000 Business Partners At IBM' (Bij IBM drieduizend zakenpartners), *De Volkskrant,* 22 March 1997

14 *Intellectual Capital, The New Wealth of Organizations,* Thomas Stewart, Doubleday/Currency, 1997, page 205

15 'Intel's Amazing Profit Machine', David Kirkpatrick, *Fortune,* 17 February 1997

16 'Transforming The Practice Of Management', Peter Senge, Paper Presented At The Systems Thinking In Action Conference, 14 November 1991

17 *Intellectual Capital, The New Wealth of Organizations,* Thomas Stewart, Doubleday/Currency, 1997, page 105

18 'Keeping Control Of The Brain' (Het brein de baas), P. Spaninks, *Management Team,* 24 February 1997

communities *Continued*
of interest 153–4
of practice 20, 154
companies, enhancing value
52–7
competencies 160, 162–4,
209, 218–20
core competencies 55, 56,
120–1, 219
pay-for-competence systems
180, 181
competency-based team
management 177
competitive advantage 57
complexity 5, 6, 48–9, 60, 191
computers with brain level
complexity 93–5
and quantum computing
96–7
compromises 114
computers
with brain level complexity
93–5
quantum computing 92,
94, 95–100
connectivity 34
consulting services 6, 7
content 139–40, 209, 211
context 186, 191
continuous learning 224
control and planning 197–9
core competencies 55, 56,
120–1, 219
corporate centres 137–8,
148–50, 151–3
corporate processes 218
cost of websites 44
creating value 32–5
creation of knowledge 26, 29

creativity 65–6, 89, 158, 164,
194
critical mass 134
culture 15–16, 123, 186
curricula vitae (CV) database
167
customer loyalty 6, 26
customer response networks
195
customer satisfaction 6
customer segmentation 45
customers, enhancing value
to 57–8
customers lifetime value 56–7
customized mass production
24
CyberSURFR modem 14

Dalkon Shield 85
data mining 193, 196
data storage 95–6
data warehousing 193, 196
databases 196
decentralization 214, 216–17
decision making 82, 89–90,
184
demand-based knowledge
management 201
depth reward systems 179–80
dialoguing 164
diffusion of knowledge 157
direction of knowledge 19–21
discarding knowledge 198
discontinuities 118–19
discussion tools 196
distributing knowledge 198
double helix of teamwork
145–6
downsizing 4–5

merchandising and sales in
e-commerce 43, 45
mergers and acquisitions 56
merit pay *see* reward systems
meritocracies 22
metaphors 186
microchips 47
mind-set in global companies
82
mindmaps 193
mission 108–9
motivation 167, 169–74, 209,
211, 221
for knowledge management
21–2, 30
multi-skill based reward
systems 179–80
multinational companies
79–80
multiple strategy
development 109

national states 85–6
nature of work 62–3
networking 164
networks 19, 20, 153, 205–6
hard and soft 159
normal intelligence work 69

offices without hierarchies 71
Oklahoma City disaster task
force 144
operational knowledge 12–17,
187, 191–3, 205–13
implementing 206–8
operational processes 135, 218
OR thinking mode 88–9
organizational architecture
105, 133, 134–5

organizational charts 126, 127
organizational design 106, 133
organizational structure *see*
structure
outsourcing 71–2

paradigms 127–9, 186
paradoxes 95, 97
pay *see* reward systems
pay-for-competence 180, 181
pay-for-skills 180, 181
performance appraisal
systems 167, 174,
174–6, 178
performance goals 172–3
performance indicators 143
performance, productivity
performance 157
performance-related pay 178
personal accountability 220
pharmaceutical industry 26
planning and control cycle
197–9
PRIME-MD 70
problem solving 105
process management 23, 28,
132–3, 135–40
business process
reengineering 4, 135
commitment to 136–7
corporate processes 218
focusing efforts 139–40,
218–20
operational processes 135,
218
scenarios 137–9
strategic processes 135,
138–9, 218
team-based process-
organization 215